UNIVERSITY OF NORTH CAROLINA AT CHAPEL HILL
DEPARTMENT OF ROMANCE LANGUAGES

NORTH CAROLINA STUDIES
IN THE ROMANCE LANGUAGES AND LITERATURES

Founder: URBAN TIGNER HOLMES
Editor: FRANK A. DOMÍNGUEZ

Distributed by:

UNIVERSITY OF NORTH CAROLINA PRESS

CHAPEL HILL
North Carolina 27515-2288
U.S.A.

NORTH CAROLINA STUDIES IN THE
ROMANCE LANGUAGES AND LITERATURES
Number 282

THE POLITICS OF FARCE IN CONTEMPORARY
SPANISH AMERICAN THEATRE

THE POLITICS OF FARCE
IN CONTEMPORARY
SPANISH AMERICAN THEATRE

BY
PRISCILLA MELÉNDEZ

CHAPEL HILL

NORTH CAROLINA STUDIES IN THE ROMANCE
LANGUAGES AND LITERATURES
U.N.C. DEPARTMENT OF ROMANCE LANGUAGES

2006

Library of Congress Cataloging-in-Publication Data

Meléndez, Priscilla.
 The politics of farce in contemporary Spanish American theatre / by Priscilla Meléndez.
 p. cm. – (North Carolina studies in the Romance languages and literatures ; no. 282).
 Includes bibliographical references and index.
 ISBN 0-8078-9286-6 (alk. paper)
 1. Spanish American farces–History and criticism. 2. Spanish American drama–20th century–History and criticism. I. Title. II. Series.

PQ7082.D7M45 2006
862'.052320806–dc22   2006040059

Cover design: Heidi Perov

© 2006. Department of Romance Languages. The University of North Carolina at Chapel Hill.

ISBN 0-8078-9286-6

DEPÓSITO LEGAL: V. 1.189 - 2005

ARTES GRÁFICAS SOLER, S. L. - LA OLIVERETA, 28 - 46018 VALENCIA

To my 9 year-old son Andrés for his courage and spiritual strength

To Aníbal for loving Andrés and me so intensely

To my sister Mildred for being my very best friend

CONTENTS

	Page
ACKNOWLEDGEMENTS	11
INTRODUCTION: TOWARDS A CHARACTERIZATION OF SPANISH AMERICAN FARCE	15
CHAPTER 1: JOSÉ TRIANA'S *REVOLICO EN EL CAMPO DE MARTE*: FARCE AND CUBA'S REVOLUTIONARY HISTORY	43
CHAPTER 2: (IN)DECENCY AND (DIS)PLEASURE: WOMEN AND FARCE IN SABINA BERMAN'S *EL SUPLICIO DEL PLACER*	87
CHAPTER 3: TRANSCRIPTION, TRANSGRESSION AND POWER IN VARGAS LLOSA'S *KATHIE Y EL HIPOPÓTAMO*	137
CHAPTER 4: POPULAR CULTURE AND CLASSICAL TRADITIONS: FARCE AND INCEST IN *QUÍNTUPLES* BY LUIS RAFAEL SÁNCHEZ	173
CONCLUSIONS: BINDING THE UNBOUND	213
WORKS CITED	218

ACKNOWLEDGEMENTS

Growing up in a family where my father was always joking and teasing us, and where my mother meant every word she said and had no sympathy for jokes was quite a polarizing experience. I was never sure to which side of the family I gravitated. At certain points of my life I thought I had developed my father's good sense of humor, and at other moments I perceived myself as someone more like my mother; a proper and serious woman who in front of an impertinent police officer called herself a "ciudadana proba," and whom I have always looked up to. The real "crisis" came when two important events happened in my life: I met the person who has been for fifteen years my husband–a formal, serious, proper man– while at the same time I began to write about humor and farce in Spanish American theatre. I realized then that I was mixing and matching in my life and in my research both the serious and humorous styles, discourses, and approaches to communication and language, to reality and fiction, that I inherited from my parents. But more importantly, I realized that my plural identity regarding humor and seriousness in the context of family affairs, was closely linked to my understanding and approach to the study of Spanish American farce.

It is by now a cliché to publicly recognize the interdependence between the personal and the professional, the emotional and the intellectual, particularly when my husband is also my colleague. Nevertheless, after spending a decade in this project, I cannot separate any more the laughs from the tears, the joys from the vicissitudes, the frivolous from the political, since these supposedly opposing forces are now woven through the tapestry of life and work. If my parents' diverse perspectives on life are somehow the responsible forces for this study on Spanish American farce, fortunately it does not seem to have stopped with me. My parents' opposing styles are still playing a significant role in my son's life: Andrés is now the recipient of Abuelo Willie's funny jokes, and also of Abuela Zory's wisdom and spiritual strength.

I wish to express my immense gratitude and love to two wonderful friends and colleagues whom, during moments both rosy and dark, encouraged me unconditionally. For many years, the support of John W. Kronik and Jacqueline Bixler have been immeasurable. I suspect that when John finished reading my doctoral dissertation 20 years ago, he thought it was the end of editing my work and telling me to spare on double adjectives and on long flowery sentences. It was only an illusion, since he has never been free of these burdens. Needless to say, his keen advice twenty years ago and now have been immensely valuable. My good friend Jackie Bixler has always been willing to "dismantle" my ideas and rhetorical language with an incredible sense of humor, and with the sole purpose of inciting me to reach higher standards. Not for a minute has she stopped encouraging me to polish and publish my work. I am most privileged to have two outstanding and faithful friends who took the time to read this manuscript with patience and encouragement.

Years ago, my friend Patricia Lunn from Michigan State University helped me translate parts of the chapter devoted to *Quíntuples*, and my graduate student from Penn State University, Andrew Wolff worked on a first version of the chapter on Vargas Llosa's *Kathie y el hipopótamo*. I wish to express my gratitude to both of them for initiating a difficult process, and my assurance to the readers that these two friends are not responsible for any errors that may remain. To my compatriots Mercedes López-Baralt, Luce López-Baralt, and Arturo Echavarría I wish to express my gratitude for their joyous and unconditional friendship, and for always supporting my work.

A special thanks must also go to the two very perspicacious and anonymous readers of this manuscript. Their suggestions and insightful comments helped me a great deal and pushed me to strive for clarity throughout the manuscript. I can only hope to someday thank them personally for their careful reading and their stimulating comments.

To my beloved husband Aníbal González, I wish to express my deepest love and gratitude for sharing a life and a profession with me. I feel blessed that the threads of our lives and our work are so beautifully woven, and in the coming years, I can only pray that together we complete the tapestry.

Introduction

TOWARDS A CHARACTERIZATION OF SPANISH AMERICAN FARCE

> Hegel remarks somewhere that all facts and personages of great importance in world history occur, as it were, twice. He forgot to add: the first time as tragedy, the second as farce.
>
> Karl Marx, *The 18th Brumaire of Louis Bonaparte*

> Farce is at the bottom of everyone's list of forms.
>
> Russ McDonald, "Fear of Farce"

IN an era when the studies on the theory and practice of performance have revitalized the field of Spanish American theatre and galvanized those who examine this region's theatrical and socioartistic manifestations, a study on genre–in this case the frequently disparaged genre of farce–may be located on the margins of modern and postmodern thought and creation. "To persist in paying attention to genres may seem to be a vain if not anachronistic pastime today" is Todorov's first sentence in "The Origins of Genres," a statement that many theorists have inevitably had to confront and that Todorov disputes as he embarks on the examination of genres in discourse. More significant to us, as critics working at the beginning of a millennium, is Ralph Cohen's summary of what many believe is the role of genre theory in postmodern literature:

> Critics and theorists who write about postmodern texts often refer to "genres" as a term inappropriate for characterizing postmodernist writing. The process of suppression results from the claim that postmodern writing blurs genres, transgresses them, or unfixes boundaries that conceal domination or authority, and that "genre" is an anachronistic term and concept. (241)

Adena Rosmarin, in her book *The Power of Genre*, also confronts the historical mockery of the discourse on genre as she reminds us that the dissolution of genres began with the Romantics and has continued since then: "To be a modern writer and to write generically is a contradiction in terms" (7). Furthermore, the fact that genre studies primarily focus on textuality seems to clash with the emphasis on performance in the last decades and its once overtly antagonistic relationship with the text.

Before I attempt to characterize farce in a culturally diverse region such as Spanish America, or even before I explain the parameters and goals of this project, I should note that because this study explores discourses frequently considered marginal, an ironic apologetic tone will necessarily underlie the discussion, prompted by the need to legitimize the examination of Spanish American farce in the context of postmodernity and "antigenre" theory.[1] Instead of downplaying this apologetic tone or silencing what some consider an outdated discussion, the problematic language of marginality and victimization will proliferate throughout this introduction with the explicit purpose of creating an environment of tension between farce and other genres, between Spanish America and other regions, and between Spanish American farce and other Spanish American literary genres.

This strategy of framing Spanish American farce within an antagonistic relationship with its context might appear at first sight to hinder an exploration and understanding of it. But the task here will not be to reposition farce in Spanish America, to alter the place where critics and the audience have put it, but to engage in the process of understanding the historical, political, and metaphorical implications of placing marginality at the center of farce, which is obviously another contradiction in terms. What will be recognized in the plays examined in this book is that farce exploits this characterization of marginality and victimization. Spanish American farce is not only capable of dismantling any position it has been forced to occupy, but is also willing, as part of its iconoclastic game with authority, to transgress its traditional identity as meaningless, frivolous and intensely physical, as well as the contemporary view that it is a more serious and even politically committed genre than was thought before.[2]

This book analyzes four plays by major contemporary Spanish

---

[1] Throughout this study I use the term *Spanish America*, although other critics sometimes use the more encompassing term, *Latin America*.

[2] The goal here is not to understand farce in a negative light or attempt to define it only in its relationship with other genres. As Jessica Milner Davis states: "When farce is examined for its own sake in the context of plays which make no claim to be anything *other* than farce, its formal parameters can more easily be grasped" (6).

American playwrights: José Triana's *Revolico en el Campo de Marte* (Cuba 1972, published in 1995), Sabina Berman's *El suplicio del placer* (Mexico 1978, revised version 1994), Mario Vargas Llosa's *Kathie y el hipopótamo* (Peru 1983), and Luis Rafael Sánchez's *Quíntuples* (Puerto Rico 1984). These plays, written and published in the last decades of the twentieth century, represent a particular trend where Spanish American farces transgress their past identity as a disparaged genre, but in the light of this past identity, they also question the attempt to reveal its serious connotations and meaningful criticism. These farces' particularity is that they refuse to conform to being stereotyped as laughing machines that are "purely ephemeral in interest" (Hurrell 426), or as a form of theatre solely focused on physical movement. Neither do they submit to the possibility of becoming indirect vehicles for specific sociopolitical agendas. If Spanish American farce, as represented by these four plays, has an agenda at all, it is to expose and transgress its multiple identities and its contradictory expressions. In the process, farce embraces marginality as a mechanism to question its identity as art, as a theatrical expression, and as part of a canonical and authoritative view of the artistic and the political.

In the context of a discourse on marginality and of farce's conscious manipulation of its "victimized" position, as almost every critic has stated, the study of theatre in Spanish America "remains a relatively marginal activity, notwithstanding the dramatic rise in the quantity and quality of the plays produced since the late 1950s" (Taylor, *Theatre of Crisis* 12). Spanish American theatre has frequently been overshadowed by the prestigious Spanish American narrative and has received less critical attention than both the novel and poetry. Among the many reasons that can be ventured for the unprivileged position of theatre within Spanish American literature are the limitations imposed by economic constraints not only on publication but, more saliently, on representation in developing countries, and by the censorship historically triggered by governmental repression throughout the twentieth century, particularly of a genre characterized by its physical dimensions and its human presence (Meléndez 11).[3] Nevertheless, the publication since the early

---

[3] Among the many notorious cases of censorship in Latin American theatre, one stands out: Griselda Gambaro's. It is well known that Gambaro's *Información para extranjeros* [*Information for Foreigners*], written in 1973 and not published until

1990s of important books devoted to the exegesis of Latin American theatre is ample proof of the continuous critical interest that this theatre has generated both inside and outside its boundaries. [4]

Just as we have remarked on the traditionally secondary status of theatre in Spanish America, it is necessary to revive the old discussions of the place of this region's literature within Western culture, which has frequently been characterized by terms such as *marginality, periphery, dependency, displacement, otherness,* and *Third World.* The role of *positionality* becomes central to the discussion of farce because the study of Spanish American literature in Europe and the United States–notwithstanding critical attention to the novel and to poetry– is still largely overlooked by literary scholars and theorists. [5] Farce's origins in Western theatre and culture, and its lack of classical antecedents (Davis 13), also underscores this issue of positionality.

In the case of Spanish American theatre, the indifference towards this genre is not limited to those in the *center,* that is, to those that

---

1987, circulated first outside Argentina, since a play about violence and cruelty in a confined space could not be staged or published during the Dirty War (1976-1983) without threatening the security of the author. It is not surprising that Jacqueline Bixler begins her essay "Games and Reality on the Latin American Stage" with the following statement: "With an ax of censorship hovering over them, many contemporary Latin American dramatists have discovered in the inherent playfulness of theatre a means of revealing non-playful aspects of their daily reality" (22).

[4] Some of these important studies are by Severino Albuquerque, Heidrun Adler and Kati Rötter, Jacqueline Bixler, Frank Dauster, Elena de Costa, Catherine Larson and Margarita Vargas, Gerardo Luzuriaga, Marina Pianca, Osvaldo Pelletieri, Diana Taylor, Adam Versényi, Judith Weiss, and the works of critics of the magnitude of Sandra Cypess, Kirsten Nigro, Juan Villegas, Beatriz Rizk, and George Woodyard.

[5] It is surprising, for example, to discover in Barbara Foley's *Telling the Truth: The Theory and Practice of Documentary Fiction* (1986), no discussion of the overtly documentary and historical character of Latin American literature. It is also worrisome to discover still in the 1991 edition of the otherwise useful *History of the Theatre* by Oscar G. Brockett, the absence of or even allusion to the existence of Latin American theatre. Although Brockett acknowledges that "since 1968 the consensus approach to history and the hegemony of patriarchal, white, European-derived culture have come under strong attack" (637), to a certain extent his text perpetuates the misconceptions of the old critical forms. The omission of such theorists as Augusto Boal and Enrique Buenaventura, significant contributors to the history of Western and non-Western theatre, continues to evoke questions of positionality, hegemony, and intellectual oppression. Addressing this point, Jean Franco begins her essay "Beyond Ethnocentrism: Gender, Power, and the Third-World Intelligentsia" with the following statement: "Anyone involved in Latin American studies knows what it is to be placed last on the program, when everyone else has left the conference. Latin America (and third-world societies) generally occupy some exceptional and therefore awkward position in mainstream scholarship. Indeed, they are not yet 'in' it at all" (503).

represent the hegemonic forces, but, as Diana Taylor reminds us, is also displayed by those in the margins: "Though theatre in general receives less critical attention than do the narrative and poetic genres, it remains even more obscure in Latin America than elsewhere. . . . The lack of mutual awareness and understanding between the many Latin American countries, however, reflects . . . a host of misconceptions, prejudices, and skewed priorities resulting from internalized colonialism" (*Theatre of Crisis* 12-13). That is, the marginal position of both Spanish America and its cultural and artistic manifestations does not preclude the development of an internal hierarchy ("meta-marginalization") that situates theatre on the intellectual outskirts of the region's literary production. Once the hierarchical mode has been established, the pattern of marginalization takes over, suggesting not only the preeminence of the hierarchy *of* modes–"tragedy is more profound and significant than comedy"–but also the hierarchy *within* modes–"*de casibus* tragedy is less exalted than Greek" (McDonald 77). The marginalization of theatre within Spanish American literature can be interpreted then as the extension of a larger social and cultural bias against this region in general.

Jean Franco's questioning of the metropolitan intellectuals' notion that the "Third World is not much of a place for theory" (503) sheds light on one of the principal issues related to the marginalization of Spanish American literature. Regardless of the "central" position acquired by the *Boom* writers during the 1960s and 1970s, their inclusion in mainly theoretical discourses has been limited to internal consumption among Spanish Americanist scholars. Franco goes a step further in her characterization of the Third World's marginal position by adding:

> Metropolitan discourses on the Third World have generally adopted one of three devices: (1) *exclusion*–the Third World is irrelevant to theory; (2) *discrimination*–the Third World is irrational and thus its knowledge is subordinate to the rational knowledge produced by the metropolis; and (3) *recognition*–the Third World is only seen as the place of the instinctual. ("Beyond" 504)

It is not surprising that Debra Castillo uses this quotation in her attempts to establish the relationship and dialectics between "Anglo-American and French varieties of feminist thought" (*Talking*

Back 2) and the emerging feminist theories in Latin America. She problematizes this perception of Latin American literature as lacking theoretical ground and also stresses the questionable response to this marginalization by well-known Third World writers: "Strikingly, in this era of gender and race consciousness, the first world continues to subject the third to analyses that relegate its cultural production to that group of activities traditionally associated with the implicitly inferior feminine realm. Even more strikingly, prominent Third World and Third-Worldist writers seem to participate *uncritically* in this subordination" (*Talking Back* 3). For Castillo, the perverse notion of Latin America "as the land of emotion and practice rather than critical thought" becomes more destructive when this stereotype is internalized by Latin Americans themselves, reinforcing "a kind of pan-Latin inferiority complex, most destructive when most subtlety masked" (*Talking Back* 4).

This very brief discussion on the issue of marginality in Spanish America, particularly in cultural terms, forces us to ask: What, then, is the position of Spanish American farce (frequently accused of lacking a strong theoretical frame) within this hierarchical structure, once it has been stated that "farce is at the bottom of everyone's list of forms" (McDonald 77)? What are the artistic and critical consequences of the indifference of Western literature and culture toward Spanish American literature when Spanish American literature itself shows disinterest in the study of theatre and, in turn, theatre critics avoid considering the last item on the canonical list of dramatic forms, that is, farce? When Taylor states that "surprisingly, the aesthetic richness and originality of this theatre [of the late 1950s] have been underestimated by commentators" (*Theatre of Crisis* 12), what is actually stressed is the marginalization of a genre within an already marginalized literature and region.

Once this labyrinthine, if not pathetic, web of displaced voices is acknowledged, it is necessary to confront the "universal" lack of critical prestige accorded to farce, as well as the role and position of farce within Spanish American theatre, particularly in comparison to the overtly politically committed plays that have frequently occupied center stage. [6] Given the social and political instability of Spanish

---

[6] When critics talk about socially and/or politically committed Spanish American plays, although they accept their diversity, they frequently allude to such works as Rodolfo Usigli's *El gesticulador* (Mexico 1937) and *Corona de sombra* (1943); René Marqués's *Los soles truncos* (Puerto Rico 1958); José Triana's *La noche*

America—an area that constantly has been threatened by colonialism, revolution, dictatorship, guerrilla movements, and foreign intervention—it is important to examine why serious and well-known dramatists from this turbulent region engage in the exploration of a critically disparaged genre such as farce.

An immediate response to these quandaries could rely on statements connected to the "psychology" of the audience: "farce has flourished during times of stress and war as audiences prefer to forget their dread and sorrow and enjoy the brief escape afforded in the theatre" (Schutz 10). Some could argue that the violence, poverty, oppression, and other evils that, in the minds of many characterize Spanish America, justify an escape into a false and farcical world capable of sheltering these victims from their painful everyday lives.

Another response to the interest in farce could be the desire of Spanish American dramatists to connect with a broader audience who, in contrast to the traditional scholarly position towards farce, considers it a highly popular and entertaining genre. Farce's connection with the audience through humor, physical movement, and its emphasis on popular culture, invokes the influential notions of the role of carnival in medieval life as examined by Mikhail Bakhtin. In *Rabelais and His World*, for example, Bakhtin forcefully stresses that "carnival celebrated temporary liberation from the prevailing truth and from the established order; it marked the suspension of all hierarchical rank, privileges, norms, and prohibitions" (10).[7] It could be argued that the "free and familiar contact [that] reigned among people [during carnival] who were usually divided by the barriers of caste, property, profession and age" (Bakhtin 10) is one of the phenomena explored by farce, particularly in societies with traditionally strong hierarchical structures. That is, farce's connection with an audience, which has been frequently linked to the popular strata of culture and society, represents both a literal and

---

de los asesinos (Cuba 1965); Egon Wolff's *Flores de papel* (Chile 1970); Isaac Chocrón's *La revolución* (Venezuela 1972); Griselda Gambaro's *El campo* (Argentina 1967); Eduardo Pavlovsky's *El señor Galíndez* (Argentina 1973); Vicente Leñero's *Martirio de Morelos* (Mexico 1981); and Mauricio Rosencof's *Los caballos* (Uruguay 1967), to mention just a few.

[7] In "Poética y práctica de la farsa: *La Marquesa Rosalinda*, de Valle-Inclán," Dru Dougherty connects farce with the tradition of carnival: "These inversions, which are typical of the *enredo*, bring the genre of farce closer to carnival, since the latter brings into life the logic of things 'turned upside down'. . . . In farce inversions are not transient but constant" (130).

metaphorical questioning of hierarchy and authority. But what is significant regarding Spanish American farce is that its connection to the popular dimension and its implicit search for freedom from taboos and oppressive hierarchies–freedom that can range from the personal to the social, from the artistic to the political–is also questioned by its own iconoclastic impulse. Even more ironic, as Dru Dougherty observes, is the fact that the very success of farce, particularly among the general populace, has sometimes condemned it to critical disdain, leading to its being regarded as a very minor genre in theatre histories (125).

Ultimately, this study focuses on the recognition that the plays examined here, and many other Spanish American farces of the second half of the twentieth century establish both an antagonistic and an interdependent relationship with the psychological and physical angles of farce, with its celebratory popular dimension, and with the views, frequently promoted by the intellectual and even the theatrical establishments, that underline farce's lack of seriousness. This book also examines Spanish American farce as an instrument for inquiring into artistic and sociopolitical systems of communication from a decentralized perspective.

Regardless of my previous attempts to "justify" the study of farce in Spanish America, the strong sociopolitical stance frequently identified with this region's art, specifically with theatre, can make readers of this book on farce skeptical about the underlining of the "comic" elements of a marginalized genre in a peripheral region. The plays discussed here as farce do not seem at first glance to represent the more overt ideological discourse traditionally expected from Spanish American theatre, as expressed, for example, by Sandra Cypess:

> As the twenty-first century approaches, the majority of the works [of the contemporary Spanish American theatre] are concerned with the most pressing issues of the twentieth century: institutionalization of violence, humankind's capacity for cruelty, political violence, power's corrupting influence, loss of direction in an absurd universe. Issues of class, gender, and ethnic diversity are addressed on stage just as they are being asserted in the political arena. (525)

The breakdown of expectations is actually one of the key aspects of Spanish American farce in general and of the four plays studied here in particular. As part of this breakdown the artistic and the political, the personal and the collective, the simple and the complex, the serious and the comic will be playfully juxtaposed and transgressed. Consequently, Spanish American farce is seen here as a postmodern discourse that portrays on stage a dialogue with its artistic and historical past that communicates, among other things, the complexity of art and of reality.[8] In the case of the four farces under study, the breakdown of expectations is also underscored by the fact that farce's stress on physical movement is ironically subject to the overtly verbal character of these plays.

Anyone familiar with Spanish American plays of the 1960s, 1970s, and 1980s, will readily recognize in many of them an extremely ambiguous sense of humor and a playful and double-edged masking of social and cultural issues. It is particularly noticeable that, in many instances, these works explore the complexities and contradictions of their own farcical discourse, while at the same time expanding these contradictions to the level of the sociopolitical.[9] To examine these and other Spanish American plays as farce is ultimately to reveal their tendency to self-parody, their capacity to uncover and simultaneously transgress their cultural order, their artistic, social and political rituals, their literary and cultural history. Language games, humor, parody, absurdity, the contradictions of role-reversal, the emphasis on popular culture and the questioning of textuality are just some of the essential elements of farce's identity that can be easily perceived in these plays. But it is significant that these same elements are transgressed in the process of being performed, underscoring Spanish American farce's rebellious stand against multiple levels of authority–artistic, social, cultural or political. Works such as Emilio Carballido's *El día que se soltaron los*

---

[8] By characterizing Spanish American farce as a "postmodern discourse" I am underlining some of its traits: it is double-edged, focuses on marginality, refuses to be pigeonholed, rebels against authority, and refuses to provide resolution.

[9] One can obviously find farces written before the 1960s that incorporate the features of humor, self-parody, and the masking and unmasking of social issues. Already in the 1930s the Argentine writer Alfonsina Storni (1892-1938) was writing her *Dos farsas pirotécnicas* (*Cimbelina en el 1900 y pico* and *Polixena y la Cocinerita*), where self-reflexivity and the problematization of women's issues were dramatized in an effective way. Catalina J. Artesi also reminds us in her "Una nueva forma para la farsa: *Fidela* de Aurelio Ferretti," about this Argentine author's persistent interest in farce with plays such as *Farsa del héroe y el villano* (1946), *Bonome* (1949), and *Farsa del cajero que fue hasta la esquina* (1958), among others (51).

leones (1957) and *Te juro, Juana, que tengo ganas* (1965), Hugo Argüelles's *Los cuervos están de luto* (1960), Luis Rafael Sánchez's *Farsa del amor compradito* (1961), Enrique Buenaventura's *A la diestra de Dios Padre* (1963), Jorge Ibargüengoitia'a *El atentado* (1963), Vicente Leñero's *La carpa* (1971), Rosario Castellanos's *El eterno femenino* (1975), Marco Antonio de la Parra's *Lo crudo, lo podrido, lo cocido* (1982), and Sabina Berman's *Águila o sol* (1984) force one to reflect on the abundance of the farcical in Spanish American theatre and the possible "meanings" of its existence and proliferation.[10] What seems clear is that many Spanish American playwrights of recent decades are using farce to underscore but also to undermine the traditional view of the genre as ridiculous, playful, meaningless and contradictory, while they also question the more recent attempts to use farce as a vehicle for criticism. More ironically, even the many Spanish American plays that call themselves farce, either through their titles or subtitles, question their identity as such.[11]

"The Urge to Define"

Alastair Fowler may be quite right when he acknowledges that "the urge to define is nearly irresistible. Everyone writing about a group of works seems to feel that 'he must commit himself to some kind of formal definition of the genre'" (41).[12] But in this context of unfulfilled expectations created by farce, one needs to remember that in literary analysis the examination of a particular genre fre-

---

[10] In *Convention and Transgression: the Theatre of Emilio Carballido*, Jacqueline Bixler devotes the second chapter of her book, "From *farsa de verdad* to Farce as Façade," to the study of Carballido's farces, and underlines how they "stretch the traditional parameters of farce in their seriousness of purpose, sociopolitical concerns, dark undertones, and strong and often contradictory emotional impact on the audience" (51). In addition to *El día que se soltaron los leones* and *Te juro, Juana, que tengo ganas*, Bixler examines *¡Silencio, pollos pelones, ya les van a echar su maíz!* and *Acapulco, los lunes* (1969) in the light of the problematics of farce. As one continues encountering farces and the farcical in Spanish American plays, one realizes that framing plays within this particular genre and offering a catalog of them–although extremely tempting and what many readers might expect–could easily become a self-defeating task.

[11] Regarding the problematic identity of farce, Dru Dougherty acknowledges: "In the face of the variety of appearances of farce, and the plurality of its goals, the problem of the genre's coherence is raised" (126).

[12] Fowler quotes Paul Delany's *British Autobiography in the Seventeenth Century* (1).

quently becomes the study of the innumerable departures from "traditional" definitions of this genre: "To be a modern writer and to write generically is a contradiction in terms. Genre works against the text's exalted stature and, what is much the same, its power to inquire into the stature and dynamics of its own writing" (Rosmarin 7). In this tug-of-war between framing or not framing, categorizing or not categorizing, defining or not defining farce, it is both significant and somehow humorous that, for example, in a 464-page book entitled *Farce: A History from Aristophanes to Woody Allen*, Albert Bermel acknowledges quite early on that he will not attempt to offer a definition of this genre but will rather "describe and analyze farces in plural":

> Being a destroyer and detractor, farce is a negating force, hard, if not impossible, to trap and pin down. . . . Definitions in the arts are occasionally of some use, but they oblige a writer to start out by reinterpreting every word as he wants it understood and to end by defending the definition against encroachment–mending its fences to keep out poachers. If he's conscientious, he must revise his wording from time to time so that it covers new work which obstinately refuses to conform to definitions, compelling definitions to make the adjustments. If he's honest, he ultimately writes a new definition or forswears the old one. (14)

Among the multiple definitions and attempts to characterize farce, one of the recurrent issues that critics have addressed is farce's secondary position in relation to other genres and other dramatic forms. By 1959 critics were more systematically denouncing the inadequacy of traditional definitions of farce:

> [C]riticism . . . dearly loves a hierarchy, and farce, having once been relegated to the lowest level of the series headed by tragedy, has been continually taken for granted as something if not actually beneath criticism, at least beneath the need for critical discussion. Everybody knows what happens in farce: a dozen definitions in standard reference books testify to the fact that it is a "low" form of theatrical presentation, the sole object of which is to excite laughter. It is inferior in every way to "true" drama: it makes use of excessively complicated plots, improbable situations, and type characterization. It is highly unrealistic, purely ephemeral in interest, and no fit subject for serious consideration as dramatic literature. (Hurrell 426)

Much of the recent criticism of farce begins its discussion either by summarizing and dismantling the critical literature on the subject up to the 1960s or by denouncing the equivocal definitions of farce offered by dictionaries and encyclopedias. Jessica Milner Davis, for example, begins the first chapter of *Farce* (1978) with the following statement: "When the newly created Poet Laureate Nahuam Tate set out to defend farce in 1693, his literary colleagues were accustomed to employ the word as a term of contempt" (1). Davis adds: "For many people today farce is still a pejorative term" (1). In "Error in Comedy: A Psychoanalytic Theory of Farce" (1980), Barbara Freedman underlines the common but, to her, unacceptable rejection of this genre: "The widespread assumption that farce is light, inherently meaningless comedy derives from a no less reputable source than the *Oxford English Dictionary*. Here we learn that farce is 'a dramatic work (usually short) which has for its sole object to excite laughter'" (233). In a parallel fashion, Robert Williams, in "Play and the Concept of Farce" (1988), discredits the standard and simplistic definitions of farce: "[F]arce has long been considered the poor relation of comedy, if not the village idiot of the performing arts. For instance, the 1974 *Encyclopaedia Britannica* describes farce as 'a dramatic genre having no pretensions beyond provoking laughter ... it is good-natured, pointless horseplay and is aesthetically and intellectually inferior to comedy'" (58). In "Fear of Farce" (1988), Russ McDonald also considers farce's lack of prestige in the light of Shakespeare's studies: "Most literary critics have little occasion to think about farce, and those who concern themselves chiefly with the creator of texts such as *Macbeth* and *Coriolanus* do their best to avoid the form" (77). As a final example, Dru Dougherty begins his article on Valle-Inclán's farce *La Marquesa Rosalinda* by mentioning the title of Jacinto Grau's essay, "Un gran teatro en desuso, la farsa" [A Great Theatrical Form in Disuse: Farce].

At least a decade before the previous statements about farce, W. Stanley Schutz, in his 1967 doctoral dissertation "The Nature of Farce: Definition and Devices," had already summarized the persistent belief that farce's main purpose has been to arouse or produce laughter: "[F]rom Brander Matthew's 1894 essay to Leo Hughes, in a letter to this writer dated February 6, 1966, this basic purpose has been repeatedly verified. For over seventy years laughter has been recognized as the paramount purpose of farce" (125). After Schutz briefly quotes Matthew, Eric Bentley, Avery Hopwood, Maurice

Valency, Louis Kronenberger, and Elmer Blistein's ideas stressing the importance of laughter and comic catharsis (125-28), and after quoting several standard definitions of farce from Bernard Sobel's *The Theatre Handbook* (1950), Wilfred Granville's *A Dictionary of Theatrical Terms* (1952), and Bowman and Ball's *Theatre Language* (1961) (130-31), he concludes: "The indifference or prejudice reflected in such definitions can only confirm the long-standing but erroneous belief that farce is inferior drama" (131).

More recently, and even when portrayed in a positive light, farce has continued to be placed on the margins of conventional literature. Dougherty, for example, sees the displacement of farce as part of its historical reality and its strength and proposes four traits or general codes that are typical of farce: the characters of a farce are inflexible and maniacal, without psychological depth; blows and beatings are common; the spectators are emotionally detached from the play's actions; there is a pact between author and spectator that stresses the playful nature of farce (128-29):

> Everything leads us to believe that farce is a borderline theatrical form. It occupies a space between the conventional genres, allowing seemingly incompatible elements to combine within it. One indication of its liminality is the name given to Cervantes' farces–*entremeses*–and the longstanding custom of staging these between the acts of longer plays. This custom offers the first clue to be followed: it confirms that farce originates in the interstices of the theatre, in the empty spaces left by more elaborate and better regarded genres. Farce is thus engendered by theatre itself, more precisely, by what theatre lacks. One may surmise that farce provides something that theatre needs and that it manages to create only in those gaps *between* its great semantic zones–comedy, tragicomedy, drama, melodrama, etc.–. Farce therefore requires the tense but tolerant coexistence of contrary elements in their purest state. (126-27)

We have seen up to this point that critics of farce have long debated the "purpose" or "intentions" of this genre and its position and (lack of) prestige in relation to other literary forms. From this study's point of view Robert Williams's observations are among the most enlightening:

> The very substance of farce–its *telos*, if there is one–is disruption of our phenomenal world by sudden joltings, outrageous turns,

even as it gives the illusion of being involved in sane, coherent representation. Or, as Derrida might say, farce is always in a state of tension, always an interplay between form and formlessness, restraint and freedom, control and chaos. The essential dynamic of farce is its genuine playfulness, manifest in its indeterminate nature, its seemingly perverse refusal to offer glib certainties. . . . [F]arce plays not only with us but with its own game. (65)

This study proposes that one of Spanish American farce's most complex aspects and its central force lies in its attempt to transgress the traditional perception that it is an antiaesthetic, anti-intellectual, anticritical, stripped of sociopolitical agendas, unrealistic, unpretentious, solely humorous and playful genre, while simultaneously questioning the opposite attempt to stress farce's more serious and "meaningful" purposes. Ultimately, this study is concerned with the iconoclastic and transgressive stands taken by plays that not only disregard genre and gender expectations, literary and cultural traditions, and textual and political authorities, but also construct multiple voices centered on the act of unmasking rather than defining, on creating a disperse image of the self rather than on a codified and stable one.

Although the ambiguous position and antagonistic relationship of Spanish American literature with respect to the West has been emphasized in the first part of this introduction, it is obvious that any attempt to characterize Spanish American farce will be aided by important essays that examine Western expressions such as Classical, French, Shakespearean, or Victorian farce, to mention only a few.[13]

---

[13] This tug-of-war between the identification of farce as part of a long tradition of Western theatre and the overt rejection and antagonism of its Spanish American counterpart in terms of expectations and significance reflects not only this region's historical, social, and political dependence on the West but also its long-standing resentment. Focusing her study on Latin American plays of the second half of the 1960s, Diana Taylor suggests that "rather than squeeze this theatre into the so-called 'Western' tradition (the term alone relegates Latin Americans to the nonspace of the non-Western) and continue to analyze it as an offshoot of the theatre of the absurd, or Brechtian epic theatre, or Artaud's theatre of cruelty, it proves more productive to relate this discourse to other minority or marginal discourses inside and outside the West" (*Theatre of Crisis* 8). Later on, and while questioning the validity of the term "new theatre" to refer to changes in quantity and quality in the Latin American dramatic scene from the 1960s onward, Taylor explains: "'New theatre' criticism, rather than exploring alternative modes of theatrical discourse, usually legitimates *one*, the Brechtian, claiming that new theatre is epic theatre, collective theatre, and so forth. The repeated critical appeal to specific models or methodologies proves

The historical development of farce as part of the Western tradition, with its complex origins and history, becomes, then, part of the transgressive identity of Spanish American farce.

In her concise and important book *Farce*, Jessica Milner Davis traces the complex origins and history of farce:

> What little is known about the antecedents of classical Greek drama . . . suggests that Athenian dramatists of the fifth century B.C. drew upon an earlier tradition of comic village performances, which were popular among the Dorian Greeks. . . . Like Athenian Old Comedy itself, Dorian farce may well have had its roots in Dionysian festivities. Quite possibly, the ritual invocation of the wine-god and his spirit of fertility called for burlesque impersonation of gods, heroes and even local characters. The act of mimicry often instinctively takes on a comic shape; perhaps by virtue of its licensed status as play, perhaps in acknowledgment of the gap between playful image and serious reality. (2-3)[14]

Davis also reminds her reader of the origins of the term –"derived from the Latin *farcire*, 'to stuff'" (7)–and underlines its linguistic link with the Latin liturgy of the Roman Catholic Church in the period between the ninth and twelfth centuries (7). Davis continues to describe the role played by the celebration of religious feasts in France such as the Feast of the Fools or Feast of the Ass, Feast of St. Stephen, Feast of the Holy Innocents, and Feast of the Circumcision, all of which represented "an opportunity to celebrate freedom from normal discipline and to mock those sober souls who resisted this topsy-turvy reign by the 'fools,' or devotees of the ass" (9). By the middle of the fifteenth century, these feasts became more secularized (though not completely), and as a consequence "townsfolk took it over and formed their own secular societies of *sots* to perpetuate the reign of folly" (Davis 9-10).[15] Nonetheless, Davis

---

limiting. It fails to account for the multiple anti-Aristotelian, antihierarchical forms that sprang up after the 1960s: *loas*, farces (by definition an anarchic genre), *el grotesco*, the *sainete*" (*Theatre of Crisis* 43-44).

[14] Schutz also traces the origins of farce to the Golden Age of Greek drama: "While 'farce,' as a theatrical term has existed only since 1670, the comic theatre of farce predates the term by hundreds of years, very likely to the dawn of the Golden Age of Greek drama" (29).

[15] Davis describes the transformation of these feasts in the fifteenth century: "Texts from the early fifteenth century show that a typical French religious play–a *mystère* (mystery) or a *vie de saint* (saint's life)–might very well include a comic episode which was explicitly intended as comic relief" (10).

explains that comic episodes within religious plays created problems with the law and "brought about the generic distinction between the *farce* and the *sottie* as the two kinds of comic performance given by the *compagnies des fous*" (11-12). "The *sottie*," remarks Davis, "was an allegorical satire," while farce "embodied a more tolerant attitude towards man's stupidity" (12). Farces, already linked to comic mimicry, the laughable, the merry, and the lack of a formal structure (Davis 12-13), were printed in large numbers during the sixteenth century. Throughout that century, writes Davis, farce continued to be seen as "a loose genre, neither tragedy nor comedy nor pastoral, which could be easy-going precisely because it lacked classical antecedents" (13). The growth and popularity of the *commedia dell-arte* in sixteenth-century Italy, with its "visual mixture of mental rigidity and acrobatic elasticity" (Davis 15), impacted the development of farce. Davis then observes that in the England of 1660, after the Restoration period, "farce was novel, chic, amusing, probably decadent and certainly daring" (17), and during the eighteenth century "the farce-afterpiece became a regular part of the theatrical bill" (19). In the case of the English farces of the nineteenth century, Davis notes that "their fun is derived from the way in which the normal train of domestic events is transformed into a whirlwind of confusions and mistaken identities" (20). But by the end of the century and under the influence of Parisian farce, British farces began to incorporate more explicitly sexual themes (Davis 20). At this junction most critics allude to George Bernard Shaw's negative reaction to this genre: "To him, farce was merely a rarefied but not very refined form of malicious pleasure at the sufferings of others" (Davis 22). Davis's and other critics' response to this discourse of contempt against farce is not only to say that "from the Feast of Fools to the Marx Brothers, farce permits an indulgent regression to the joys and terrors of nonsense," but to underline that "its illogicality is most logical" (Davis 23). Finally, Davis attempts a characterization of the genre:

> Farce is indeed mechanical and its mechanical manipulations of plot and character distinguish it clearly from other, more flexible comic forms. Like all comedy, farce is both aggressive and festive. At its heart is the eternal comic conflict between the forces of conventional authority and the forces of rebellion. (24)

Although it is unquestionably necessary to travel to the past in search of the origins of farce, it is important to emphasize that the definition of farce derived from the works of well-recognized farceurs such as Aristophanes, Plautus, Terence, Shakespeare, Molière, Gogol, Chekhov, Feydeau, Jarry, Pinero, Synge, Shaw and Wilde, to mention a few, is part of the aforementioned tug-of-war between Spanish America's marginal position and the power and authority of the West. Part of my argument is that farcical elements in the Spanish American plays are not exclusively a consequence of Western European and US traditions of farce, and that the particular insertion of Western artistic forms into culturally and racially diverse societies during the first centuries of colonization, followed by four centuries of colonialism and political turmoil, transformed the essence of everything that was imposed on the "new" space. More explicitly, as Adam Versényi has suggested in his examination of the intertwining of religion, politics, and theatre in Latin America, a *syncretic* form of satire and burlesque was already used in sixteenth-century Nicaragua, in a play entitled *El güegüense*, to make fun of civil authority, ultimately pointing "to [a] strong indigenous influence":

> The play was written in a mixture of Nahuatl, Mangue, and Spanish, and incorporates a great deal of comic wordplay and dance as the Governor Tastuanes attempts, and finally succeeds, to bring a notorious trickster, *El güegüense*, to heel. The numerous dances interspersed throughout, the repetition of phrases in a formal manner akin to the *Rabinal Achí*, and the continuous action, all point to strong indigenous influence. (40)

It is also pertinent to allude here to Julie Greer Johnson's book, *Satire in Colonial Spanish America: Turning the New World Upside Down*, as an example of a study of a complex, problematic genre that, although linked "to ancient forms of discourse that challenged tradition and officialdom," grows in the New World "out of an extraordinary set of circumstances" (15). Johnson underscores those circumstances from the beginning and focuses on the "contrapunteo" or tug-of-war between the Europeans' high expectations inspired by the discovery of America and the disillusionment of those that began to recognize and experience the "discrepancies between the glowing visions of the New World and its strikingly distinct reality..." (1). Johnson immediately states that it is from this latter group that "the earliest writers of Spanish American satire emerged" (1).

To some extent, this synthetic view of the development of another genre (with comic overtones) in Spanish America sheds light on the suggested transformation of farce within a diverse and distinct context, and the challenges it poses regarding positionality and power. That is, from this study's point of view, Spanish American farce is consciously undermining its historical relationship to the European and US forms of the genre by transgressing its traditional generic language and conventions and constructing its own pseudo-comic and, most of all, self-conscious version of the genre.[16] The use of farce by Spanish American dramatists reveals, on the one hand, the heavy burden placed upon their cultural and literary shoulders by Western tradition and, on the other, the attempt by Spanish American theatre to establish a dialogue, to reason, to interact with the West, and, consequently, to free itself from this source of oppression. In an article on the role of history in the Third World as represented in one Latin American and one African novel (García Márquez's *One Hundred Years of Solitude* and Ouologuem's *Le devoir de violence*), Edna Aizenberg observes: "Instead of seeing the historical engagement of postcolonial fiction as evidence of Euro-North American literature's 'new desire to think historically,' with the specter, once again, of the 'center' absorbing the 'margins,' one might argue that the 'center' has finally caught up with the 'margins'" (1238).

It is indeed accurate to say that Spanish American farce takes from its Western counterpart its dual nature. But this duality reflects not so much the subjection to the center by the marginalized other as the split identity of Spanish America's art and its past and present political reality. From the perspective of a dialectic identity of farce, the study of *Revolico en el Campo de Marte*, *El suplicio del placer*, *Kathie y el hipopótamo*, and *Quíntuples* establishes an interplay among various factors: the history of farce (its origins and development); the antagonism between center and periphery in artistic and

---

[16] Self-consciousness on the part of the characters and on the part of Spanish American farces is a key element in this region's theatre. For example, when Andrea Labinger discusses the Chilean play *El delantal blanco* in her essay "The Cruciform Farce in Latin America: Two Plays," she confronts this issue of self-consciousness in the context of Davis's notions of farce: "Jessica Davis insists that the farcical character is totally unselfconscious and lacks insight into his own motivation. 'Farce,' writes Davis, 'risks its immunity when its jokes become shame-faced about their aggressions'" (224).

sociopolitical terms; and a sense of humor ambiguously related to comic catharsis and to a desire to unmask the sources of oppression–call them social, political, familial, economic, and/or artistic.[17] It should be noticed that the frequent absence of solutions in Spanish American farces, that is, their unwillingness to propose authoritative and coherent alternatives to the problems of oppression that they frequently but subtly present, flirts with the notion of farce as an apparently meaningless theatrical form. At the same time, many of these Spanish American farces avoid falling into other oppressive structures that can restrict even further the freedom of those texts to attack and unmask violently and playfully. By at times ridiculing and unmasking themselves as meaningless, and by emphasizing their ambiguous position, Spanish American farces create their own disenfranchised discourse and space, where attacks on artistic forms of communication and on social and political systems become a source of laughter and self-exposure as well as of reflection and self-examination.

The relative power of farce in Spanish America to distort, destroy, dismantle, expose, attack, rewrite, and erase lies in its experience as a victim of such acts and in its desire to redefine a discourse traditionally associated with an oppressive culture and region such as the West. The use of self-destructive and irreverent structures consciously maintains the Spanish American expression on the margins of literary studies but, by the same token, keeps it from becoming another artistic and cultural oppressor. Spanish American playwrights, obsessed with the artistic and political control exercised upon them, have realized that farce's "lack of power" and marginality can be a resourceful way to confront censorship and external aggression and a mechanism to reject the possibility of becoming part of the oppressive center. But they insist on this serious action at the same time that they play with farce's satirical and ironic sense of the self and of meaning. Ultimately, this questioning of the self and of meaning, and this absence of power, mirrors the peripheral history of Spanish America, of theatre within Spanish American litera-

---

[17] Eric Bentley stresses the connection between Aristotle and Freud by suggesting that through comic catharsis the spectator reveals repressed desires, that through jokes and laughter "inhibitions are momentarily lifted, repressed thoughts are admitted into consciousness, and we experience that feeling of power and pleasure, generally called elation" (230). This, in turn, allows Bentley to emphasize the "immense contribution of humor to the survival of the species" (230).

ture, and of farce within both Spanish American and Western literary traditions.

To resort to farce and simultaneously to move away from its conventions, as a considerable number of Spanish American playwrights are doing, is to recognize the reality and power of laughter and the fictional, deceitful source of such joy.

Throwing Bombs or Pies?

Although it needs to be acknowledged that many Spanish American plays labeled as farce, and those with farcical elements, say as much about the complex reality of their theatrical discourse as about the political and social realities of the region, it is not the purpose of this book simply to pose the traditional quandary of how these plays "combine" humor and sociopolitical criticism, that is, pies with bombs, or simply favor one over the other.[18] As Bentley clearly states: "If it is dangerous to attempt a compromise between the two conflicting opposites of a dialectic, it is disastrous to accept one and forget the other. Sheer aggression is just oppressive.... Sheer flippancy is just boring" (244). More significantly, what Bentley and other critics in the last decades have attempted to do has been to emphasize the dialectic of farce, its dual nature, its simplicity and simultaneous depth, and above all, the recognition that this dialectical relation between aggression and flippancy in farce "is one of active conflict and development" (Bentley 244), not one of reconciliation or fusion. It is in this conflictive environment that the transgressive aspect of farce has been recognized, while identifying the conventions, rules, and expectations that frame it.

The goal of this study cannot be limited, then, to identifying recurrent preoccupations and strategies of a group of Spanish American plays that exhibit important features of the genre of farce, features that, if one follows key aspects of Bentley's characterization of this genre, are of a thematic, theatrical, and philosophical nature.

---

[18] Andrea Labinger uses the pertinent phrase "to throw pies, rather than bombs, in the face of the oppressor" (219) in her article "The Cruciform Farce in Latin America: Two Plays," as she discusses the emergence of farce in the midst of a troubled region. This phrase and its context are alluded to later.

Among these features Bentley includes such issues as the problematization of the family structure, or better, its desecration (226); the cathartic nature of jokes and humor linked to the "gratification of the forbidden wish" (230); the role of violence and aggression in what could be considered "laughable" social and theatrical contexts (222-24, 240); the dialectic between farce's simplicity and its depth (241); between its gaiety and its gravity (241-42), between masking and unmasking (242); issues about the intensity of movement and the body (247-48); and about the characterization of extremes (243) and of absurdity (245).[19] Many of these features will be encountered in the four plays discussed here–and those related to farce's dual nature will be particularly stressed. Nevertheless, and to paraphrase Joseph Farrell's statements regarding Dario Fo's adaptation and parody of farce (311), this study is rather interested in the persistent dialectics of some Spanish American plays between its various artistic, ideological, and social discourses and the humorous and absurd aspects of these same discourses. From an iconoclastic angle, the plays discussed here can be characterized as engaged in "politicizing humor," that is, they launch a sardonic laugh at their serious attempt to legitimize and impart seriousness to a discourse that historically has been marginalized and considered a second-class genre.

Although I will argue that Triana's *Revolico en el Campo de Marte*, Berman's *El suplicio del placer*, Vargas Llosa's *Kathie y el hipopótamo*, and Sánchez's *Quíntuples* are particularly concerned with their identity as artistic works and as language what is political about them is their capacity to question the authoritative ideological prevalence of the plays' discourses. Farce, as many contemporary critics have suggested, is not necessarily or exclusively a laughing matter (see Farrell), and even if laughter prevails, it does so only after farce in Spanish America has transgressed its artistic identity and explored its darker and serious side.

This paradoxical angle of farce leads us to inquire into how the apparent duality emerges between the traditional wit, humor, and

---

[19] In addition to Bentley's well-known chapter entitled "Farce" in his book *The Life of Drama*, anyone dealing with either a narrow or a broad profile of farce needs to examine such essays as "Farce" by Meyerhold, "A Note on Farce," by Hurrell, "Philosophy as Farce, or Farce as Philosophy," by Perret, "Fear of Farce" by McDonald, "Play and the Concept of Farce" by Williams, Davis's book *Farce*, Bermel's *Farce: A History from Aristophanes to Woody Allen*, and *Farce: Themes in Drama* edited by Redmond.

superficiality of farce and the tendency of this discourse in Spanish America to engage in social, cultural, political, artistic, and philosophical commentary. Critics have acknowledged the borderline nature of farce: "Farce might be said to exist on the lunatic fringe of comedy and on the ludicrous fringes of tragedy and melodrama" (Bermel 52). Part of the irony of this complicated process in which a text contradicts its own expectations and codes is that the apparent meaninglessness of farce is counteracted by an irreverence before the literary establishment, before the traditional rules that define farce. The irony goes a step further when one recognizes that the breakdown of the literary establishment, which lays bare the underlying political and social content of the work, is in turn satirized together with the uncovered discourse. As Labinger has suggested, the problematic nature of Latin America's history has been dramatized by both the "serious" theatrical forms and by the humorous ones:

> Latin American theatre, like the troubled societies it represents, is no stranger to brutality, violence and humiliation, either in its unadulterated form–tragedy or melodrama–or in more ebullient guise.... While admittedly most Latin American playwrights rely on black humor, heavy-handed satire and the grotesque to communicate their dissatisfaction with social and political realities, the occasional farceur does surface now and then to relieve the bleakness and to throw pies, rather than bombs, in the face of the oppressor. (219)

What is persistently seen in Spanish American farces is the transgression of the plays' theatrical structures as well as of their ideological ones through an iconoclastic dramatic construction.

Labinger's essay discusses the cruciform structure of the Chicano work *Las dos caras del patroncito* (*The Two Faces of the Boss*, published in 1971) by Luis Valdez and of the Chilean drama *El delantal blanco* (1964) by Sergio Vodanovic. This cruciform structure involves a temporary role reversal between a character with status and power and a character who is lowly and powerless (219-20). For Labinger, the operating principles of humiliation and ridicule represented by role reversal, particularly by the transfer of external trappings from one character to another, become primary in these two plays since they "can topple the entire social order, while at the same time eliciting our laughter" (220). In the case of Spanish American farce this dual nature allows it to speak various languages simultaneously, address various audiences, and playfully undermine its apparent lack of meaning while dramatizing issues of historical and political relevance. Therefore, the "farcical dialectic of hostility and festivity," as Labinger says, quoting Jessica Milner Davis (219), portrays the nonhierarchical and apparently noncommitted position taken by Spanish American farce, all the while that it is engaged in a hostile attack on both the vehicle of communication and the content communicated. The symbolic image of two characters exchanging their dramatic roles–for example, their social positions in *El delantal blanco* and their sexual ones in Berman's *El suplicio del placer*–is emblematic of an exchange of identities and artistic, social, and sexual icons dramatized in Spanish American farce. Nevertheless, in the discussion of role-reversal in Berman's play in chapter 2, I argue that this exchange is incessant and does not attempt merely to substitute one voice, discourse, or oppressor for another but to discredit the power that displaces as well as the act of displacement.

In addition to the incisive analysis of *Las dos caras del patroncito* and *El delantal blanco* in Labinger's article, there is a less explicit recognition among critics that Latin American farce does not necessarily respond to traditional expectations of the genre: "If as Davis insists, farce is obliged to use jokes for their own sake and not 'primarily as dramatic vehicles for satirical comment upon the way of the world,' then *The White Uniform* falls slightly outside the boundaries of this *genre*. Yet, it seems unfair to exclude from the domain of farce a piece which so obviously contains many other farcical characteristics" (223). Although Labinger rejects exclusion and rigid definitions, she fails to state clearly that farce in Latin America creates and stresses its own particular features that may or may not coincide with the Western traditions of farce. Many of these plays' farcical character surfaces as they formulate their own deconstructive rules by using and questioning the genre and by searching for an independent and (self)iconoclastic voice.

SELF-DEPRECATING HUMOR

One of the most overt ways in which identification with a genre can be achieved–in this case the identification with farce–is by including the genre in the title. If, as has been stated, farce carries an ambiguous baggage in terms of popularity among large audiences *versus* its lack of reputation within the literary sphere, the act of self-identification can also be equated with self-deprecation and self-destruction. Farce's "infliction" upon itself of ambiguous and supposedly negative characteristics should be interpreted as a double-edged, playful act of constructing and questioning its own discourse.

On the one hand, it is important to recognize the implications of plays that identify themselves as farce: Alfonsina Storni's *Dos farsas pirotécnicas* (1932); Salvador Novo's *Don Quijote: Farsa en tres actos y dos entremeses* (1948); Emilio Carballido's *El día que se soltaron los leones: Farsa en tres jornadas* (1960) (the author later referred to it as *farsa didáctica*); Luis Rafael Sánchez's *Farsa del amor compradito* (1961); Jorge Ibargüengoitia's *El atentado* (1962), labeled by the dramatist as *farsa documental*; Rosario Castellanos's *El eterno femenino: Farsa* (1975); and, more playfully, Agustín Cuzzani's *Los indios estaban careros* (1958), subtitled *farsátira en tres actos*. On the other, it is equally significant to study under the rubric of farce and from these same artistic, political, and philosophical angles other plays that lack this self-identification, such as Sergio Vodanovic's *El delantal blanco* (1964), Enrique Buenaventura's *La audiencia* and *El menú* (1977), Sabina Berman's *El suplicio del placer* (1978) and *Águila o sol* (1984), Mario Vargas Llosa's *Kathie y el hipopótamo* (1983), Luis Rafael Sánchez's *Quíntuples* (1984), and Griselda Gambaro's *Real envido* (1984).[20] Obviously, the presence of the word *farce* as part of the title or subtitle of a play does shed light on

---

[20] Labinger recognizes *El delantal blanco* as borderline farce but nonetheless chooses to highlight the farcical features of the play (221); Taylor refers to *La audiencia* as judicial farce (190) and to *El menú* as "farce dedicated to democracy and social integration" (*Theatre of Crisis* 192); Ríos describes *Quíntuples* as the exception in the traditionally solemn Puerto Rican theatre (50); and the last chapter of this book examines the play as farce and the relationship of farce to incest. Boling stresses what Gambaro herself had stated in an interview, that is, the appropriate use of farce in *Real envido* to talk about greed and about the voracity and stupidity of power (Boling 77).

the playwright's attempt to call the audience's attention to the question of genre and to the play's attempt to place itself within a complex artistic dialogue. It might even serve to manipulate the audience's expectations. But what seems to link these Spanish American plays regardless of their acts of self-identification and self-deprecation is, on the one hand, their unwillingness to commit themselves to a single view of art and to a consensus understanding of social and political forms and, on the other hand, their refusal to conceal this lack of commitment. They respond uniformly neither to a particular historic-artistic pre-text nor to a dogmatic and authoritarian perception of the contextual and diverse reality of Spanish America.

Spanish American farce constitutes an expression capable of exploring its questionable nature as a form of entertainment and of denouncing in the process the grotesque parallelism between its marginal position and the internal and external isolation of Spanish America. What is observed in these four plays and in other Spanish American farces is their capacity to transgress the "rules of the game" and expose the meaningful contradictions of the genre. The possibility of playing with the notion of meaning (placing, replacing, displacing it) might not be significant for some. But it explains why Spanish American dramatists use, to describe this region's already ambiguous history and reality, a complex genre that has traditionally lacked prestige among critics and scholars and whose capacity to communicate is constantly questioned. The farcical elements of *Revolico en el Campo de Marte*, *El suplicio del placer*, *Kathie y el hipopótamo*, and *Quíntuples* offer both a view of artistic and political worlds that lack ulterior meaning and a mordant criticism of those apparently meaningless worlds.

SPANISH AMERICAN FARCES OF THE 1970S AND 1980S

Following a chronological order, but not attempting to establish a historical development of farce, the first chapter, "José Triana's *Revolico en el Campo de Marte*: Farce and Cuba's Revolutionary History," discusses José Triana's play written in 1972 and revised and modified by the author for its 1995 publication in the journal *Gestos*. One of the goals of this chapter is to confront the permeable nature of farce in its relation to other genres or discourses, particularly as it pertains to (semi)humorous artistic and cultural forms. That is, this chapter explores the implications of *Revolico*'s interaction with other similarly evasive, marginal, and fragmented forms such as the theatre of the absurd, the *esperpento*, the Cuban buffo, and the *choteo* within the context of the also ambiguously perceived and far less humorous Cuban Revolution. This study deals with the play's "contrapunteo" between a revolution and a *revolico* and shows how this counterpoint reveals Triana's critical yet playful stand with respect to the sociopolitical and ideological reality of Cuba's colonial past and revolutionary present.

Regarded as one of the most distinguished playwrights of contemporary Mexican theatre, Sabina Berman stages in 1978 what is going to be the first version of *El suplicio del placer* under the title *El jardín de las delicias*, and expands the play with an additional segment in the 1994 edition. The second chapter of this book entitled "(In)Decency and (Dis)Pleasure: Women and Farce in Sabina Berman's *El suplicio del placer*," fixes on the dialectics between issues of genre and gender and demonstrate that, in the case of a farce that deals with women's and feminist issues, these discourses become antagonistic but also complementary. That is, farce and feminist writings coincide in aspects such as aggression and transgression of norms, but in their actual interaction they unmask and parody each other's inconsistencies, underline each other's weaknesses, and defy any attempt at definition. Paradoxically, this mutual antagonism is exactly what makes them similar entities. In Berman's title, *El suplicio del placer*, antagonism and displacement become the keystones of the fragmentary nature of the play, and to some extent, these features of the play, in conjunction with the dialectics between farce and feminism, can be linked to Rosario Castellanos' *El eterno femenino* (The Eternal Feminine, 1975). Chapter 2 also explores the interaction of the notions of textual and sexual pleasures with the conventions of farce and with the discussion of the role of woman in a male-dominated society.

Although the Peruvian Mario Vargas Llosa's theatre has been accused of producing neither tears nor laughs (Pérez Blanco 207), the third chapter, entitled "Transgression, Transcription and Power in Vargas Llosa's *Kathie y el hipopótamo*," analyzes the parodic and farcical aspects of the act of communication—written, oral, and representational—and the process of artistic creation that culminates in the transcription of the inner realities of both the characters and the fiction. The complexities of communication portrayed in *Kathie* will take the analysis to an examination of rhetorical strategies, such as the abundance of metaphors and the persistent use of ironic language, and to the problematics of translation as a means to transform one type of discourse into another. Vargas Llosa's emphasis on linguistic and communicative structures also unmasks how the play confronts issues of dominance and hierarchy in artistic, social, political, and gender terms. Particularly in regard to authority and power, chapter 3 examines the way in which these issues establish an intertextual relation with narrative discourse in general (including Vargas Llosa's own novels) and with the dictator novel in particular. That is, the chapter will establish a farcical relationship between the image of the one who dictates in *Kathie* and the political dictator, between the artistic creator and the authoritative figure, between the scriptwriter and the dictator's secretary. The chapter also shows that when narrative discourse is confronted with theatrical language in farce, the play becomes a mechanism for questioning the traditionally authoritative position of narrative, even as it affirms its marginality as farce.

Finally, moving into the realm of Puerto Rican theatre and bearing in mind Rubén Ríos's humorous remarks about the lack of levity in the island's dramatic production–"Puerto Rican theatre, which is accustomed to plays that end with women setting themselves on fire, machines swallowing the protagonist, or crazed prostitutes on their way to the madhouse, does not possess an extensive tradition of farce, parody, or humor" ("Del teatro ambulante al libro")–, the fourth chapter, "Popular Culture and Classical Traditions: Farce and Incest in *Quíntuples* by Luis Rafael Sánchez," explores the tendency of farce to self-parody and to betray expectations. The chapter examines farce's capacity to dismantle its cultural order, its artistic and social rituals. The familiarity with farce by the Puerto Rican playwright and novelist Luis Rafael Sánchez dates back to his 1960 play *Farsa del amor compradito*, wherein he utilizes the characters of the *commedia dell'arte* to explore the nature of theatre and to propose a sardonic view of human and social relations. In 1984, Sánchez returns to farce with *Quíntuples*, and in a different and subtle way touches issues similar to those of his first published play. Parallel to *Farsa del amor compradito*, the farcical elements of *Quíntuples* emphasize both the dual and contradictory character of family relations (family seen in both social and political terms) and the dramatization of theatre's mask and falsehood. To some extent, neither the Morrison family nor the genre of farce are willing to conform to traditional views and expectations. Therefore, contradiction, as we will attempt to demonstrate, is at the heart of *Quíntuples* both as a strategy to examine the play's complex understanding of identity and power (artistic, communicative, social, sexual), and as a means of playing with and escaping from restrictive and authoritative forces (family, father, sexual codes, historical and political influences). As part of this generic, structural, and philosophical complexity, *Quíntuples* dramatizes the explosive interaction between the overt elements of contemporary popular culture present in the play and the oblique mythical and literary traditions of the classical past. Specifically, the use of monologue in *Quíntuples* will be linked to both traditions–postmodern performance and ancient Greek tragedy– and will also allow us to unmask the problematics of incest (notions of identity, familiarity, otherness, love, sexuality, plurality vs. singularity, parricide, and violence) in the context of farce. In other words, the final chapter attempts to demonstrate the way in which both incest and farce represent grotesque and hyperbolic expressions of love and art, and how they both aim to transgress theatrical and social communication in Sánchez's play.

This chapter and the remaining ones devoted to the exegesis of four Spanish American farces seek to demonstrate that this genre, despite its historical stigmas and contradictions, has developed a capacity to deconstruct the rules of its own game, thereby revealing its critical power. Spanish American farce is much more than a mere "laughing machine"; it is also a fearless genre that exposes, assimilates, and critiques the most powerful discourses in society.

CHAPTER 1

JOSÉ TRIANA'S *REVOLICO EN EL CAMPO DE MARTE*: FARCE AND CUBA'S REVOLUTIONARY HISTORY

¿Hubo en el mundo tal trueco?
¿Pensó el diablo tal novela?
En la invención de la tela
verán como fue embeleco
el pensamiento en que dio.
Diz que tela pueda haber
que la pueden unos ver
claramente y otros no.

Llega el legítimo y vela,
llega y no la ve el bastardo...
Yo sólo la tela aguardo;
veamos quién ve la tela.
Porque si ella se ejecuta
y la llegamos a ver,
maldito el hombre ha de haber
que no sea hijo de puta.

Lope de Vega, *El lacayo fingido*

At this point a mania set in. The rest of 1920 was passed, day by day, in a dream-like atmosphere more reminiscent of a film comedy than real life. Up, up, up, went the prices. On 2 March, sugar sold at 10 cents; on 18 March, at 11 cents. . . . The "dance of the millions" continued.

Hugh Thomas, *Cuba: The Pursuit of Freedom*

To see or not to see the Emperor's new clothes is a key metaphor in the examination, from a farcical point of view, of *Revolico en el Campo de Marte* (1972) by the Cuban dramatist José Triana (1931).[1] The possibility of recognizing what is implicit and what is

---

[1] Thanks to the generosity of my colleague Diana Taylor, of New York University, I had access in the early 1990s to a copy of Triana's manuscript, at that time unpublished. In 1994, the first version (in Spanish) of this chapter–"*Revolico en el Campo de Marte*: Triana y la farsa esperpéntica"–was published in *Palabras más que comunes: Ensayos sobre el teatro de José Triana*, edited by Kirsten Nigro, but since then both Triana's play and my own understanding and critical comments on it have gone through important revisions. The changes that Triana made for the 1995 publication of *Revolico* in the pages of the journal *Gestos* revealed his recognition that this linguistically and theatrically complicated play needed more stage directions, which could help both reader and director to disentangle the playful and witty "enredos" created in this work. Triana has indicated that the play was actually written in 1972, and the copied manuscript indicates that it premièred in reading form on December 4, 1981, at the Warner Bentley Theatre under the direction of the author and interpreted by the students of a Spanish course at Dartmouth College. José Triana was born in 1931 in Camagüey, Cuba, and after returning from exile, he began publishing his plays in 1960. It was during this decade that he published one of the best-known plays in Spanish American theatre, *La noche de los asesinos*

explicit, what is literal and what is metaphorical, what is direct and what is indirect, but, more importantly, what is revolutionary and what is a mere *revolico* (that is, something of a pseudopolitical chaotic act) in this Cuban play written in the early 1970s, reveals farce's complex mechanisms of communication, in particular its persistent dialogue with other marginal discourses. The multifaceted character of farce has been acknowledged by critics and is evidenced in the tensions between form and formlessness, control and chaos, gaiety and gravity, appearance and reality, and between symbol and object, among other polarized structures (Williams 65, Bentley 241-42). This tug-of-war between opposite forces, which has become characteristic of farce, has also entered an overtly political sphere that, in the case of *Revolico en el Campo de Marte*, underlines the grotesque parallelism between past and present events in Cuban history, of which the Revolution of 1959 represents a watershed. However, what needs to be emphasized in the context of Spanish American theatre is that farce's serious but also iconoclastic dialogue with other discourses, mainly political and social ones, emerges from its relationship with marginality, not from an attempt to occupy center stage or to search for legitimacy.

The particularity of farce as constant violator of its rules and as an antagonistic force against oppressive discourses derives in the context of Triana's *Revolico* from its interaction with other similarly evasive, marginal, fragmented, and grotesque artistic and cultural expressions and (semi)humorous forms such as the absurd, the *esperpento*, the buffo, and the Cuban *choteo*. To some extent, farce's dialogue with these already iconoclastic forms will comment succinctly on these discourses' internal ambiguities and disparities, their responses to political issues, and their lack of a fixed and homogeneous voice inside Triana's play. That is, this dialogue stresses the play's mechanisms of communication from a decentralized

---

(1965), in addition to *El Mayor General hablará de Teogonía* (1960), *El parque de la Fraternidad* (1962), *Medea en el espejo* (1962), and *La muerte del Ñeque* (1963). With *La noche de los asesinos*, Triana received the Premio Casa de las Américas in 1965, and in 1967 *La noche* became the first Latin American play staged by the Royal Shakespeare Theatre in London. Twenty years later, his play *Palabras comunes* (1987) was also staged by the Royal Shakespeare Theatre. Triana actively participated in Cuban cultural life after the 1959 Revolution, but, as Taylor reminds us, he was gradually marginalized, ceased to publish, and in 1980 again went into exile (*En busca* 3-4). *Ceremonial de guerra*, written between 1968 and 1973, was published in 1990, *Cruzando el puente* in 1993, and *La fiesta o comedia para un delirio* in 1995.

viewpoint, where, beyond the obvious historical and formal differences between farce and the aforementioned expressions, the connecting thread among them is their struggle against unchangeable linguistic, artistic, and political codes and against oppressive artistic and sociopolitical tendencies. More importantly, the presence in Triana's play of these popular and nontraditional discourses creates a unique brand of farce that shows its awareness of the artistic past, calls attention to basic denominators of humor and entertainment, and simultaneously reveals oppressive social and political structures.

The aim of this chapter is, then, to unmask in *Revolico en el Campo de Marte* both the revolutionary character of farce in its relation to other (pseudo)humorous artistic forms while also unmasking the farcical character of the ambiguously perceived and far-less-humorous Cuban revolutions of the twentieth century: one that led to Cuba's independence in 1902, and the other the widely known Cuban Revolution of 1959. This chapter attempts to prove how the explosive interaction between farce and the absurd, the *esperpento,* the buffo and the *choteo* becomes a metaphor for the scattered and violent social actions and volatile characters (evocative of revolutionary acts) in Triana's *Revolico*, which in turn reveals farce's capacity to integrate and transform the artistic and the political, past and present. Triana's play reveals farce's capacity to redefine and show both the interdependence and the conflict between a revolution and a *revolico*.

Regarding the political dimensions of *Revolico en el Campo de Marte*, some could argue that in contrast with other plays by Triana, such as *La noche de los asesinos* (1965) and *Ceremonial de guerra* (1987), where the idea of revolution has serious repercussions in artistic and political terms, in *Revolico* certain aspects of the revolutionary act are not only questioned but are represented in a frivolous light. It will be demonstrated that the identity of farce in Triana's play surfaces in the process of unmasking the tension between the supposedly serious notion of revolution and the frivolous world created by a *revolico*. That is, this study concerns the play's tension between a "sudden, forceful, and violent overturn of a previously relatively stable society and the substitution of other institutions for those discredited" (Burns 196), and a messy, confusing, chaotic, senseless, and indecipherable event. As used by Triana in his title, *revolico* refers to a grotesque and buffoonish deformation, to a frivolous overturn of a society without the possibility or intention of any substitution, but always in a tense relation to the "real" act, to the "authentic" sociopolitical and economic upheaval. Nevertheless, this so-called "real act," as Taylor reminds us, has become in the case of Cuba another repressive institution: "Revolution/repression, self-determination/colonization, progress/repetition, triumph/extinction–the dream of differentiation collapses into a nightmare of monstrous sameness" (*Theatre of Crisis* 51).

The idea of a revolutionary reality is stripped of its transcendental character, and the counterpoint between a revolution and a *revolico* is portrayed through two means. First, through the fusion and confusion of farce with other artistic and cultural expressions that traditionally have either been linked to lack of meaning, to senseless humor, or defined as marginal and grotesque (the aforementioned theatre of the absurd, the *esperpento*, the Cuban buffo and its relationship to *choteo*), all of which represent diverse moments in history. Secondly, the tension between a revolutionary act and a *revolico* is also portrayed through the juxtaposition between Cuba's "successful" achievement of political independence from Spain several years after the Spanish American War in 1898, and the frivolous and constantly changing amorous relationships that prevail among the characters, their greed, their immoral behavior, and their desire to deceive others precisely in the postrevolutionary republican Cuba of 1917. Regarding this political level one wonders what is implied by this contrast between a struggle for independence and dignity apparently achieved in 1902 and the characters' struggle for money, sex, and power in a Cuba enjoying the so-called "dance of the millions" two decades after becoming a republic. Is the implication that serious sociopolitical acts charged with moral overtones and goals will end up having messy, irreverent, and antisocial consequences? Is the play suggesting that this transformation of the revolutionary process for independence in Cuba into a mere *revolico* is nothing but a mirror image of the eventual transformation of the Revolution of 1959 into another materialistic, corrupted and frivolous era? Only in the desacralized context of a *revolico* can the spectator accept that violent acts (reminiscent of the political struggles of the end of the nineteenth century) are capable of turning into caricaturesque ones. This transformation is evident when one of the characters of Triana's play, Enrique, shoots his gun in the middle of a scene of jealousy, what comes out is not a bullet but "chorros de tinta roja" (III, i: 125) [a spurt of red ink]. The fact that violence is the product of jealousy and not caused by political struggle reveals a radical change of focus, but what makes this ridiculous act seem even more meaningful is the transformation in meaning from violent to funny, from dangerous to harmless, from the threat of death to the joy of play. Ultimately, the irony consists not in the substitution of the concept of revolution for that of *revolico*, but in the interaction and dependency between these two images that represent artistic, social, and political change.

What surfaces, on the one hand, is that farce's blatant use of liminality as it plays with antagonistic realities–humorous, artistic, political, philosophical–transgresses in *Revolico en el Campo de Marte* its own generic rules and establishes a tense dialogue with other semi-humorous and sociopolitical discourses. The tension in this dialogue arises not only from these discourses's questioning of their identity but also from their questioning of the others' through parallel discrediting and desacralizing means. On the other hand, while Triana's play exposes its fragmented nature and the disjointed links among its parts, it also uncovers political history as a series of apparently systematic though grotesque repetitions. It is significant that a play written in 1972 (a period of economic growth in the postrevolutionary Cuba) recreates events placed by Triana in the first two decades of the twentieth century. That the Cuban author stresses ambiguity regarding the specific historical time of the action –"Época: Principios de 1900 o 1917" (140) [Time: Beginning of 1900 or 1917]–suggests that *Revolico* is playing with important moments in the political and economic history of Cuba. In both cases–the Cuba of 1900 or of 1917–Triana underscores how political revolutionary events such as the Cuban War of Independence of 1898 and the 1902 establishment of the Republic of Cuba became degraded and lost their revolutionary implications through the establishment of a US protectorate in the first case, and through rampant corruption in the second case. It should be recalled that the years around 1917 have been considered an explosive economic moment in Cuban history: the so-called "dance of the millions" was characterized by an increase in the price of sugar mostly due to the collapse of European markets during the First World War, by strong foreign economic intervention, and by an environment of corruption and immorality in Cuban government and society (see Thomas 536-

43, 544-56).[2] In *Cuba: The Pursuit of Freedom*, Hugh Thomas describes the years of the Young Republic, from 1909 to 1932, and focusing on the first year of this period (1909), he stresses the economic and social progress of the next decade:

> The Cuba which Magoon handed over to José Miguel Gómez was by no means the ruined country which limped out of the war of independence with U.S. help. All provinces had increased their population.... Economic recovery from the war and improved medicine and health were partly responsible, but immigration from Spain was almost as important.... There were about five theatres in Havana, where every winter outstanding international actors and singers would appear. (497-98)

But in conjunction with this economic and social boom, Thomas also describes the increased corruption directly linked to President Gómez (nicknamed *Tiburón*): "Pardons, sewerage, telephone concessions, bridge building, barracks, all yielded lavish profits to those who surrounded the president.... Under José Miguel Gómez there began an advanced system of political corruption whereby all newspapers were recipients of government subsidies and so could never be regarded as arguing their own point of view" (504-05).

It should be clear that the frivolous attitudes of the characters in *Revolico en el Campo de Marte*, their disorderly life, their lack of dignity and sense of loyalty throughout are linked to the economic boom and to the corruption of the first decades of the twentieth century. Ultimately, this link between the social, the economic, and the political brings to the surface the parallel reality between this Cuba and the postrevolutionary one of the early 1970s when *Revolico* was written, a period characterized by a forced attempt to create an economic boom accompanied by the same deceit and corruption traditionally denounced by revolutionary governments and societies. As Taylor asks rhetorically about *La noche de los asesinos*: "Is revolution the awaited radical upheaval or yet another repetitive cycle, one more substitution?" (82).

What is of interest to us of the early 1970's is that in the midst of an economic downturn–"The harvest of 1969 was described by

---

[2] I place greater importance on 1917 because it can be seen as a culmination of a process of political and social corruption that began with the US protectorate in 1899.

Castro as 'the country's agony'" (Thomas 1437)–Castro, nevertheless, strives for an economic boom by launching the so-called 'year of Decisive Endeavor' (1969-79) which is a project "especially geared to the production of ten million tons of sugar" (Thomas 1436). The mix of this "bizarre undertaking" (Thomas 1437) with the official attempts to disguise its failure makes this period particularly significant when compared to the Cuba of the first two decades of the twentieth century, which was characterized by its economic development and corrupt environment: "In the middle of May 1970 Castro bitterly admitted that this target could not after all be achieved and that nine million would be the maximum possible.... It is also unfortunately conceivable that the figures were falsified and, providing Russia assists in the deception..., there is no means of checking the truth of the announcement" (Thomas 1437). The notions of failure, deceit, disorder, greed, economic power, and falsification seem to be recycled and "revalued" precisely after revolutionary movements have created new realities and expectations.[3]

In sum, through the emphasis on a cyclical historical structure the play indirectly evokes two parallel instances and attitudes in the history of twentieth-century Cuba: the emergence after the establishment of the republic in 1902 of a bourgeois environment that became stronger in 1917 with the "dance of the millions," and the emergence of a new, highly bureaucratized, *petit-bourgeois* (the Cuban equivalent to the Russian "nomenklatura"), created during the early years of the 1970s. Regarding this period, Carmelo Mesa-Lago states in his *Cuba in the 1970s: Pragmatism and Institutionalization*:

---

[3] Regarding the initial historical moments of the twentieth century and taking into consideration the circular view of history implied in *Revolico*, we focus on the similarities of two parallel intances in Cuban history –the 1917 "dance of the millions" and the economic growth of the first part of the 1970s. Hugh Thomas has stated in "Menocal reigned for another four years also, more or less as a dictator, governing largely by decree, drawing huge private profits for himself and his family, while Cuba itself embarked on a drive for unprecedented wealth–1917 was the year when the great new sugar plantations of Oriente began to bear fruit for the first time...." (531). For his part, Franklin Knight, discussing the economic development of the first half of the seventies, states: "Orthodoxy in the 1970s paid handsome economic dividends.... In the mid-1970s, with consumer lines shortening, the Cubans had good reason to believe that they had turned the corner. For one brief shining moment it seemed that the good times had finally arrived, justifying the revolutionary sacrifices of a decade" (250-51).

> My contention is that the Revolution has come of age and, learning from its mistakes and under Soviet influence, has become increasingly pragmatic and institutionalized. The former personalistic-charismatic regime is being transformed by delegation of power from the "maximum leader" to technocrats. . . . The romanticism of the 1960s has apparently come to an end, resulting in disillusion for permanent revolutionaries and devoted idealists. . . . The appealing, quixotic attempt to skip the transitional phase of socialism and rapidly create a "New Man" in an egalitarian communistic society through the development of consciousness, the use of moral incentives, and labor mobilization has been quietly halted. (ix-x)

Revolutions are meant to create radical social and political changes, but when they turn into *revolicos* many of their most fundamental beliefs disappear. Therefore, *Revolico en el Campo de Marte*'s portrayal of a farcical and dysfunctional social and moral reality within a politicized moment in the life of the twentieth century Cuba, and the integration within this farcical discourse of other artistic and cultural expressions are the play's most important mechanisms to deal with the issue of freedom and authority in Cuba's past and present history. These issues of freedom and authority are expressed in *Revolico* through questions of legitimacy, level of commitment to radical change, social struggles (for example, gender interaction), the syncretism of cultural and religious beliefs, and literary traditions, among other vehicles. Therefore, what is being suggested is not only that *Revolico en el Campo de Marte* criticizes the trivialization of revolutionary acts but that the author chooses to dramatize this process by displacing the supposedly serious, collective, and transcendental goals that incite a revolutionary act with the particularities and intrigues of socially and morally dysfunctional characters of postrevolutionary societies.

Revolico en el Campo de Marte is a play written in verse and divided into three acts, each internally divided into *cuadros* and scenes. The first act takes place mainly in a private space, that is, Luis's house, while the second act alternates between private and public space, between the fair taking place at the Campo de Marte and events at Luis's house. The final act occurs in its entirety in the carnavalesque environment of a fair in the Campo de Marte, and it is in this act that the notion of a *revolico*–an action that portrays images of chaos, violence, moral disorder, abuse–achieves its highest point.

Set in the Havana of either 1900 or 1917 (see note 2), the play dramatizes the story of a series of dysfunctional and greedy characters (husbands and wives, friends, siblings, lovers, members of a gang), revealing the incongruities and disharmony of social and economic relations. For example, one notices that the most prevalent element that connects one character to another is money. Luis, who is married to Alicia, lusts after Anita the maid, but he ends up falling in love with Magdalena, with whom Enrique is infatuated, but Luis has also looked at Marieta with desire, who, even though married to Enrique, is attracted to Renato. Benjamín, Luis's brother, initially seems to be drawn to Alicia, but before he ends up in the arms of Magdalena and finally stays with Marieta, he flirts with Anita, with whom Felo the servant is madly in love.

The chaotic nature of this play, filled with distrust and jealousy, furtive encounters, masquerade and ambushes, hypersexuality and obvious trickery, is exacerbated by the presence of Rosa, the *santera*, who at the request of Magdalena prepares a magic spell that will awaken Luis's desire for her:

> ROSA. Sigue punto a punto hechizo
> de albahaca, miel y granizo
> de las aguas del Leteo.
> Fíjate que es importante
> no olvidar escoba amarga
> ni el perejil ni la adarga
> del ojo abierto y brillante.
> ¡Ah!... Y otra cosa se me escapa:
> pon dos clavos por si acaso
> en medio del cielo raso
> con bufidos de siguapa. (I, iii: 145)[4]

[ROSA. Follow point by point the spell of basil, honey, and hail from the waters of the Lethe. Notice that it is important not to for-

---

[4] Because of the difficulty of translating verse and because of the highly figurative nature of Triana's language, I offer my translations of *Revolico en el Campo de Marte* in prose. I include the Spanish original to give the reader the opportunity to experience the level of complexity, the chaotic and playful construction of Triana's language, and the text's humor, which are explicit elements of this play. Translations in this chapter are mine, save where otherwise indicated.

get the bitterbrush or the parsley or the *adarga* with the wide and shiny eye. Oh!... I forgot something else: put two nails, just in case, in the middle of the ceiling while you snore like a barn owl.]

This spell will incite all the characters to the war of sex, where, not surprisingly, physical attraction is disguised as love. The sudden and unexpected infatuations will unmask both the frivolity of relationships among characters and the superficiality of their commitments.[5]

Most important, it is in the unique figure of Rosa that the fusion occurs between the traditional characterization of the Celestina type and the Afro-Cuban religious elements. In Rosa, the social and formal structures of the Golden Age comedies are linked to one of the most significant aspects of Cuba's cultural and religious syncretism, that is, *santería*. Cuban *santería* is based on the coexistence of forms and formulas of the African religious heritage and the rituals of Spanish Catholicism. One of *santería*'s most significant manifestations is the masking of Afro-Cuban deities behind Christian saints.[6] Therefore, it is not surprising that many of the characters rely on the

---

[5] Kirsten Nigro cleverly compares *Palabras comunes* with *La noche de los asesinos*, underlining the theatrical games, the sexual and political levels, and the issue of class in both plays. Interestingly, these same strategies and preoccupations are dramatized in *Revolico*, written more than a decade before *Palabras comunes*. Therefore, it is also possible to establish a "contrapunteo" or interplay between these two works. For example, Triana's literal and metaphorical interest in Cuba's transitional years, from Spanish rule to quasi- or pseudopolitical independence in the latter part of the century and the beginning of the present one, is evident in the fact that the historical period portrayed in *Revolico* (1917) covers the years immediately after those of *Palabras* (1894-1914), just when the moral and economic structures of the nation were rapidly changing. But more significant–and also humorous–is that the characters' obsession with order, cleanliness, and decency in *Palabras comunes*, and the apparent rejection of everything that is "sucio, desordenado, indecente" (Nigro, "Orden, limpieza y palabras comunes" 70) is unabashedly exalted and comically dramatized in *Revolico*. Disorder and indecency are the order of the day in *Revolico*. Nevertheless, in both cases, and also in *La noche de los asesinos*, cleanliness and dirtiness, order and disorder, and decency vs. indecency in theatre, politics, sexual relations, and class structures share a common space, making these polarities almost impossible to distinguish.

[6] Robert Lima states the following about the masking and subsequent coexistence of religious values and images in Cuban society: "Spanish-speaking countries of the Caribbean have come to call the worship of the Orishas *Santería*, a term which signifies the syncretic nature of the religion in the region, the result of dressing the African gods in Christian garb in order to circumvent the prohibition of their worship under Catholic structures in place since colonial times. Rather than abandon their deities when priest and master demanded conversion to Christianity, the slaves associated the Orishas with saints whose colors, accouterments, functions or other aspects were the same or resembled those of the African gods, gender notwithstanding" (34).

powers of the supernatural, nor is it unusual to hear in Marieta's speech how she, indistinctly and simultaneously, conjures deities from diverse religious traditions:

> ¡Nada jures!
> *(Contemplando a Renato, en un hipnótico desenfreno.)*
> ¡Perfecto cuerpo, Dios mío!
> La piel del escalofrío
> me empuja a que te conjure
> a Shangó y Yemayá. (I, iii: 145) [7]

[Swear nothing! *(Gazing at Renato in hypnotic frenzy.)* Such a perfect body, my God! The goosebumps on my skin make me conjure Shangó and Yemayá.]

To some extent, this persistent syncretism of religious beliefs reveals the characters' iconoclastic attitude toward authority and tradition, their willingness to express a freedom that is unorthodox and chaotic.

At another level, but also related to this coexistence of traditions and to the rampant chaos in the amorous arena, it is important to examine what incites Alicia to disguise herself as a man and Felo as a woman, or what incites Alicia to tell Anita to dress up with her clothes, that is, as a woman from a higher social class. In their eyes, disguising themselves as someone of the opposite sex or of another social class to reach amorous acceptance will turn their wishes and desires into reality. In *Revolico* the trick of the woman disguised as a man, and vice-versa, not only evokes Golden Age comedies such as *Don Gil de las calzas verdes* (1615) and *La villana de Vallecas* (1620), both by Tirso de Molina, but above all, it singles out the interplay of identities as a persistent preoccupation of Cuban society, culture, and literature. This emphasis on the act of disguising not only surfaces at all levels of the play–sexual, political, cultural–but poses questions about truthfulness, accuracy, identity, and integrity that are important when dealing with the counterpoint between a revolutionary act and a *revolico*. To some extent, then, the coexistence of religious and secular traditions, the particularity of Cuba's religious syncretism, the "exchange of attire" allusive to

---

[7] Shangó is the god of fire, thunder, war, and the drums; Yemayá is the deity of the sea catholicized as *Nuestra Señora de Regla* (Cabrera 88, 321).

Golden Age comedies but also to the disguise of Afro-Cuban deities, establish a relationship between the deceitful notion of sexual and religious identity, and political deceit, where instances of corruption and greed recur throughout Cuba's history and where a revolution ironically becomes a *revolico*. Triana's *Revolico en el Campo de Marte* produces a specific literary and cultural syncretism that, within the parameters of farce, becomes a succulent *ajiaco* wherein heterogeneous and apparently antagonistic structures, epochs, and dramatic forms share a common space.[8]

Revolico en el Campo de Marte's hyperaction does not diminish as it arrives at its closing moments. Towards the end of the play, there is a sudden and unexpected exchange of partners, and the magic spells–real or fictitious–seem to have acquired a life of their own by following their unique courses and whims. Luis, who lusted after Magdalena, suddenly falls in love with Marieta, and Magdalena, who cast a spell on Luis to attract him, stays with Benjamín, Luis's brother. Enrique, who was seeking revenge for his unfaithful wife, Marieta, finally stays with Anita the maid; and Felo, who was initially after Anita, ends up admiring and consoling Alicia, Luis's wife, who asks herself at the end:

> ¿Qué pasa?... ¿Estamos soñando
> acaso el sueño de un loco?
> ¿O los hechizos cambiaron
> y dislocaron antojos?
> ¿O nuestros ardides fueron
> máscaras de otros rostros
> que no pensamos ni vimos
> transformarse en azoros? (III, xx: 204)

---

[8] In *The Cuban Condition: Translation and Identity in Modern Cuban Literature* (1989), Gustavo Pérez Firmat explores Fernando Ortiz's metaphorical use of the Cuban *ajiaco*, or stew, which, in conjunction with the concept of transculturation, Pérez Firmat uses as principal ingredients to explain the Cuban condition: "[W]orks of critical criollism willingly get caught up in a *contrapunteo* between the native and the foreign. The best among them ... find interesting and innovative ways of resolving the counterpoint.... Fittingly enough, Fernando Ortiz imaged the results of process with a culinary metaphor: the *ajiaco*, a Cuban stew characterized by the heterogeneity of its ingredients. In the best cases, the translational, contrapuntal performances of critical criollism produce a savory linguistic and literary *ajiaco*: food for thought, words of mouth" (10).

[What's going on? Are we dreaming a madman's dream? Or did the magic spells change and twist our caprices? Or maybe our ruses were masks of other faces that we never imagined would turn into ghosts?]

Nevertheless, at the end of *Revolico* there is still another surprise which can be easily linked to the world of dreams: Triana winks to the (double) audience of the play as the characters themselves reveal that, all along, the action has been a theatrical game, a comedy performed by actors and witnessed by an audience that has been interacting in a carnivalesque and greedy environment:

> SASTRE. *(Mientras bebe de una botella.)*
> ¡Eyey!... Un momento, señores,
> que mi entrada ahora llega,
> que debo decir dos cosas,
> o tres tal vez....
> *(Gritos y parloteo, al fondo, entre los participantes de la comedia.)*
> Pero no..., aunque sí..., quizás...
> Todo acontece en escena,
> lo visible y lo invisible,
> pues el teatro es sorpresa,
> es exorcismo y es magia.
> *(Los actores comienzan a patear y silbar al unísono.)*
> ¡Muy bien! ¡Calma! ¡Como quieran!
> *(Al público. Secreteando.)*
> ¡Horda de fascinerosos! (III, xxi: 204)

[TAILOR. *(While drinking from a bottle.)* Hey, hey! Just a minute, kind sirs. Now comes my turn, and I must say two things, or maybe three.... *(Shouts, chatters, in the background, among the actors of the comedy.)* But no..., although yes..., maybe.... Everything happens on stage; things visible and invisible, since theatre is a surprise, it is exorcism and magic. *(The actors begin to kick and whistle in unison.)* All right! Take it easy! As you wish! *(To the audience, in secret.)* Bunch of hooligans!]

The indecipherable, hilarious, and absurd reality of the play leads to the constant rediscovery of amorous relationships among the characters. In consequence, this particular "reality" is determined by various of traits that underline the contradictory and iconoclastic view of society in general and of those relationships in particular: the apparent absence of meaning; the outrageous and crazy behavior of the characters; the possibility that the supposed reality is only a bad dream, or simply a play; the result of the magic spells; the trivialization of the "real" meaning of love; the overexcitement caused by desire; the carnivalesque environment; and the prevalent role played by the characters' literal and metaphorical masks and disguises. Significantly, Triana includes as one of the three epigraphs to his play a quotation from the Cuban novelist and poet José Lezama Lima that underscores the use of disguises as a paradoxical means of recovering one's identity: "Con el disfraz del peluquero podemos bailar las propias danzas" [With the hairdresser's disguise we can dance our own dances] (140).

But this complex, humorous plot also disguises other aspects which establish an antagonistic relationship with the messy love affairs and the continuous exchange of partners that characterize the play. This supposedly hidden level is based on a contradictory process in which both the hidden and the overtly dramatized levels of the play are transgressed on stage. That is, the incorporation in *Revolico en el Campo de Marte* of specific social, cultural, artistic, and political codes, texts, and structures that define the play is counterbalanced by the transgression on stage of these same codes, texts, and structures. One can recognize in this farce –with its clear integration of elements of the absurd, *esperpento*, buffo, and *choteo*–not only the formulas and conventions of traditional comedy with its grotesque characteristics, but the parodic and deconstructive dialogue of a work that displays a profound awareness of its own theatrical, cultural, and sociopolitical history.

To see or not to see a plurality of dramatic levels in *Revolico*, such as the intricacies of love, infidelity, sexual desire, witchcraft, violence, deceit, or greed–along with other quandaries involving where, when, and under what circumstances these levels can be seen or recognized–depends not only on the spectators' power of interpretation and familiarity with the underlying artistic and sociopolitical texts and contexts of the play but also on language's conscious (re)creation and transgression of meaning. In *Revolico en el Campo de Marte*, the apparent meaninglessness of language and action, with its idiosyncratic use of verse, its frivolous characters and relationships, and its constant mixing and matching of identities, can be interpreted as a meaningful, multifaceted response to artistic and political oppression and censorship and, ultimately, as an effective instrument of communication. Patrice Pavis's statements about farce's emphasis on movement also shed light on farce's communicative force:

> Such rapidity and force give farce a subversive nature–subversion against moral or political authorities, sexual taboos, rationalism and the rules of tragedy. Through farce the spectators have their revenge on the constraints of reality and reason; liberating laughter and drives win over tragic inhibition and anxiety, in the guise of buffoonery and "poetic license." (148)

It is not surprising that throughout the play Triana incorporates other artistic and cultural discourses which are related to linguistic games and nuances, to communicative means associated with the tension between what is meaningful and what is meaningless, what is metaphorical and what is literal, implicit and explicit, tragic and comic. In the case of the theatre of the absurd, as is well known, the action centers on problems of communication–"the *fabula* of absurd plays is often circular, guided not by dramatic action but by wordplay and a search for words" (Pavis 1)–while the *esperpento* centers, among other things, on the deformation of reality through language. In buffo theatre the popular and caricaturesque language takes center stage, and is linked to the *choteo*'s humorous and vulgar language and double entendres. Throughout *Revolico* Triana uses an array of words that reveal a great deal of linguistic fluidity and pomposity on the speakers's part but that carry a desacralizing tone and the appearance of lack of meaning. While "trápala" is a person who speaks a lot but without substance (María Moliner 2: 1367), "parlanchín" is one who speaks in excess and indiscreetly says what should be left unsaid (María Moliner 2: 644). "Pamemas," which is the crossing of "pamplina" and "memo," refers to a meaningless and simplistic phrase, to something unimportant even when someone attempts to make it a significant statement or issue (María Moliner 2: 618). Meanwhile, "monserga" refers to language that is confusing and misleading (María Moliner 2: 448). In other words, "trápala," "parlanchina," "pamemas," and "monserga" are just some of the words displaying the humorous, affected, and superficial qualities of language and of communication that Triana persistently dramatizes in *Revolico en el Campo de Marte*, while at the same time they shed light on a world that has moved from the depths of political transformation (the Cuba of 1902) to the shallow waters of sexual innuendoes and disputes.

As part of this caricaturization of the communicative medium, one recognizes how the pseudopoetic and consequently parodic character of the play is dramatized by the use of octosyllabic verses sporadically interrupted by hendecasyllabic sonnets, both of questionable literary value.[9] In addition to the indirect link between Triana's play and Valle-Inclán's and Lorca's farces, the popular, humorous, farcical, and even anachronistic use of verse reminds the spectator of the Golden Age comedies. As Charles Aubrun has stated in discussing the preferential treatment of verse in the Spanish comedy of the seventeenth century:

> There is nothing surprising in such a total rejection of prose as a vehicle of dramatic expression. First, Spanish theatre is both tragedy and comedy: between the traditional verse of the former and the possible, but not obligatory, prose of the latter, the balance favors the more elevated and pathetic mode. Second, . . . [comedy] is addressed to a mainly illiterate, but cultivated, audience. For them, verse is easier to remember. . . . Finally, the use of verse accentuates the distancing effects between reality and fiction, between theatre and stage, between life and the transference . . . to dramatic adventure. (31-32)

Versification in *Revolico en el Campo de Marte*, in addition to invoking the tone of the cloak-and-dagger plays and the comedies of intrigues, creates a popular and farcical atmosphere that parodies the most important structures of Cuban literature, culture, and society. The musicality of the octosyllabic verse (which the Cuban buffo mixes with prose) characterizes the rhythmic and desacralizing tone evident in Triana's play.[10] The active interaction and exchange of

---

[9] Throughout *Revolico* it is possible to connect the use of hendecasyllabic sonnets with moments of introspective reflection on the part of the characters. They seem to have recourse to a more intellectual verse form when they are by themselves and are attempting to understand their feelings and the world in which they live (*Revolico* II, vii: 176).

[10] As Rine Leal notes: "the buffo language . . . becomes a rhythm, a manner, a sound and a tongue different from that of Spain" (18).

identities among the characters in *Revolico* reproduces a particular environment where the musical aspects of the dramatic work and the pantomimic movements become the emblems of (linguistic) communication and action. It is possible, then, to recognize the dual role of verse: on the one hand, it evokes and theatricalizes important literary systems from both the Hispanic tradition and the Afro-Cuban and popular one; on the other hand, it parodies those systems as it recontextualizes them within an absurd plot and within contemporary Cuban theatre and society.

As Valle-Inclán had done before in his cycle of farces in verse, Triana fuses the sentimental with the grotesque, which in the literary production of these two playwrights turn out to complement and contradict each other by overtly dramatizing the way language is used (see Ruiz Ramón 111). Ruiz Ramón, reflecting on the use of language in Valle-Inclán's farces, states: "The coarse and vulgar language responds to a stylistic norm that is, naturally, not only a reflection of a degraded world which the author presents on stage, but also the most effective instrument of alienation between the author and his dramatic world" (114). Ultimately, the distancing effect between reality and fiction created by the use of verse places the attention on theatre as theme. That is, it focuses on the characters' disguises, on their masks, on their pseudopoetic and farcical language, on the interplay of movements, and on the caricaturization of violence as a way to question the social and political system, which, ironically, supports and controls the artistic one. The sudden disclosure at the end of the play that the characters are actually actors of a comedy takes the distancing effect even further, since it leads to a reinterpretation of the frivolous action, the bizarre relationships among the characters, their use of disguise, and the issue of communication (meaning or lack of it). But even after this revelation there is yet another transgression: the Sastre announces the end of the comedy as determined by the author: "Y en llegando a este punto/ se termina la comedia,/ dice el autor y se mete/ en el cáliz de una adelfa" (III, xxi: 204) [Having reached this point there ends the play, says the author, as he hides himself in the chalice of an oleander]. But the Tailor also announces his intention to add his own ending, his own view of the coexistence between reality and the world of dreams: "Y tomando este pretexto/ yo decido cornamenta/ de un discurso que he soñado/ soñando que alguien me entrena" (III, xxi: 205) [Taking this as a pretext, I'll decide how to crown a discourse I have dreamt while dreaming that somebody's training me"].

Farce is then contradictory and transgressive in nature and constantly rejects possible conclusions. Through language, gestures, and caricaturization, farce is capable not only of characterizing a world lacking ulterior meaning, but also of launching a mordant criticism of that same meaningless world. The fragmentation or distortion through farce of social rituals that are more or less familiar to all, are represented in *Revolico* through the parody of traditional love, "amorous" relationships, and social hierarchies. As Bermel reminds us:

> Farce does at least two things with, and to, [familiar social ritual]. It borrows or recreates it from life, rigidifying it, making it look exaggeratedly schematic, and therefore ludicrous. . . . Farce will then often subvert the ritual, giving it an unforeseen, disorderly ending. Art is said to pluck order out of chaos. Possibly so, but in farce the orderly ritual has a way of degenerating into chaos. (8)

The emphasis on the interplay between the absence and the proliferation of meanings and angles proposed by the farcical nature of *Revolico* can be linked to the same interplay that characterizes the theatre of the absurd. Pavis underlines the historical relationship between the absurd and farce in his definition of the former: "Among the theatrical precursors to the contemporary theatre of the absurd are farce, parades, grotesque interludes in Shakespeare and Romantic *drame*, playwrights who defy categorization such as Apollinaire, Jarry, Feydeau and Gombrowicz" (2). In Triana's play the tug-of-war between what is meaningful and what is meaningless appears as a collage of palimpsests, which tend to dismantle the more literal dimension of the action frequently identified with the clumsiness and stage tricks of farce. But at the same time, it is the questioning of the superficial plane that gives a deeper meaning to the use of farcical elements in *Revolico*. Significantly, the fact that, as Pavis indicates in his definition of the absurd, "Man is a timeless abstraction incapable of finding a foothold in his frantic search for a meaning that constantly eludes him. His actions have neither meaning nor direction" (1) demonstrates that it is only when searching for a meaning that it becomes clear that it cannot be found.

In an attempt to establish a parallelism between the parodic and farcical character of Triana's play and the plurality of levels of communication and meanings that characterizes the absurd (including the lack of meaning), the structural and philosophical aspects of the play coexist with the sociopolitical in an implicit realm. More importantly, *Revolico*'s reflections on its complex identity as farce establishes a dialogue with the absurd, which, in the case of the Spanish American tradition, has struggled in a parallel way with its plural meanings and its political commitment. The complex interaction between *Revolico*'s farcical tone and the strong tradition of the theatre of the absurd in Cuba since the late 1940s–notwithstanding its eventual rejection during the postrevolutionary period–underscore the common elements of these two discourses and their particular artistic and ideological distinctions.[11] It is clear that *Revolico* distances itself from the so-called pure aesthetic of the absurd in vogue before the Cuban revolutionary period and during the first years of the Revolution (Montes Huidobro, *Teatro puertorriqueño* 455).[12] But this distancing does not occur simply by changing from the implicit antidoctrinal use of absurdist features to their explicit functional and referential use, that is, from the aesthetic to the ideological.[13] Rather, this distancing that emerges *from* both extremes becomes the *raison d'être* of the work. As suggested, the success of Triana's play consists in the counterpoint between *revolico* and revolution, between carnivalesque upheaval and a radical sociopolitical change.

It is precisely as part of the tension between the subtle presence of ideology and its more overt stand within the absurdist expression of theatre that this study will briefly compare *Revolico en el Campo de Marte*'s absurdist features with those of the play *Carnaval afuera*,

---

[11] In 1949 the Cuban dramatist Virgilio Piñera published what is considered the first play of the new theatre of the absurd in Spanish America, *Farsa alarma*. Terry Palls reminds us that the publication of this play in the journal *Orígenes* (vols. 21-22) predates the eventually prestigious European absurd theatre of Samuel Beckett and Eugène Ionesco (26).

[12] Since I later allude to Matías Montes Huidobro's *Persona: Vida y máscara en el teatro cubano*, but most of my quotations are from his book *Persona: Vida y máscara en el teatro puertorriqueño*, I will identify them in parentheses with the last part of their respective titles: *Teatro cubano* and *Teatro puertorriqueño*.

[13] The antidoctrinal stance of the prerevolutionary absurdist theatre is one of the reasons the Cuban literary revolutionary establishment rejected the theatre of the absurd and considered it suspicious (Montes Huidobro, *Teatro puertorriqueño* 455-56).

carnaval adentro (1960) by Puerto Rican dramatist René Marqués. Although these two plays fluctuate between the discourse of farce and that of the absurd, the interaction of these two discourses varies in degree, intensity and, above all, perspective.

In *Persona: Vida y máscara en el teatro puertorriqueño* (1986), Montes Huidobro focuses on *Carnaval afuera*'s particular codes and their relationship to the theatre of the absurd. More significantly, he compares them with those of Cuban absurdism: "The tragic paradox of the absurd is that it begins as an antibourgeois reaction, but since it has a plurality of meanings, it never responds to strict political norms. Marqués's play distances itself considerably from the *implicit* connotations of language to become in many cases *explicit* and functional: therefore, it also distances itself from the antidoctrinal norms of the Cuban absurdism" (456, my emphasis). For Montes Huidobro, *Carnaval afuera* and the Cuban theatre of the absurd differ in the explicit didactic and ideological development of Marqués's play in contrast to the implicit levels of political commitment of the Cuban expression.

More specifically, *Carnaval afuera, carnaval adentro* allegorizes the destructive subordination of Puerto Rican values to the powerful and oppressive economic, political, and social forces of the United States. Regarding the allegorical nature of many Spanish American plays, Tamara Holzapfel observes: "This tendency to allegorize national as well as universal reality seems to me to be the distinctive mark of absurd drama in Spanish America. A strong critical sense toward an unjust social order has traditionally permeated Spanish American literature, and given the present-day socioeconomic situation and political conditions, it is not surprising to encounter the 'denuncia en el aquí y el ahora' even in form-conscious literature such as the new novel and the theatre of the absurd" (40). Through the use of festive and farcical elements, such as the presence of *vejigantes* or carnivalesque figures, drum music, linguistic absurdities, change of roles or identities, pantomime, and others, René Marqués creates a codified artistic world that mirrors and parodies the values of a society that subjects itself to appraisers and is willing to sell itself to the highest bidder.[14]

---

[14] While Zalacaín's underscores *Carnaval afuera*'s self-referentiality, he also recognizes the political stands of the play as he decodes its allegorical plot: "Little by little, the Puerto Rican has sold everything that identified him with his reality in

The brief comparison of this Puerto Rican play with the Cuban absurdist expression suggests that *Carnaval* is overtly concerned with sociopolitical themes and linked to ideological rigidity, while the Cuban form of the absurd reflects–at least until the first years of the Revolution–a stronger commitment to its traditional aesthetics. Cuban absurdism is characterized by its exploration of language and human communication, its antidoctrinal tendencies, its nonrevolutionary thematic development, and its nonrealist stylistic construction (Montes Huidobro, *Teatro puertorriqueño* 455-56; Palls 26).[15] In comparison with this aesthetically oriented view, Montes Huidobro argues that although the aesthetic code was more important in the Cuban absurdist theatre than the revolutionary one, "the multiple meanings of the key elements of the absurd clash with the strict doctrinal systems: therefore, many of these approximations are conditioned by the political reality of the historical processes" (*Teatro puertorriqueño* 455-56).

The pertinence of these comments regarding *Carnaval afuera*'s relationship with the theatre of the absurd in general and with *Revolico* in particular is that *Carnaval*'s emphasis on the doctrinal and on the politically explicit distances it from the plurality of meanings traditionally expected in absurdist expression. Critics have fre-

---

exchange for cement and the machine..., sacrificing his innocence, his art, and his liberty for material benefits" ("René Marqués" 36-37). One should also stress that *Carnaval afuera*'s double ending reflects the supposed conclusion of the farce that has been represented, but not the actual end of the play. Both Tía Matilde and Ángel acknowledge that, after the actors and audience leave the theatrical illusion and the theatre, they are walking into another farcical reality, that of a carnivalesque and senseless country:

> ANGEL. ...The farce has ended! *(He open his eyes and realizes that he is in front of the audience. Slowly he puts down his arms, bitter.)* But...! Yes, yes, I should have imagined it. You. For you, out there, the carnival continues. *(He smiles weakly.)* Always that carnival of yours! *(He laughs heartily.)* (III: 128)

Tía Matilde closes the (second) play saying: "Let us all be humbugs and hypocrites, like them! Bow, actors! Bow!" (III: 130).

[15] Montes Huidobro, who notes that *Carnaval afuera* was initially rejected for representation in Puerto Rico for political reasons and was premièred in Havana in 1962 clarifies: "The exaggerated caricaturization of the Cuban exile was appropriate for a pro-Castro audience, although in stylistic terms it arrived at an inadequate moment, since the climax of the Cuban theatre of the absurd had already vanished" (*Teatro puertorriqueño* 454-55). Montes Huidobro then adds that during the Revolution the Cuban absurd theatre lost significant terrain and became quite suspect, since it did not reflect the objectives of the new social, political, and economic movement (*Teatro puertorriqueño* 456). See Palls 27 and Holzapfel 40.

quently noted that the absurd theatre in Spanish America does not limit itself to social criticism and to portraying the existential anguish of human beings in modern societies but is actively engaged in political issues.[16] What Montes Huidobro argues is that *Carnaval* removes itself even further from the implicit and antidoctrinal stands of the European-like theatre of the absurd, and in the examination of the play he stresses the ideological dogmatism and the serious limitations imposed on the literary analysis by the reinforcement of basic (political) clichés (*Teatro puertorriqueño* 465). If, as Montes Huidobro suggests, "the absurd is a stage clue that functions in opposition to logic" (*Teatro puertorriqueño* 455), then everything that is predictable and deliberate (with the exception of the "anticonventional logic itself") will reflect the mimetic, explicit form of representation that the Cuban theatre of the absurd has frequently avoided.

This discussion regarding a Puerto Rican play with absurdist touches and its counterpart the Cuban theatre of the absurd, underlines both the plural character of this theatrical expression and the multiplicity of meanings in Triana's *Revolico en el Campo de Marte*. If we follow closely the aforementioned development of absurd theatre in Cuba, Triana's play should at least in theory have distanced itself from the antidoctrinal and implicit Cuban theatre of the absurd prior to the Revolution, and it should have revealed explicitly its political stand. But ironically, part of the revolutionary aspect of the play is its reconsideration of this earlier notion of the theatre of the absurd as implicit and antidogmatic though not politically

---

[16] Several important studies that address the distinction between the development, antecedents, and major exponents of the European theatre of the absurd and the Latin American expression, and that address the existential and social preoccupations of the former vs. the politically oriented aspects of the latter, are Daniel Zalacaín, *Teatro absurdista hispanoamericano* (1985; see also "René Marqués, del absurdo a la realidad," 1978), and Raquel Aguilú de Murphy, *Los textos dramáticos de Virgilio Piñera y el teatro del absurdo* (1989). Zalacaín suggests that for René Marqués "reality is chaotic only in so far as the supremacy of the United States over Puerto Rico continues; once this influence ceases, reality would offer hope," and then he adds, "Marqués always deals with the absurd in terms of Puerto Rico's sociopolitical reality" ("René Marqués" 35, 36; also *Teatro absurdista* 79). Tamara Holzapfel, in "Evolutionary Tendencies in Spanish American Absurd Theatre" (1980), identifies the absurd theatre as "diverse and unprogrammatic," stressing in this way its multiple manifestations and the various directions that this theatre has followed (see 37). Holzapfel adds that "it is increasingly meaningless to distinguish between socially committed and avant-garde dramatists" (37).

neutral. In other words, *Revolico*'s antagonistic view of the Cuban Revolution revalues the codified prerevolutionary understanding of absurd theatre, particularly its notion of a plurality of meanings that coexist within the text and in opposition to an explicit commitment to the political and ideological.[17] Triana's significant contribution is that his play breaks with prescribed patterns: on the one hand, it distances itself from the theatre of the absurd's connection with aggressive artistic transgressions and disdain for politics. On the other, *Revolico* breaks with the Cuban postrevolutionary theatre's rejection of the artistic and linguistic experiments of the theatre of the absurd. This also implies a rejection of Cuban postrevolutionary theatre's emphasis on the political "reality" that surrounds the action. By distancing itself from both extremes, *Revolico en el Campo de Marte* creates a dialectical relationship between past and present in artistic and political terms, in which the implicitness of the artistic past coexists with the explicit ideological commitment of the artistic present.

As part of the relationship between farce and the absurd, it is possible to recognize certain parallelisms between these two dramatic expressions and the discourse of the *esperpento*, especially as we focus on the personal and collective deformation of the characters' reality and actions, and on the sociopolitical implications of this deformative process: "¡Oh torcida suerte!,/ de un gigante o

---

[17] In his analysis of Triana's *La noche de los asesinos*, Eduardo Lolo examines critics' emphasis on the ambiguity and plural meanings of the play, particularly as most of them discuss the historical space that *La noche* occupies and attempts to recreate (35-37). At a primary level, Lolo supports the view that *La noche de los asesinos* portrays the end of the 1950s and the first part of the 1960s, and not Batista's Cuba from 1952 to 1958. But by the end of Lolo's essay, the opposing critical positions regarding the historical space are less explicit than was previously suggested: "[I]t is now evident for me that the promoters of both interpretations were exaggerating their respective endorsements. I don't deny the logic of their differentiating characteristics, but I question their excluding features" (43). Lolo believes that if *La noche* had been written during the 1950s, the young people oppressed by the Batista government would have interpreted the play in a fashion similar to that of the oppressed youngsters under Castro's regime ten years later. For Lolo, both the parents and the children in Triana's *La noche* are the same characters, extracted from different periods and juxtaposed within the fictional time of the play: "[T]hey were, in other words, the oppressed youngsters of the 50s confronted with their own image as oppressors in the 60s. . . . There is no dichotomy in *La noche de los asesinos*, but juxtaposition; no ambivalence, but synthesis. A synthesis that, to escape from Castro's censorship, disguises itself as ambiguity, but whose end result has been universality" (44).

más bien zorro/ soñábame sostenida/ existencia y desemboco/ en ridículo esperpento" (III, xix: 202) [Oh twisted fate! I dreamed I was a giant or better yet a fox, and I end up as a ridiculous esperpento]. It is not mere coincidence that Francisco Ruiz Ramón stresses both the artistic and the social dimensions that gave birth to the *esperpento* and its intrinsic relationship with the absurd: "The deformation and disjointment that are instrumental in the *esperpento* would be the only way to show a specific reality critically, provoking a direct awareness of the absurd character of that reality" (126).

We turn here to the discourse of the *esperpento* as a way to underscore *Revolico*'s emphasis on grotesque and caricaturesque actions and relationships. This emphasis, in turn, unmasks the play's reflection on the similarities between the social and political chaos of the Cuba of the first decades of the twentieth century and the chaos and hypocrisy of the revolutionary Cuba of the seventies. The play's emphasis on showing the deforming and degrading side of the characters' personal and collective reality (their materialistic, selfish, and corrupted behavior) reflects the carnivalesque nature of a world that seems oblivious to the struggles for freedom and dignity of its revolutionary history and gives preference to deception, to fraud, to swindling:

> SASTRE. A esto se llama chantaje
> y es una inconsecuencia.
> ROSA. ¡Asúmete!
> *(Vuelve a repetir el registro: ahora de otro modo, hasta que logra quitarle el dinero.)*
> ....
> *(Guardando el dinero en sus bolsas, con mucho orgullo y desplante.)*
> Bien sabes que soy brujera
> y si mi trabajo ignoras
> pregúntale a las señoras
> del Cerro y de la alta esfera
> que me consultas..., y espera...,
> *(Gritando.)*
> que me voy, ay, que me iré
> en la escoba de la fe
> y la cachimba soplando...

SASTRE. *(Gritando.)*
  ¡Aguanta!...
ROSA.   Me está empujando
  el muerto de Mamá Inés.
  *(Se va volando en una escoba. El Sastre corre detrás
  de ella. La música apaga a veces el ruido de relám-
  pagos esporádicos.)* (III, xv: 198)

[TAILOR. This is blackmail, pure and simple, and also an inconsistency.
ROSA. Get ready!
(She again repeats her inspection, now in another fashion, until she manages to take his money.)
....
(Stashing the money in her bags, proudly and boastfully.)
You well know that I'm a witch; and in case you don't know, just ask those ladies on the Hill and the upper levels...and wait... (Shouting.)
I'm going, aiee!, I'll go in my faithful broom and puffing on my pipe...
TAILOR. *(Shouting.)* Wait!
ROSA. I'm being pushed by the dead man of Mama Inés!
(She flies off on a broom. The Tailor runs after her. The music at times overshadows the thunder of occasional lightning.)]

Critics have identified the *esperpento* with terms such as "distancing," "theatre of the absurd," "antitragic theatre," "degrading vision," "theatre of protest," "defamiliarization" (see Ruiz Ramón 118). Therefore, what is interesting about this artistic manifestation in the context of *Revolico en el Campo de Marte* is the perception of a world where the marginal prevails, where characters and actions are constantly displaced, decentralized, questioning in this way the artistic and cultural structures of the past, as well as the social and political structures of the postrevolutionary present. It is even more important to recognize that the characters' inclination to simulation and disguise is an explicit sign of the play's attempt to communicate at various levels. On the one hand, *Revolico*'s messy and caricaturesque portrayal of the characters' relationships and social reality emphasizes trickery, language games, making a fool of the other and laughing on the other's behalf. On the other hand, this emphasis on simulation and disguise forces us to question *Revolico*'s playful and comical environment. It forces the spectator to look for what is behind the mask, behind the disguise, even behind the historical façade. In Rosa's double-edged conversation with the Tailor the struggle between the appearance of honesty and the reality of hypocrisy is more than evident:

> SASTRE. *(Balbuceante.)*
> ¡Tú!...
> ROSA. ¡Atrevido!
> *(Otro tono.)*
> ¡En el anzuelo cayó!
> SASTRE. Si usted desea...
> ROSA. ¿Que yo
> deseo?... ¡Me has confundido!
> Sólo te pido servicio
> de amistad, y a la verdad...
> Pero si tu honestidad
> no accede... Mil beneficios
> me debes, tú, Caricato...
> ....
> Si me falla no sé lo que hago.
> Como sorda, como muda
> me fingiré... *(Pausa.)* ¡Sangre suda
> Cristo! (II, v: 168-69)

> [TAILOR. *(Stammering.)* You!
> ROSA. How dare you! *(In another tone of voice.)* I've hooked him now!
> TAILOR. If you desire...
> ROSA. Me, desire? You've misunderstood me! I'm only asking you for the service of your friendship, and in truth... But if your honesty doesn't allow it... You still owe me a thousand favors, Caricato...
> ....
> If this fails me, I don't know what I'll do. I'll pass myself off as a deaf-mute. By Christ's bloody sweat!]

From this study's perspective, the interaction between farce and the *esperpento* in *Revolico* not only underscores its intertextual dialogue with other theatrical forms that are transgressive, iconoclastic, plural, and marginal in nature, but also questions the truthfulness of the actions and intentions of the characters and of their world. Are these characters merely caricatures who live in a senseless and trivial world? Or should the spectator interpret the deceitful nature of their actions as a way to question the play's apparent frivolity? This level of contradiction and uncertainty about the communicative levels of the play can be linked to the identity of the *esperpento*. For example, even after offering a synthesis of the theories of the *esperpento*, Ruiz Ramón asks himself: "is the *esperpento* tragic or anti-tragic?" (126), a quandary which reveals the plural interpretive approaches to this artistic form. In the case of *Revolico* this plurality and uncertainty of meanings is expressed in the dichotomy between the rational and the irrational, the *ser* and the *estar* as the tailor questions what is real and what is not:

> SASTRE. Y la realidad es como un río
> y en tu sueño su realeza
> de *razón y sin razón*
> urde castillos de fiesta.
> La máscara da un sentido
> a tu proverbial extrañeza
> de *ser y estar*, porque el tiempo
> es la máscara que sueña
> y que te viste los huesos
> en su variable estridencia,
> y *ser y estar* es lo mismo
> que el tiempo que desencerra.
> (III, i: 128, my emphasis)

[TAILOR. And reality is like a river, and in your dreams its realism of reason and unreason conjures up festive castles. The mask gives meaning to your proverbial strangeness of being and seeming, because time is the mask that dreams of and dresses your bones in their variable stridency, and to be and to seem is the same as time, which uncovers everything.]

The interaction between farce and the *esperpento* in *Revolico en el Campo de Marte* stresses the attempt to address the contradictory identity of these two discourses as vehicles of artistic and sociopolitical revolutions and as parodies of themselves and of others. And in more concrete terms, the fact that Triana's farce establishes this dialogue with the *esperpento* suggests the play's awareness of its covert political overtones, while at the same time showing its desire to confront and carnivalize its ambiguous connection to ideology and political revolution. One could say, then, that in Triana's play the end product is a hybrid, where revolution as instrument of artistic and social change and *revolico* as the carnivalesque and chaotic transgression of these changes all coexist in a single space questioning each other's intentions and identities.

It is in an environment of disorder, lack of values, excessive histrionics, racial and social conflicts, political corruption, and amorous intrigues that *Revolico en el Campo de Marte* directs the attention to one of the most important theatrical manifestations in Cuba's dramatic development: the buffo. The abundance of intertexts in Triana's play, the already established relationship between farce, the theatre of the absurd, and the *esperpento*, and the implicit and explicit allusions to artistic forms of the past, all open the door to the phenomenon of the Cuban buffo (with its racial and class implications). Significantly, Cuban buffo had its initial impulse at the end of the 1860s, when a colonial Cuba was experiencing economic and political crises: "1867-8 was a year of revolutionary formation" (Thomas 242). [18] It is clear, then, that *Revolico* has not only explored the farcical and parodic elements of the action by creating a dialogue with various literary and cultural discourses from various traditions, but it has also established a link with multiple historical realities in Cuba's political trajectory such as the years after the founding of the Republic of Cuba in 1902 and the 1959 Revolution. Not surprisingly, as we reflect on the Cuban buffo in Triana's *Revolico* we are forced to reflect on the revolutionary movement with which it coincided. Cuba's struggle against Spanish colonial power at the end of the 1860s and the annexationism of some who wished to join Cuba to the United States underscores the island's cultural and political turmoil, which would have its repercussions in the two Cuban revo-

---

[18] Regarding the origins of the Cuban buffo, José A. Escarpenter and José A. Madrigal comment: "On Sunday, May 31st, 1868 the *Bufos habaneros* theatre company makes its first appearance in the Teatro Villanueva in Havana, an event that will mark the starting point of a new mode of Cuban popular theatre" (15). Escarpenter and Madrigal add: "The titles and some of the texts that have survived display four main trends in buffo genre: the parodic vein, the *campesina* (or peasant style), the *catedrática* (which parodied intellectual pretensions), and the *costumbrista* (or comedy of manners)" (16). One can see that the origins of the Cuban buffo in 1868 forces us to think of the political events of that year. The *Grito de Yara* of 1868, which began with the planters of the east rising against Spain (Thomas 245), had, as one of its concerns, the abolition of slavery, but as it turned out this subject could not be addressed immediately, and it was not until 1882 that slavery was finally abolished in Cuba.

lutionary movements of the twentieth century. Therefore, it is evident that *Revolico en el Campo de Marte* shares parallel structures and themes with the theatrical form of the Cuban buffo while at the same time is linked to a period of political instability. Rine Leal defines Cuban buffo in the following terms:

> It is a genre that includes music and dance. It is parodic and popular. *It desacralizes the major themes of the past.* Caricaturesque, it lacks any moralizing intention. It is a reflection of daily life, the history of a people without history. It is a scene based on circumstances, satire and *choteo*. It lacks literary anxiety and the desire of immortality. It is more representational than textual, it is intention more than literature. (23, my emphasis)

José A. Escarpenter and José A. Madrigal underscore in their characterization of the Cuban buffo the focus of this popular expression on the theatrical rather than on the literary, on the comical rather than on the serious (19). For the buffos the spectacle was not only more important than the text, but their purpose was to entertain with plays which would make fun of the popular customs of the day (Escarpenter and Madrigal 19). Undeniably, some of the elements characteristic of the Cuban buffo are present in the farcical, parodic and caricaturesque nature of Triana's play. The popular dimension of its language ("tremendo vacilón," "ninfa pitoflera," "vieja pelleja," "cabeza de pirulí," "pan de piquito") and the ridicule of social relations and amorous feelings coincide with some fundamental themes of the Cuban buffo, which throughout its history also experienced important transformations.

Another dimension of buffo theatre alluded to by Rine Leal is the presence of the *choteo*, which in the case of *Revolico* can be connected to its carnivalesque environment, to the abundance of sexual innuendoes, to a disorderly world, to a lack of dignity, and to the rejection of authority (see Mañach, *Indagación del choteo*).[19] In the

---

[19] Not surprisingly, the Cuban *choteo* can be closely linked to the contradictions and excesses of *Revolico*. As defined by Jorge Mañach and glossed by Pérez Firmat, the *choteo* exemplifies the persistent dichotomy evident in Cuba's history and in the Cuban sense of humor: "No matter what the angle of approach to *choteo*, and there are many–etymology, psychological causes, environmental influences, social consequences–Mañach proceeds by first making distinctions and subsequently placing *choteo* on both ends of the dichotomy. One major example: much of *Indagación* is given over to a discussion of whether *choteo* is pernicious or salutary; after weighing both alternatives, however, Mañach concludes that it is both" (Pérez Firmat 54).

second act Triana offers the following stage direction as he describes a scene between the scoundrels Felo, Rufo, Pito, and Curro: "Divertido, mientras Felo se desnuda. La escena toma por momentos, un aire de franco choteo" (II, 5: 173) [Amused, while Felo undresses. The scene takes on, at certain moments, an openly mocking tone]. It is evident that *Revolico*'s action is primarily motivated by the characters' sexual drives and caricaturesque desires (Benjamín experiences an amorous trance, and Anita wants to appease his desire with water, I, xi: 156), and it is also evident that most of the dialogues are permeated by humorous and vulgar double entendres:

> OLEGARIO. ¿Y dónde me sitúo...?
> CANDELARIO. ¿El pito?
> *Largas risotadas, barullo.*
> OLEGARIO. ¡Huevos, berraco!
> CANDELARIO. ¡Huevitos!
> *Otras risotadas. Aumenta la confusión entre los seis hombres.*
> (II, v: 171)

> [OLEGARIO. Where do I place...?
> CANDELARIO. Your weewee?
> *Intense laughter, uproar.*
> OLEGARIO. Eggs, beast!
> CANDELARIO. Small eggs!
> *More laughs. The confusion increases among the six men.*]

For Mañach, "*choteo* is a desire for independence that is externalized in a mockery of every non-imperative form of authority" (41).[20] But the incompleteness of this definition from Pérez Firmat's viewpoint leads to his own addendum: "*Choteo* is a tropical tropism that unmasks the *culo* behind every *cara*, that bares the other cheek; it is this anatomical downturn that Mañach's essay attempts, but does not quite manage, to arrest" (74). To some extent, the unmasking to which Pérez Firmat alludes also takes place in Triana's *Revolico* in terms of the play's questioning of its farcical and buffoonesque identity and its reminder that at the same time the Cuban buffo is established, a significant segment of Cuba's population is

---

[20] "El choteo es un prurito de independencia que se exterioriza en una burla de toda forma no imperativa de autoridad" (Mañach, 41). I use Pérez Firmat's translation of Mañach's definition of *choteo* (56).

striving for independence and for the abolition of slavery through revolutionary action. In other words, through the direct characterization of Cuban buffo, Triana again brings to the surface the issue of an apparently disparaged and theatrical expression which lacks serious expectations and motivations. But what proposed is that this anti-intellectual stand and the statement that buffo theatre "lacks moralizing intention" is going to be questioned. Triana continues to emphasize marginal discourses as a mechanism to expose social and political criticism.

It is pertinent to mention Anthony Caputi's historical outline of buffo as the genius of vulgar comedy, particularly as he discusses its antecedents and folkloric backgrounds, its transformation, and its persistent characterization within the European theatrical context. Just as Leal identifies Cuban buffo's lack of a moralizing intention, Caputi states that this expression "points to the comic and the laughable, but to the comic and laughable as they exist apart from such sophisticated issues as irony, satire, wit, parody, and burlesque. It designates an instinctive, uncritical, frenetic species of fun..." (20).[21] It is significant that Caputi's attempt to characterize the buffo forces him to establish the difference between vulgar comedy and farce. In his own words:

> "Farce" is the term usually used for the village square comedies of the Middle Ages and for such recent work as *Charley's Aunt*, yet not all critics would accept it as a description of the Dorian mime or certain examples of English pantomime. Moreover, as a critical term it is usually applied to dramatic wholes, while I shall sometimes be concerned with bits and pieces of plays. (16)

But beyond either the subtle or explicit differences between farce and buffo, what is of interest in *Revolico en el Campo de Marte* is the play's eagerness to explore multiple theatrical expressions of the comic as it simultaneously subverts the standard expectations of

---

[21] Caputi chooses the term "vulgar comedy" to identify a subtype of comedy and mentions the insufficiency of various names with which it has also been identified–popular comedy, farce, low comedy. He then comments on the identity of this expression: "vulgar comedy does not stimulate serenity, or a wise, sophisticated acquiescence, or an enlarged idea of life. It is unintellectual and unphilosophical. Instead of a residue of thought, it leaves a tingle in the blood" (16-17).

both farce and the buffo, particularly their so-called instinctive and uncritical nature.[22]

The indirect allusion to buffo theatre in Triana's play is an attempt to signal and question its supposed lack of a "moralizing intention." That is, at a primary level the presence of buffo elements in *Revolico* not only represents a significant recognition of Cuba's theatrical past but also undermines the implicit seriousness of the play's "messages." Ironically, this lack of seriousness, as Leal suggests, is the buffo comedian's principal virtue, "since they worked in a country that did not seem to take life seriously" (17). In an absurd and grotesque way, the revolution becomes a *revolico*–violence takes place in the *fair*, in the *park* of Campo de Marte–where, in addition to collectively celebrating an event, "common people launch their criticism and parodies of the powerful" (Leal 20). Inevitably, this carnivalesque upheaval still carries within its linguistic and artistic connotations the consequences of radical and extreme political violence. Therefore, in contrast with Caputi's definition of the buffo, where the comic and laughable exist "apart from such sophisticated issues as irony, satire, wit, parody, and burlesque," and where "it designates an instinctive, uncritical, frenetic species of fun" (20), the double irony in Triana's play is revealed when buffo elements *do* stress central issues of social, historical, and political importance. Although, as already stated, Cuban buffo portrays its lack of a "moralizing intention" and of a "desire for morality" (Leal 23), Leal himself states: "When the buffo comedians define themselves with a different *morality* from that of the colonialists, when they disdain and parody the melodramatic scheme, when they satirize and transform a popular sensibility and reverse their values, they are creating a different *morality* that negates the social hypocrisy behind which the colony hid a class structure and an imperial objective" (18). It is clear then that *Revolico* actively plays with its contradictory artistic and social identities, attitudes, and discourses, problematizing its different levels of interpretation. That is, while it overtly displays its

---

[22] One of Caputi's main characterizations of the buffo, which will be questioned later as it pertains to the Cuban expression, is the notion that it is "an instinctive, uncritical, frenetic species of fun..." (20). Rine Leal, in contrast, does underscore the parodic aspects of the Cuban buffo: "Through parody, charming guarachas and *choteo*, that genre destroyed the very foundations of the *morals* of a society still nostalgic about slavery and still singing the praises of [King] Pelayo and Columbus" (18).

supposed meaninglessness and lack of moralizing intention, it plays with its meanings and morality, which in the case of *Revolico* are linked to the incongruities between a frivolous and humorous world and a violent and revolutionary one. For example, when Alicia discovers Luis's infidelity and decides to pay him back with the same coin, Anita wonders what the Church would say about this act of revenge and what the Catholic ladies would say. Alicia responds:

> ¡Refresquemos la cabeza!
> Detesto las antiguallas,
> los garabatos venales
> y esas prédicas pacatas
> de caridad y piedad
> que dislocan y disfrazan
> pensamiento y sentimiento,
> describiendo como cábalas
> pasajes del bien y el mal. (II, ii: 164)

> [Let's clear our heads! I detest old fashioned things, corrupted scribbles, and that prudish preaching of charity and piety that twists and masks thoughts and feelings, describing in a confused manner scenes of good and evil.]

Within these dichotomies, the satiric tone of *Revolico* and the frequent incorporation of insignificant characters (Leal's "history of a people without history") reveal the play's concern with popular structures, both literary and social: the use of the octosyllabic verse, the antididactic tone, the recycling of popular figures from the literary tradition, the caricaturization of the racial and socioeconomic profiles of characters, and the iconoclastic stand towards the major themes of the past. From a social and racial perspective one identifies the presence of a group of scoundrels, among them a *curro*, who underline the buffoonery and violent atmosphere of the play. In *Revolico* the spectator can see how Enrique, the district's sergeant, is about to gather his friends to take revenge for the infidelity of his wife Marieta, who has left with Renato. Among Enrique's friends there is Curro, who is immediately identified with the *negro pendenciero*, or quarrelsome black, a real and literary character of nineteenth-century Cuba. Not surprisingly, an excellent definition of the *curro* appears in Cirilo Villaverde's *Cecilia Valdés,* one of the most influential texts of Cuban nineteenth century literature and culture (many of this novel's violent acts take place in the park called *Campo de Marte.*) The narrator of Villaverde's text defines the *curro* as follows:

> We have here sketched with a coarse brush the living image of a gallant of *el manglar* [curro de Manglar] in the outskirts of rural Havana, memorable during the period of our history. The dandy in Andalusian dress is not original with us. He is nothing more or less than some young Negro or mulatto living in this quarter or two or three other similar ones, a devil-may-care bully, living on neither work nor charity, quarrelsome by nature and by habit, by occupation a thief, brought up in the streets, living on the proceeds of thievery, and who seems from birth to be cut out only for the whip, the ball and chain or a violent death. (*Cecilia Valdés or Angel's Hill* 454) [23]

In *Revolico*, when Benjamín is captured by the scoundrels, Curro gives instructions to his men as he copiously drinks and shows his bad blood and violent temperament by whipping Benjamín without mercy (III, i: 114). But more significant is to link the *curro* with a particular space where violent deeds prevail. The third act of *Revolico* takes place entirely in the Campo de Marte during a fair, and it is here where physical encounters and intrigues among antagonistic characters reach their highest expression. Although most of the characters of *Revolico* are not *curros*, they somehow share the aforementioned characteristics of this social outcast: greed, arrogance, and desire to deceive.

It is possible, then, to establish a causal relationship between the violent acts that permeate Triana's play, the presence of the *curro*, and the type of action or *revolico* that develops in the Campo de Marte as reflection of a problematic racial, social, and political atmosphere. In *Revolico*'s farcical and grotesque scheme of things, everyone's agenda is both similar to and opposite from the other person's goals: everyone attempts to conquer an individual of the opposite sex who, in turn, aspires to conquer someone else. Control, authoritarianism, power, trickery, deceit, corruption are forces that prevail in the (im)moral and (hyper)sexual worlds of the characters of *Revolico*, but these same forces are also prevalent in the political atmosphere of the

---

[23] Translated by Sydney G. Gest.

time and space in which these characters live. The fact that the Cuba of 1917 is experiencing an economic boom (1917 is one of the two possible dates in which Triana sets his play) is reflected in the attitudes and priorities of the characters as they center on their own well-being, pleasures, and desires, and are oblivious to any sense of the collective. What began as a revolutionary search for freedom and independence in different moments of Cuban history has become a *revolico*.

This environment reproduces a space where the alteration of order–the revolt, the revolution, or, better, the *revolico*–becomes both an artistic symbol and the representation of specific moral and sociopolitical issues. The rebellious act is again twofold: at one level, Triana's farce represents a daring attempt to transgress the stiffness and rigidity of dramatic creation, wishing to provoke an artistic revolution. At another level, it violently reverses the results of transcendental political actions, such as the establishment of the Republic of Cuba in the early part of the twentieth century, while it also parodies the (moral) results of the Cuban revolution of 1959. It is possible to argue that in the midst of the artistic control and repression prevalent in the Cuba of the late 1960s and the 1970s (the play was written in 1972), the most precious concept–that of revolution–is redefined in Triana's play and given contradictory meanings. [24] Significantly, the Campo de Marte hosts both a fair with music, dance, and costumes and a "boxing ring" (which ironically resembles a theatre stage) where amorous offenses are argued and violently approached. *Revolico*'s multiple revolutions, among them the use of farce and its significant dialogue with the absurd, the *esperpento*, and the buffo, represent an opportunity for artistic renewal whose radicalization consists of rejecting fixed and conventional viewpoints. But from the perspective of a political revolution, Triana's play portrays its corrupted side, the evils of conventionalizing and institutionalizing it, since revolutions traditionally represent antibureaucratic and antiestablishment perspectives.

If one takes into account this particular characterization of the concepts of *revolico* and revolution, it is no coincidence that in *Cecilia Valdés* most of the action among the characters of lower

---

[24] As suggested in note 15, after the 1959 Cuban Revolution the theatre of the absurd in the island was openly rejected, since it was considered inadequate to promote the new political principles.

classes (mulattos and blacks) is linked to the Campo de Marte, to the presence of *curros*, and to their respective acts of violence. [25] But above all, both in *Revolico* and *Cecilia Valdés* the violent disputes that are frequently provoked by the attraction to a woman, by uncontrollable sexual desires, and by jealousy are also linked to sociopolitical issues of their respective times. For instance, when Curro asks Pito in *Revolico* if he has seen anything particular at the fair, Tabo responds: "Ratas, gatos/ y algunos perros que celan/ a sus perras de otros perros" (III, viii: 189) [Rats, cats, and some male dogs who guard their females from other dogs]. Ultimately, the desacralizing tone in *Revolico* is the result of the *esperpento*-like, grotesque, and absurd coexistence of literary, cultural, and social structures that not only evoke the farcical and produce signs of rupture but also evoke referentiality (past and present).

Throughout this book, the economic marginalization of Spanish America, the conflictive position occupied by its literature, the general indifference to its theatrical production for economic and artistic reasons, and farce's lack of prestige within the larger appraisal of politically committed theatre have been (and will be) considered in the light of oppressive and hierarchical conditions attempting to silence the *other*. We have so far, and will continue to insist in examining Spanish American farcical plays within the discourse on marginalization and underlining their deliberate attempt to use and affirm this position to their artistic and political advantage. But as Diana Taylor suggests, if there is something that allows Latin America to position itself and many of its political and artistic voices at center stage, it is revolution: "The revolutionary movement promised to cast Latin America in a leading role on the world's political and cultural stages. The 1960s provided a new theatrical infrastructure for the marginalized, the oppressed, and the repressed" (*Theatre of Crisis* 47).

Revolution has been clearly an important theme in Triana's dramatic production, and in the article "Framing the Revolution: Triana's *La noche de los asesinos* and *Ceremonial de guerra*," Taylor

---

[25] A pertinent example is the scene where the *curro de Manglar*, whose name is Malanga, encounters Dionisio Jaruco in the area of the Campo de Marte; Jaruco has been stabbed by Pimienta for having offended Cecilia Valdés. Both the dance among the mulattos and blacks (*gente de color*), where Cecilia is insulted, and the fight between Pimienta and Dionisio, take place in the Campo de Marte (part 2, chap. 17).

offers a renewed, more complex vision of the theatricality of revolution, of the potential for a theatrical revolution, and of theatre about revolution in the works of the Cuban playwright: "[These two plays] are particularly interesting in that they are among the first works to raise the most urgent questions about the nature and meaning of revolution from within the frame of the revolutionary movement itself" (83).[26] The increased urgency of Triana's questions regarding revolution in both *La noche de los asesinos* (1965) and *Ceremonial de guerra* (1968-73) reflects the disruption of revolutionary ideals and the dismantling of political myths. According to Taylor, "Contradictory images, formulated in some of the major plays of 1965-70, reflect the beginning of an ideological crisis. . . . As early as 1965 Triana's *Assassins* was already suggesting a disenchantment with revolution in general and with the Cuban revolution in particular, insinuating that 'revolution' did not necessarily mean 'liberation'" (*Theatre of Crisis* 50). Taylor finally describes the disillusionment of some with the Cuban Revolution and the perception that this important sociopolitical and economic movement has been betrayed: "Dreams of liberation and self-determination gradually gave way to a new authoritarian order, but one which (like the Mexican Revolution) integrated the revolutionary vocabulary and images–new images that also proved re-creations of the old. . . . For many writers who believed that revolution could free the oppressed, the Cuban revolution became another repressive institution" (*Theatre of Crisis* 51). It is clear that this recreation of the old–the repetition of ingrained bad habits–becomes in *Revolico* a source of parody and is what transforms the revolution into a *revolico*. Not surprisingly, in the instances that the play overtly speaks about politics and of the political, it refers to them almost exclusively as a means of amassing wealth. When Luis is wondering how he is going to sustain his house economically, he recognizes his boss's wisdom by quoting him:

> "¡Hay que meterse en política!
> Palabras que son constancia
> de una verdad invencible...
> Puesto que si no..., te aplasta
> el estar como una hormiga
> trabajando sin ventajas." (I, v: 148)

---

[26] See also Taylor's *Theatre of Crisis* 45-51 and 64-95.

[We have to get into politics! Words that are proof of an invincible truth... Because if not... working without profit like an ant will crush you.]

To a great extent, an ironic form of role reversal takes place in *Revolico* when there is an exchange of codes between the traditional disparagement of farce and the seriousness of a political revolutionary act. One might conclude that the goal of this apparent deflation is to redefine revolution within multiple antagonistic discourses at chronological, ideological, and artistic levels. *Revolico* not only fluctuates between the absurd, the farcical, and the sociopolitical approach, but it also fluctuates, in chronological terms, between several periods of Cuban history: the indirect allusion to the 1868 attempt at independence against Spain; the portrayal of the Cuba of the early twentieth century with the establishment of the Republic of Cuba in 1902 and later the so-called period of the "dance of the millions"; the Cuba of the 1959 Revolution; and finally, the Cuba of the early 1970s, when some of the most questionable attitudes that prevailed half a century before were repeated. These attitudes included the rise of a new bourgeois-like element in society, political and economic corruption, moral degradation, and, above all, the *disillusionment* with the high expectations aroused at the end of the nineteenth century by Cuban independence and the ideas of José Martí, and after 1959 by the Castro revolution.

In other words, the unorthodox relationship that Triana establishes between revolution and farce in *Revolico en el Campo de Marte* becomes both antagonistic and complementary. On the one hand, radical and fundamental changes in the political and socio-economic situation of a country or region are usually devoid of humor and always have serious consequences regarding the life and death of their participants. On the other, Triana recognizes the potential of a revolutionary act to become a circus, a pandemonium, an unstable situation where it is almost impossible to identify the performers and their respective ideological stances. That is, it seems difficult to distinguish the "true" revolutionaries from the defenders of the *status quo*, and to know which one leads to the emergence and existence of the other. The suggestion is that, after the triumph of the revolutionary ideology–which came into being in reaction to the clownish, chaotic, historical immediate past–the now-powerful revolutionary rulers will become as reactionary as the former leaders and will not only suppress and silence all attempts at change, but will become as corrupt as the ones they replaced. The linkage between farce and revolution in *Revolico* is then based on notions of instability, polarization, contradiction, chaos, and, above all, role reversal, wherein, ironically, farce reveals more overtly its rebellious and profound nature, while revolution unmasks its caricaturesque dimensions and its capacity to mislead. Ironically, Diana Taylor's fear of simply "reducing the revolution to a spectacle" (*Theatre of Crisis* 47) is accomplished in *Revolico en el Campo de Marte* in literal and metaphorical terms, when ridiculed and senseless repetitions characterize the revolutionary act. The play ends with the words of the tailor (maker and "un-maker" of garments and perhaps also of identities), with his reflection on the interaction between past and present, between the new expectations and the probable failures that mirror previous ones:

> SASTRE.   Eres tiempo y nada más.
> Un tiempo que se entremezcla
> con las hebras de otros mundos
> y en el presente es espuela
> que abre añicos de visiones
> de plenitud y demencia
> –posible de un imposible
> que hacen sueño tu existencia. (III: 205)

> [TAILOR. You are time and nothing else. A time that mixes with the threads of other worlds, and in the present it is a spur that creates fragmented visions of plenitude and madness–the possibility of an impossibility, which turns your existence into a dream].

"Can revolution ever break out of the repetitive cycle? Rather than profound social upheaval, does revolution signal circular repetition, as in the revolutions of the earth around the sun? Or does it denote substitution, the process by which one power figure merely replaces another?" (*Theatre of Crisis* 89-90). It is particularly significant that these unanswered questions posed by Taylor in relation to Triana's *La noche de los asesinos* not only shed light on *Revolico*'s farcical characterization of revolution but also parody the impossibility to answer them. The rhetorical character of these quandaries as they relate to *La noche de los asesinos* reflects the grotesque substitution of the problematics of revolution dramatized in this play for the problematics of *revolico* in Triana's later piece. Nevertheless, the capacity to recognize in *Revolico en el Campo de Marte* the circular nature of history (the revolutionary governments are as corrupt as their predecessors) is dismantled by parodying any possible pattern that portrays a systematic, repetitive structure. The chaotic aspect of the action acknowledges the rampantly incoherent upheaval that destroys communication, meaning, social structures, family relations, sexual and economic arrangements, and even the supernatural dimensions portrayed through the presence of the *santera* and her spells. Farce's struggle against fixation seems to play tricks even on the notion of reversing the transcendental role of revolution in the lives of its participants, turning it into a comedy of intrigue and errors. The tension between portraying and dismantling revolution in artistic and political terms leaves the spectator with the idea of anachronistic, incoherent, and apparently meaningless transgressive action.

What we have seen through the dichotomy of revolution and *revolico* is that *Revolico en el Campo de Marte* scrutinizes traditional linguistic and artistic codes, which are represented in the persistent characterization of duality through opposing pairs: love/money, man/woman, revolution/*revolico* (carnivalesque upheaval), good/evil, married couples (Alicia/Luis, Enrique/Marieta), servants (Anita/Felo), siblings (Luis/Benjamín, Magdalena/ Renato), and a variety of daring combinations. But in Triana's play, the evident dichotomies aim less at underlining the extremes than at stressing the emptiness of that intermediary space between existence and language. For example, the hyperbolic, false conception of love presented in *Revolico* establishes a paradoxical link with the valorization of money. That is, the notion of purity, faithfulness, and idealism connected with the Platonic idea of love is disparaged and becomes directly linked to greed and economic ambition and power. Ironically, these two essentially antagonistic elements–love and money–can represent, at different levels, similar structures of power that are capable of revealing their multiple and false masks. In *Revolico*, love and money can fuse their conflictive realities and also confuse the traditional role that each of them plays in the lives of the characters. For instance, Luis's marriage to Alicia is evidently the product of economic interest, and he recognizes it: "Mal pensé que el amor era/ acomodo y otra fruta/ desmadejada . . ." (II, viii: 179-80) [I wrongly thought that love was comfort but it turned out to be an enervating fruit]. Meanwhile, Alicia also acknowledges that if Luis had been someone with prestige and power, she would have kept up appearances and would not have been concerned with his infidelities: "¿Luis?... Si él fuera el Presidente/ o un tipo de importancia/ bien le guardara la forma" (II, ii: 164) [Luis?... If he were President or someone of importance, I would treat him politely]. As a result, the standard meanings of love and money are parodied and substituted with notions of excessive sexuality, arbitrary exchange of partners and resources, sexual harassment, exploitation, and the use of both violence and magic spells to achieve control over the desired person or, better, object. Consequently, what is initially characterized as *love* is in fact lust, physical attraction, sex; and what is understood as a basic instrument of commercial transactions becomes a source of greed. In the final scene, the tailor states as a sort of moral: "Y si el dinero entorpece,/ más envilece la guerra/ del sexo que se disfraza/ del amor en su contienda" (III, xxi: 205) [If money damages, the war of sex, masked as love, degrades even more]. In other words, one recognizes that, beyond the purer, more abstract meanings of love, what ultimately prevails is the battle of the sexes –expressed through the disturbing nature of physical desire–and the possibility of fulfilling these desires through monetary means. This transgression of the ideal notion of love suggests the extent to which another ideal notion such as political freedom can become subjugated to the power of money and corruption.

In *Revolico en el Campo de Marte* the relationship between money and sex (not only between money and love) is one of the focal points of the play, since throughout the action, the first pair develops closer and comfortable links between its elements. Frequently, the characters' wishes–or, rather, sexual caprices–can be fulfilled only through the economic remuneration of an intermediary, who will intercede with tricks and subterfuges to unite the pairs, while the notions of love and freedom are left too weak to confront greed, sexual desire, and exploitation. In the initial scenes of the play, Luis's conversation with Rosa, the *santera*, is dominated by two images: one visual and one auditory. The visual one is portrayed by Luis's persistent action of counting money, putting his wallet into his pocket and pulling it out. The auditory one is represented by Rosa's constant shaking of a bag of money while she discusses with Luis his amorous afflictions. Rosa's implicit suggestion is that by trusting her with his money his now-unfortunate love life can drastically change

(I, i: 141-42). Nevertheless, even the immense power of money seems to have its limits and its own devastating consequences:

> ENRIQUE. ¿Es el dinero la causa
> del grotesco quita y pon
> o sirve de colofón
> o es el barniz de una pausa?
> Si es así, ¿por qué desgrano
> obstinados resquemores? (II, iii: 165)
>
> ....
>
> LUIS. ¿O es el dinero el que atranca
> y deforma y prostituye
> en odiosa zarabanda? (II, iv: 166)

> [ENRIQUE. Is money the cause of this grotesque give-and-take, or does it function as a colophon, or is it the varnish of a pause? If this is the case, why do I feel such persistent suspicions?
>
> ....
>
> LUIS. Could it be that money hinders and deforms and prostitutes in a hateful and disgusting dance?]

Throughout Triana's *Revolico en el Campo de Marte* the artistic aspects of the play and the Cuban sociopolitical environments that are evoked (the Cuba of the first two decades of the twentieth century–1900 or 1917– and the Cuba of 1970) become mirrors capable of reflecting a broad spectrum of angles from which to observe–but above all, judge–the multiple, ambiguous, contradictory realities of revolutionary acts recreated and parodied by this dramatic work. The farcical dimension of Triana's play attempts to reveal its chameleonic role. It pretends to be everything that it is not, and ends up becoming a conglomerate of appearances and evasions of what it could actually be: maybe a theatrical game, or the reflection of the pseudocircular and ironic nature of history, or a mordant criticism of the Cuban revolutionary present, or a parodic imitation of the literary past, among many others. The unmasking act characteristic of *Revolico en el Campo de Marte*, which lays bare artistic experiments, the mixing of dramatic genres, the inconsistencies of the Cuban revolution, and its similarities to the island's corrupted historical past, does not necessarily imply the removal of one "reality" for another in which the supposed new face becomes permanent (see Ruiz Ramón 126). Instead, the unmasking will allow us to recognize the underlying cultural and sociopolitical structures of the play that demand to be interpreted, while also recognizing that these structures will also be displaced (although not necessarily substituted).

In conclusion, *Revolico*'s in-depth knowledge of its cultural and theatrical traditions and of its sociopolitical origins (the Cuban war for Independence in 1898, the formation of a Republic in 1902, the Revolution of 1959, and the circumstances of the early 1970s) is evidenced by the presence of themes and techniques that will simultaneously recreate the past as well as quarrel with it. These themes and techniques are, as noted earlier, the overt allusion to the comedy of errors and to the cloak-and-dagger Golden Age play (with its use of verse); the implicit allusion to the antislavery literature of the nineteenth century (Villaverde's *Cecilia Valdés*); the allusion to the Cuban buffo theatre of the nineteenth and twentieth centuries, with its particular characterization of language and society; the influence of African religions in Cuban culture and literature; the incorporation of absurdist elements and those of the *esperpento* with its social and philosophical overtones; and the significant role played by monetary issues that contrast with parodied traditional amorous codes.[27]

The theatricalization of these formulaic conventional themes requires not only the spectator's general familiarity with the dramatized events but also his/her recognition that these artistic and sociopolitical codes will be subject to a thorough scrutiny and parodization. That is, insertion into a modern frame of theatrical forms and themes, of structures, languages, moods, characters, and plots from various times and traditions, emphasize the simultaneous harmony and tension that will create the farcical tone of the play and will problematize the dialogue between past and present in Cuba's artistic and political history. The possible suggestion that both art and history in *Revolico* have a circular, repetitive nature is not only appealing but concrete, but it is nevertheless transgressed in the play when one recognizes that this recycling of artistic forms and this repetition of historical events are caricatured and hyperbolized. Therefore, *Revolico* seems to choose both the act of creating and

---

[27] Through parallel strategies, although for different reasons, *La noche de los asesinos* has also been described in terms of a juxtaposition of various artistic languages and forms. Eduardo Lolo, in his analysis of *La noche*, underlines, as one of the reasons for the play's universality, Triana's masterful gathering of elements of the Cuban theatre of all periods, such as the biting humor, the quasi-existentialist tone, absurdism by excess, and even elements of the radio soap operas (45).

recreating artistic forms and political acts of the past and the present, while also transgressing through parody their dramatic construction as a strategy to reveal the many disguises of the characters and of a society dishonest with their/its own commitments and beliefs.

Chapter 2

(IN)DECENCY AND (DIS)PLEASURE: WOMAN AND FARCE
IN SABINA BERMAN'S *EL SUPLICIO DEL PLACER*

> Is pleasure legitimate after all? What are its allowable forms and limits? How can the radical egoism of the pleasure principle be reconciled with an ethic of duty and unselfishness, or at least rendered innocuous to the social order that pleasure itself requires? Does pleasure degrade or enhance character?
> Christopher Herbert, "Comedy: The World of Pleasure"

> La irrupción del ahora significa la aparición, en el centro de la vida contemporánea, de la palabra prohibida, la palabra maldita: *placer*.... Cuando digo placer no pienso en la elaboración de un nuevo hedonismo ni el regreso a la antigua sabiduría sensual–aunque lo primero no sea desdeñable y lo segundo sea deseable–sino en la revelación de esa mitad oscura del hombre que ha sido humillada y sepultada por las morales del progreso: esa mitad que se revela en las imágenes del arte y del amor.
> Octavio Paz, "Crítica de la pirámide"

IN an examination of José Triana's *Revolico en el Campo de Marte* (1972), Vargas Llosa's *Kathie y el hipopótamo* (1983), and Luis Rafael Sánchez's *Quíntuples* (1984), this book concentrates on how Spanish American dramatists have constructed, through farce, a sharply critical, humorous voice in which aesthetic and social issues are questioned and transgressed. The problem with this particular approach emerges when the peripheral position of Spanish America in artistic, cultural, political, and economic terms is perceived as a homogeneous and coherent reality. The rejection of this notion of homogeneity leads the way to a reconciliation between a general conception of Spanish America and a deeper understanding of the cultural and historical diversity that characterizes this region. Diana Taylor, among others, has acknowledged this complexity in the larger context of Latin America: "It proves more constructive to think of twenty-five different countries–each with its own particular combination of races and populations, languages and dialects, traditions and cultural images–that share a similar history of conquest, colonization, economic and political instability, and continuing sociopolitical and economic dependency" (*Theatre of Crisis* 8). At a micro level, this heterogeneity is also stressed, for example, by Rigoberta Menchú in her complex and now controversial testimonial narrative, where she reminds us of the twenty-three different ethnic groups and their respective languages that coexist in Guatemala alone (1-2).

The dismantling of a homogeneous view of Spanish America's literature and history, the recognition of the diversity that exists among and within its countries, and a multifaceted understanding of artistic, social, and political marginalization form the basis for this chapter's examination of the unorthodox relationship between farce, female writing, and feminism.[1] These considerations are also the basis for analyzing the heterogeneous dimensions of various forms of discourse in Sabina Berman's *El suplicio del placer* [The Agony of Ectasy, 1978; expanded version 1994].[2] But it should be stressed from the outset that the discourses of farce and feminism in Berman's play seem always to avoid fixation by stressing their paradoxical and contradictory angles. Therefore, although the relationship between them in *El suplicio* will be addressed in terms of their aggression towards traditional views of genre and gender, neither farce, female writing,

---

[1] As a way of avoiding the homogenization of women's writing, this chapter underscores a notion of this discourse that rejects authority and rigidity; a discourse constantly willing to transgress its language, ideology, and philosophical and political stands. *El suplicio del placer* is not a doctrinaire work of feminist writing, but is instead one that questions feminism from within its own postulates.

[2] Sabina Berman (Mexico 1953), regarded as one of the most distinguished playwrights of contemporary Mexican theatre, has successfully published and staged her plays since the middle of the 1970s and on various occasions has been awarded the Premio Nacional de Teatro by the Instituto Nacional de Bellas Artes. In recent years several of Berman's plays have become box-office hits: *Entre Villa y una mujer desnuda* (1993), *Krísis* (1996), *Molière* (1999), and *eXtra* (2002). Some of her plays have been translated into English and French, and *Entre Villa* has been staged in the United States both in English and Spanish. She has also produced a television series entitled *Leyendas de México*, and in 1995 directed the cinematic version of *Entre Villa y una mujer desnuda* in collaboration with Isabelle Tardan. Since the production of her first play in 1975–*Esta no es una obra de teatro* [This is not a play]–Berman has continued to enrich the Mexican stage for more than two decades with such plays as *Yankee* (1979), *Rompecabezas* (1981), *Heregía* (1983), *Águila o sol* (1984), *Muerte súbita* (2nd version 1991), among others, and her reputation and success have continued to grow. She is also a poet and the author of two novels, *La bobe* (1990) and *Amante de lo ajeno* (1997). Adam Versényi has translated the title of Berman's play as *The Agony of Ecstasy*, and Versényi's translation of this and other plays by Berman are published by Southern Illinois UP. All translations are mine unless indicated.

nor feminism occupy a fixed and secure position at the play's so-called end. Nor will the aggressive discourses of farce and women's exploration of this discourse offer a constructive alternative for the "destruction" of a traditional literary and social order.[3]

Through *El suplicio del placer* the particular *contrapunteo*, or dialectics, between issues of genre and gender will be examined, and this examination will focus on the way in which these discourses become antagonistic to but also interdependent of each other. Some of Berman's important observations regarding farce and feminism as marginal discourses also will be compared with those of another Mexican writer, Rosario Castellanos, in her play *El eterno femenino* [*The Eternal Feminine*, 1975]. Finally, I will explore through this dialectic between genre and gender how the notions of textual and sexual pleasures interact with the conventions of farce and with the discussion on the role of woman in a male-dominated society. For now, the discourses of farce and feminism will be reviewed individually, underscoring their connections, particularly their rejection of a fixed and categorical definition.[4]

---

[3] Judith Butler's conception of gender is extremely enlightening in our discussion of Berman's *El suplicio del placer*: "[G]ender is no way a stable identity or locus of agency from which various acts proceede; rather, it is an identity tenuously constituted in time–an identity instituted through a *stylized repetition of acts*. Further, gender is instituted through the stylization of the body and, hence, must be understood as the mundane way in which bodily gestures, movements, and enactments of various kinds constitute the illusion of an abiding gendered self" (270-71). In Roselyn Costantino's study of *El suplicio del placer* she states that the dramatic structure of Berman's theatre is flexible and dynamic, devoid of absolute theses (245). Jennifer Zachman proposes that in *El suplicio* feminist identity is not only foregrounded but also questioned (38). It is not surprising either that the absence of a fixed ending in Berman's play connects it with the tradition of farce. (Berman could continue adding segments to her play, as she did in 1994 with what is now "Los dientes.") For some critics, the difference between comedy and farce resides precisely in their endings: in most comedies there is reassurance that the world "out of order will be–by the end of the play–comfortably set back in order" (Carlson 159), while "full closure violates the play of farce," that is, "farce is less a thing, a 'work,' than yet another instance in an endless chain of play with us and its own existence" (Williams 67). Joan Dean states about Joe Orton's farce: "His farce neither provides nor suggests a safe, orderly world to which his characters (or audience) can retreat. . . . Perverse and healthy, right and wrong, rational and irrational are polarities which coalesce in his plays" (485).

[4] Roselyn Costantino's contribution to the study of *El suplicio* is noteworthy, since she confronts important issues of the play in light of Michel Foucault's theories of power and sexuality, particularly how Berman's work represents an "exploration of the individual involved in amorous relations where pleasure is a mask of

It is misleading to suggest that farce's traditional struggle with literary and social conventions is limited to clear-cut entities, such as the opposition between oppressor and oppressed or between Western and non-Western traditions. The struggle is much more wide-ranging and, most importantly, it is frequently addressed to itself. Therefore, the examination of farce as a marginal genre underlines the fact that Spanish American farce persistently struggles against cultural, literary, and historical oppressive forces, and that part of its aggressive rebellion serves to ridicule its own history, expectations, conventions, and marginalization. Within this iconoclastic agenda, farce's thematic and structural development in Spanish American literature shows no tendency to position itself at the center. That is, the benefits of occupying a powerful position are not part of farce's fragmented and fragmentary project. Indeed, even the idea of a preplanned project would be unacceptable to some of the farcical texts studied here, since it would imply a "coherent" perception and an incorporation into their literary corpora of past and present "realities." [5] What is pertinent in the context of this chapter is to examine the way in which Spanish American farce fulfills a consciously ambiguous role, exaggerating and showing the grotesque side of reality misleading the spectator, and ultimately proposing that even the most serious social and artistic issues avoid prescriptive and fixed solutions.

The concept of "metamarginalization" also needs to be considered not only in the light of farce's position as the last item on everyone's list of genres (McDonald 77), but within a complex social realm where some oppressed groups become the oppressors of others. Many critics have stated that the hierarchical and oppressive patterns characteristic of first-world ideologies are themselves root-

---

what is actually a game of power" (245). I have benefited from the excellent analyses offered by Kirsten Nigro on the first segment of *El suplicio del placer* in her essay "Inventions and Transgressions: A Fractured Narrative on Feminist Theatre in Mexico," and by Amalia Gladhart's third chapter–"Playing Gender"–in her *The Leper in Blue: Coercive Performance and the Contemporary Latin American Theatre*. Zachman examines *El suplicio* in its structural, thematic, and technical relationship with *Noches de amor efímero* by the Spanish playwright Paloma Pedrero. Both plays, argues Zachman, present, question, and invert the notions of gender, identity, and power within intimate relationships (38).

[5] The irony suggested in the use of quotes implies that farce is overtly antagonistic to the possibility of coherence and to the existence of one or even multiple realities.

ed in the internal structures of many, if not all, Spanish American societies. Therefore, class, racial, and gender struggles in this region could be perceived as a duplication of patterns of exploitation frequently associated with the colonial and postcolonial eras.[6] Ironically, the fact that Spanish America occupies a secondary position in the economic and cultural so-called world order does not preclude its own rulers and authority figures from transferring these hierarchical and oppressive structures to what they consider less powerful voices in their midst. I am referring in particular to the marginalization (some would say "exclusion," others "silencing") of women in Spanish America and, as a direct consequence, of their artistic and literary productions.

The Argentine writer and critic Sylvia Molloy offers a clear example of what I have called "metamarginalization" as she compares the position of Latin American women writers with that of their male counterparts. For Molloy, phallocentric language, more than excluding women, assigns them "to a subordinate place and, from that position of authority, deauthorizes woman's word. That is, it includes that word but in a position of weakness" (García Pinto, [Interview] 143). She then mentions one of the most striking instances of this subordination, which continues to be a source of wonder and frustration for those who have seriously studied the works of the Mexican Elena Garro:

> A case in point is the very different fates of two splendid books that are surprisingly alike: *Los recuerdos del porvenir* and *Cien años de soledad*. . . . "Just look at how Elena Garro's novel, which came out four years before García Márquez's did, was set aside, ignored, while the patriarchal novel was triumphantly promoted. *Recuerdos* didn't even win inclusion in the dubious 'boom,' which is exclusively masculine, of course." (García Pinto, [Interview] 143)

---

[6] For a detailed discussion of theories of development in Latin America and on internal colonialism, see Stanley J. and Barbara H. Stein, *The Colonial Heritage in Latin America* (1970), and Jorge Larrain, *Theories of Development: Capitalism, Colonialism and Dependency* (1989). For her part, Sara Castro-Klarén reminds her reader that women's rejection of a dominant system–she refers to the rejection, dismantling, and new beginning that Susan Gilbert and Susan Gubar characterize as specific features of feminine writing in *The Mad Woman in the Attic*–is not a unique historical event, since there are parallel developments in the history of colonial societies (39-40).

To trace the distinguished role of women writers in Mexican literature and to analyze its complex history go beyond the limits of this project, since, to begin with, one would have to embark on a journey to the seventeenth century and Sor Juana Inés de la Cruz's writings. Suffice it to acknowledge the boldness, the struggles with and challenges to society, the daring examination of sexuality from a female and feminist point of view, and the iconoclastic stands of many women writers who have populated the Mexican scene, since their search has directly or indirectly contributed to the empowerment of Berman's powerful dramatic voice. In Sor Juana's footsteps, Sabina Berman, Carmen Boullosa. Nellie Campobello, Julieta Campos, Rosario Castellanos, Laura Esquivel, Elena Garro, Margo Glantz, Barbara Jacobs, Ángeles Mastretta, María Luisa Ocampo, Elena Poniatowska, and Jesusa Rodríguez are some of those literary voices that establish, in their own respective ways, "a new praxis, subverting the authoritarian language that puts them 'in their place,' dislocating it in different ways depending on the time period" (García Pinto, [Interview] 143).[7]

But the act of framing Berman's creative production in the (positive) light of other female and feminist Mexican writers should not be perceived as another form of oppression or as an attempt to limit her search for a voice. The open recognition of notions of subversion, inquiry, fragmentation, and individuality in feminist writing reveals, more than anything else, common preoccupations and strategies that frequently emerge from parallel, but not equal, histories. As suggested before, it is important to recognize that the premise from which this discussion on the topic of feminism will depart is that female and feminist writers and critics do not necessarily coincide in their understanding of their literature and criticism, since other factors, such as race, class, or sexual preference will also play a significant part in female and feminist views of mul-

---

[7] For a detailed study of the images of women in Mexican literature and of Mexican women writers, see Jean Franco, *Plotting Women: Gender and Representation in Mexico* (1989); Aralia López González, Amelia Malagamba, and Elena Urrutia's edition *Mujer y literatura mexicana y chicana: Culturas en contacto* (1990); Sandra Messinger Cypess, *La Malinche in Mexican Literature: From History to Myth* (1991); Claudia Schaefer, *Textured Lives: Women, Art, and Representation in Modern Mexico* (1992); Kristine Ibsen, ed., *The Other Mirror: Women's Narrative in Mexico, 1980-1995* (1997); María Elena de Valdés, *The Shattered Mirror: Representations of Women in Mexican Literature* (1998); and Debra A. Castillo, *Easy Women: Sex and Gender in Modern Mexican Fiction* (1998), among others.

tiple realities. In Berman's *El suplicio del placer* the concept of social and artistic imprisonment is precisely what is being initially questioned and eventually transgressed.[8]

In this attempt to consider both the orchestration of feminism and the elements of differentiation among its advocates and participants, Debra Castillo's discussion of Victoria Ocampo's letter to Virginia Woolf, sheds light on the distinction between Latin American feminism and its European counterpart: "Ocampo celebrates the room Virginia Woolf has been able to discover and unlock but recognizes that Woolf's key does not necessarily fit a Latin American keyhole; that key Ocampo has to discover herself" (*Talking Back* xv).[9] Castillo adds:

> Ultimately, then, Ocampo, herself a privileged woman, hints that it would be a grave mistake to appropriate Woolf (and implicitly, we might add, de Beauvoir or Julia Kristeva or Hélène Cixous or Showalter or any other theorist) uncritically for a Latin American critical practice, for her theories and her conclusions derive from specific conditions that may not be duplicated in Latin America, where circumstances of race, gender, class, and cultural relationships exist which may not obtain in the Anglo-French sphere. (*Talking Back* xvii)

This same careful acknowledgment of the coexistence of multiple and even antagonistic voices among first-world and third-world feminist discourses also needs to be made when considering Spanish

---

[8] Nancy C. M. Hartsock begins her essay "Postmodernism and Political Change: Issues for Feminist Theory," with the following statement: "Throughout the eighties, white North American feminist theorists have been responding to arguments originating from radical women of color that feminist theory must take more account of diversity among women" (39). Kirsten Nigro's reflection on her position as a US scholar studying Spanish American plays that deal with feminism in Mexico contrasts with the intolerance of dissenting voices within feminism. As a means of enhancing the dialogue between north and south regarding feminism and "larger projects of social reform," Nigro identifies the common challenges, purposes, and spaces between these regions: "For although feminism here [in the United States] has been dominated by white middle-class women, the struggle over the past decade has been to be less exclusionary, to accept and respect diversity, to somehow allow for both coalitional and identity politics. It is not true or fair, therefore, to insist on our extreme individualism, as opposed to the collective concerns of Latin American feminists. Despite basic cultural differences, there is a commonality of challenges and purposes that allows for a dialogue in which voices from both sides are equally vital" ("Inventions" 156).

[9] Castillo is referring to Victoria Ocampo, *Testimonios*, vol. 1.

American women's writing and feminist criticism. In the introduction to the frequently cited *La sartén por el mango*, Patricia Elena González highlights the issue of diversity (and lack of agreement) within feminism by summarizing the central aspects of an encounter among Latin American women writers and feminist critics, some of whom, like Sylvia Molloy, play both roles:

> The essence of the discussions was centered on the existence or non-existence, on the definition or lack of it, on the characterization or non-characterization, of a feminine writing. In our three-day experience, focusing on the dilemma in oppositional structures ended up in the impossibility of grasping the frying pan by the handle, and obviously, words spilled out all over. (13)

The need to differentiate among feminist discourses implies not only stressing the notion of individuality, subversion, and fragmentation but recognizing the presence of multiple voices as a paramount feature of feminist diversity in the midst of unity, and vice versa, unity in the context of diversity.[10]

Along the same lines, once the similarities between farce and feminist writing have been acknowledged in terms of their rejection of a fixed image of themselves and their opposition to authority, it is essential to pose questions regarding their possible antagonistic relationship. Up to this point, I have emphasized that farce's goal is to struggle with and subvert traditional expectations; it is simultaneously to dismantle and construct a critical space, creating around it an ambiguous and unpredictable aura. For example, the notion of role-reversal has been a constant preoccupation of both comedy and farce, and is a key element in the discussion of gender issues in *El suplicio del placer*.[11]

---

[10] In Kirsten Nigro's analysis of Rosario Castellanos's *El eterno femenino* and Carmen Boullosa's *Propusieron a María*, Nigro stresses the plays' awareness of the dangers of globalizing the critical discourse of female dramatists: "From the beginning, it would be necessary to underline what is obvious–that if one argues against essentialisms, then it is not possible to talk about *a* theatre, or about woman, or about feminism, but of theatre*s*, or women, or feminism*s*, thus allowing room for the differences in nationality, class, race, and ethnicity of women dramatists as well as their audiences" ("Para narrar" 243).

[11] Although the distinctions between comedy and farce are acknowledged in the introduction, it is still pertinent to mention here some useful ideas that critics have offered regarding women in comedy, comedy and feminism, and women's humor. See Susan Carlson, "Women in Comedy: Problem, Promise, Paradox;" Nancy

As to the position of women in relation to comedy, Susan Carlson describes critics' polarized approach to role-reversal in this genre and their perception that the relationship between comedy and society falls into one of two categories: "On the one hand, critics of comedy emphasize the temporary nature of comedy's central role reversal, study the world turned upside down, and document how such 'unnatural' inversion readies an audience for comedy's happy ending and social affirmation. On the other hand, critics highlight the opportunity comedy offers, through its inversions, for new, changing, and even revolutionary roles" (160). This dichotomy between comedy as "a socially conservative force" or comedy as "a liberating, potentially antisocial force," underlines once again the internal polarization and ambiguity of this genre.[12]

In the case of farce, Andrea Labinger expands the notion of cruciform farce as it relates to the importance of role-reversal in oppressed societies: "This X-shaped configuration is ideally suited to the needs of the Spanish American playwright because it depicts very graphically the rise of the humble and the well-deserved decline of the mighty.... Role-reversal, or the transfer of these trappings from one character to another, can topple the entire social order, while at the same time eliciting our laughter" (219-20). But beyond the dichotomy between comedy and farce and their affirmation or destruction of social norms, what is being considered is farce's aggressive attempt to parody, and even remove, the very notion of roles–fixed or exchangeable–from its discourse. Does Berman's play, or any other Spanish American farce, actually deal with role-reversal, or maybe with the possible removal of roles altogether? What would be the reaction of an audience–or even better, a society–when confronted with the absence of categorization and characterization?

The common use of role-reversal in farce puts a new mask on *El suplicio* by rejecting a mere change of position–regardless of how

---

Walker, "Do Feminists Ever Laugh? Women's Humor and Women's Rights;" and Judith Wilt, "The Laughter of Maidens, the Cackle of Matriarchs: Notes on the Collision Between Comedy and Feminism."

[12] Carlson's view is that comedy's "underlying bottom-line message is always conservative, often reactionary. Comedy does encourage us to hope for change, but this hope is perpetually undercut by the social structures that comedy assumes. Women's equality to men is not, as Meredith would have it, comedy's essential ingredient. Exactly the opposite is true. The fact that comedy's women are *never* quite equal is the key to its age-old message of joy, continuity, and hope" (160).

socially or artistically significant this exchange is—and by creating a space where the notions of hierarchy and authority, as sources of oppression, are rejected. A detailed examination not only of *El suplicio* but of other plays by Berman, such as *Un actor se repara* (1975), *Yankee* (1980), *Águila o sol* (1984), *Muerte súbita* (1988), and *Entre Villa y una mujer desnuda* (1993), shows that promoting commotion and creating a feeling of instability is one of the playwright's goals, dramatized in *El suplicio del placer* by the coexistence, comparison, and clash between farce and gender issues.[13]

This discussion of role-reversal in comedy and farce and its similarities to and differences from feminist discourse elicits even more questions: Should it be concluded that women writers, like Berman, who resort to farce are somehow inverting an already inverted and unfixed genre? What would be the result of this dual inversion? Is the woman farceur playing with the notion of an "infinite" or, at least, constant inversion of something already unstable and inverted? What is feminist discourse saying about itself and about farce in terms of their similarly contradictory natures?

Berman's premise in *El suplicio del placer* seems to be that both discourses—that of farce and that of the position of women as characters, as individuals, and as writers—defy any attempt at fixation. In Berman's text the discussion of genre and gender issues reveals their complex dimensions. Therefore, inverting the already inverted, as feminine writing does to farce, and vice versa, suggests not a return to so-called essentials or to a supposed point of departure, but the creation of a vacuum that becomes a new space for representation and social transformation. Farce and feminist writing coincide in aspects such as aggression and transgression of norms, but in their actual interaction they unmask and parody each other's inconsistencies, they underline each other's weaknesses. Paradoxically, this mutual antagonism is exactly what makes them similar enti-

---

[13] In this environment of uncertainty, Nigro states: "Confusion, of course, can breed ambiguity, and at times it is not altogether clear in *One* [first segment of *El suplicio*] whether gender roles are being reversed rather than subverted" ("Inventions" 147). From this study's standpoint, the notion of role-reversal in farce takes a new meaning in *El suplicio*, once we recognize the attempt to portray incessant inversions and, therefore, an almost inevitable subversion. Although the notion of role-reversal applies to Berman's play in its entirety, this aspect will be discussed in greater depth with analysis of the first segment of *El suplicio* ("El bigote"), where the male and female characters, *Él* and *Ella*, problematize their sexual roles and identities.

ties. From the very title of Berman's work (including the subtitle in the 1985 edition, *Tres obras en un acto sobre un tema* [Three one act plays about one theme]), antagonism and displacement become the keystones of the fragmentary nature of the play.

El suplicio del placer was first staged in 1978 under the title *El jardín de las delicias* at the Universidad Autónoma Metropolitana, directed by Teresa Valdés (this change of title will be discussed later). It was also staged in 1985, now under the new title, and directed by Martha Luna (*Teatro de Sabina Berman* 325, 327). Becky Boling reviews the staging in January 1990 of "Dos"–the second part of *El suplicio*–and alludes to the staging of "Tres"(166). In August of 1992 I saw in the Teatro Rodolfo Usigli, also Corral de las Comedias, in Coyoacán, Mexico, an excellent staging of *El suplicio del placer*, directed by Josefina Félix and staged by Grupo Espejos. The acting was consistently superior throughout the three parts, and the experimental nature of the staging mixed well with the fragmented nature of the play. More important, in the 1994 edition of *El suplicio* by Grupo Editorial Gaceta, Berman added a fourth segment entitled "Los dientes": "On January 27th, a group of no more than six people in the Foro Ghandi put on several extremely short one act plays by Sabina Berman: 'Dos' and 'Tres' of the three part text of *El suplicio del placer* (1978) and a slapstick sketch called 'Los dientes' by the same dramatist" (Boling 166). This "slapstick sketch" later became the fourth segment of *El suplicio del placer,* and this latter version will be the one examined in this chapter.[14]

The first segment of *El suplicio del placer*, informally identified by Hugo Argüelles as "El bigote" (212), is about a couple whose relationship can be described as unorthodox in terms of men and women's traditional sexual roles, particularly because of the persistent exchange of the moustache between them. In "Casa Chica," the second segment, *Ella* plays the role of the submissive mistress or prostitute, and *Él* is the typical caricaturesque and violent *macho* who exploits women and who categorizes them as objects of desire.

---

[14] The inclusion by Berman of a fourth segment in *El suplicio del placer* should not surprise anyone, since one of the features of the play is the constant blurring of its multiple and ambiguous beginnings and endings. Berman's habit of changing the titles of her plays (see note 26) can also be interpreted as another mechanism used to dismantle authority and to create an environment of uncertainty. Unless stated, all quotes will be from the 1994 edition, and the translations are mine and placed in brackets.

In the third segment, *Él* and *Ella* seem to be playing games as the only viable way to survive a long and tedious relationship. But the grotesque games are of a terrorizing nature, and the spectator can easily confuse whether madness and murder are part of the characters' lives or part of their games. The fourth segment entitled "Los dientes," presents the vicissitudes of a dental patient–Ms. Berman–who is portrayed as having a huge mouth and whom the Dentist confuses with Ingmar/Ingrid Bergman. At the end, both the Nurse and the Dentist are sucked in by the huge mouth.

El suplicio del placer introduces at the start the contradictions and ambiguities that will prevail throughout the play. Its title is the first and most overt source of discomfort and confusion: Is pleasure something that we all aim for, something enjoyable, or actually a source of pain, a torture, a punishment, a *suplicio*? Is there an attempt to cancel both terms, or rather to create a third? Can the term "pleasure" be objectively defined? Who decides what produces pleasure and what is pleasurable? Should the examination of pleasure (sexual, psychological, ethical) in Berman's drama be extended to the theoretical discussions of "the pleasure of the text," to borrow Roland Barthes's title?[15]

The complexity of the term "pleasure" is one of the central points of *El suplicio del placer*. The play's tug-of-war is created not only by framing the "serious" issues of the play (ethical or psychological hedonism, sexual relations, sexism, power struggles, madness, or criminal behavior) within a farcical atmosphere (grotesque exaggeration, caricaturization, clichés of clichés, oversimplification, repetition), but also by derailing any attempt at defining pleasure and by dismantling any attempt at constructing a well-structured view of so-called social and artistic realities. In this environment of negation and anti-authoritarianism, the use of farce, the overt characterization

---

[15] In William Alston's article, "Pleasure," published in the 1972 edition of *The Encyclopedia of Philosophy*, he summarizes people's most basic understanding of this concept: "It seems clear to most people that pleasure and enjoyment are preeminent among the things worth having and that when someone gets pleasure out of something, he develops a desire for it" (341). But ironically, in the attempt to define pleasure, most commentators make recourse to a dichotomy: "Pleasure and pain have usually been regarded as opposite parts of a single continuum" (Alston 341). In his *Diccionario de Filosofía*, José Ferrater Mora is more blatant in stressing the inherent difficulties of defining pleasure, and by underlining the multiple contexts and uses of this word, argues for an abstention from defining the term (422).

of feminist issues, and the preeminence in the play of a term such as "pleasure" demonstrate how *El suplicio* confronts authority and oppression by taking recourse to concepts that have themselves been traditionally marginalized and subjected to powerful structures.

Even though the subtitle of the 1985 edition, *Tres obras de un acto sobre un tema*, a convention that usually serves to clarify, or add information about different aspects of a play (its genre, its tone, its structural arrangement), here creates an unstable image of an already contradictory title. Should the discussion of Berman's play(s) be centered on an analysis of each one of the parts of *El suplicio* or on the proposed single theme or, rather, on the interaction among the segments? One wonders if the "single theme" should be identified as the intricacies of the concept of pleasure, or of the concept of power, or of the relationship between pleasure and power. And also wonders if the play is mostly and seriously concerned with feminist issues, or rather with a farcical view of the feminist discourse in its most iconoclastic form. In reference to the 1985 edition, Hugo Argüelles articulates the difficulty of naming the sections of *El suplicio* that he is trying to describe: "What are these three exercises, these three 'appearances,' these three theatrical propositions, these three games, these three dramatic sequences, these three short farces? Well, they are all this and more" (212).[16]

Even though this study initially examines each segment separately, the fragments are not perceived as isolated entities, but as interdependent and complementary bodies. For example, although the *Él* and *Ella* of the first three segments change identities, the audience is driven to believe that they are the same throughout the play. Only in the last segment, "Los dientes," the pattern of naming the characters *Él* and *Ella* is changed as they are identified by their professions. In "El bigote" *Él* and *Ella*, described in the stage directions as an effeminate male and a masculine woman, are not only dressed alike but look very much alike and are equally slender, beautiful, and elegant (I: 161). Nevertheless, the tension between them is quite visible. In the living room of a suite, in their identical

---

[16] To maintain the notion of unity within a fragmented structure, I will frequently identify the so-called one-act plays as segments, since this reflects the interdependence among the parts. In the 1994 edition, Berman dates the play 1984-87 (159).

pajamas and over two cups of tea, the argument between *Él* and *Ella* immediately centers on the moustache: who has it, who should have it, who had it before, why did one of them have it and not the other?

> ÉL.   Ya sé lo que tienes de raro. No traes tu bigote.
> *Ella baja el periódico.*
> ELLA.   ¿Mi bigote? Por supuesto que no traigo mi bigote. Mi bigote lo traes tú.
>
> ....
>
> ÉL.   ¿Y se puede saber por qué traigo yo tu bigote?
> *Ella baja de súbito el periódico. Lo dobla enérgicamente. Lo mira con fijeza.*
> ELLA.   ¿Se te olvidó lo de anoche?
> *Él rehuye mirarla.* (I: 162-63)
>
> [HE.   Now I know why you look so strange. You don't have your moustache.
> *She lowers the paper.*
> SHE.   My moustache? Of course I don't have my moustache. You have my moustache.
>
> ....
>
> HE.   May I ask why I have your moustache?
> *She suddenly puts down the paper. She folds it energetically. She stares at him.*
> SHE.   You forgot about last night?
> *He avoids looking at her.*]

The farcical tone is set early in the play, and the audience responds with laughter to the absurdity of the suggestion that a woman has a moustache.[17] But the tension between the characters never vanishes and contaminates both the stage and the audience.

---

[17] Nigro humorously contrasts the presence of a moustache in females and males: "that well-groomed growth of facial hair that on a woman connotes some kind of aberration, as with the moustachioed circus ladies, but that on a man's face is taken to be the quintessential sign of sexual prowess and masculine guile" ("Inventions" 145). On her part, Gladhart states that "The mustache alternately disguises, enhances, or transforms the 'real' gender behind it, working as a visual cue, or as visual performative–to wear the mustache is to become/perform a gender" (135-36). Sharon Magnarelli reminds us how Berman subtly connects *El suplicio* with another of her plays, *Entre Villa y una mujer desnuda* (1993), through the female moustache: "Emphasizing what might be read as her masculinity, Adrián is fascinated with Andrea's 'bigotito'" (68).

What is evident is that neither *Él* nor *Ella* is following respective male or female traditional roles, as would be dictated by an equally traditional society. He is portrayed as a weak and insecure man, incapable of being independent and assertive, and she as an aggressive woman determined to do only what she wants, not what others want or expect her to do. Thus, what is common or uncommon, traditional or nontraditional, expected or unexpected, normal or bizarre, decent or indecent, pleasurable or pleasureless in the lives of *Él* and *Ella* becomes the focus of the action of "El bigote," and also of the remaining segments of the play.

In this first piece, *Ella* supposedly wears the moustache to deter men from making sexual advances when she does not want them. But as she reminds *Él*, he now has the moustache because she gave it to him the night before so that he could make a good impression on a brunette sitting at the table next to theirs. Ironically, *Él* cannot remember anything about his encounter with the brunette, but *Ella* can describe her "rival" in amazing detail. Both the spectator and *Él* notice the sensual tone of *Ella*'s description of the brunette, and her attraction to other women becomes an implied –but unresolved–issue:

> ÉL. ¿Y fue a mí a quien le gustó?
> ELLA. De nuevo estás insinuando...
> ÉL. No, nada, nada. Me duele la cabeza. ¿Hay hielitos? (I: 164)

> [HE. Was it I who found her attractive?
> SHE. Again you're insinuating...
> HE. No, nothing, nothing. I have a headache. Is there ice?]

In response to *Él*'s implicit accusation of *Ella*'s bisexualism, she immediately accuses him (and men) of being capable only of admiring certain types of beauty and underscores his insatiable desire to possess, consume, and exhaust everything that he is attracted to, while she can be satisfied with contemplating from afar. *Ella* argues that being a woman is not an obstacle to admiring the beauty of other women. But what *Él* ultimately resents is that it is only he who takes advantage of their pact of independence and their so-called liberal arrangement:

> ÉL. Por eso me remuerden [tus aventuras]: porque no las tienes. Me predicas las delicias del amor libre, me predicas su

valor civil incluso: . . . pero tú nunca... No te molestes si te lo recuerdo, pero tú nunca te compartes con nadie. Te voy a pedir...

ELLA. *(Poniendo a un lado el periódico.)* ¿Sí?

....

ÉL. Te voy a exigir que por mí, por mi salud mental, de pronto, cuando estemos en público, te quites el bigote, dejes que se te acerque algún galán, y te compartas. Si yo te viera actuar como una mujer liberada no me sentiría mal por las mañanas.

ELLA. ¿Cómo te atreves? ¿Quieres limitar mi libertad, pidiéndome que actúe como una mujer libre cuando soy tan absolutamente libre que no necesito actuar como si fuera libre? (I: 172)

[HE. That's why I feel so upset about your affairs: because you don't have any. You talked to me about the delights of free love, even about its civic importance . . . but you never... Don't get upset if I remind of it, but you never share yourself with anybody. I am going to ask you...

SHE. *(Setting the newspaper aside.)* Yes?

....

HE. I am going to demand that for my sake, for the sake of my peace of mind, when we are with other people, you take off the moustache, let some handsome guy approach you, and share yourself with him. If I saw you acting like a liberated woman, I wouldn't feel so bad in the morning.

SHE. How dare you? Would you limit my freedom, asking me to act like a free woman when I'm so free that I don't need to act as if I were?]

Ella's questioning of his prejudices unmasks the farcical side of what is logical and reasonable. It is evident that forcing her to be liberal and open-minded about their relationship is as coercive as prohibiting her from being so. But why is it that this logical statement, which stresses the difference between being free and being forced to show one's freedom, sounds ridiculous and funny? For one thing, the repetition of words contributes to this effect by creating a hyperbolic version of the statement. But more so, by framing the argument of women's liberation within the parameters of farce (lookalike caricatures dressed identically and a woman with a moustache encouraging her partner to seek other women, and vice versa), the play creates a double-edged sword that can simultaneously win and threaten the new position in society claimed by women. Even though *Ella*'s argument is valid, Berman forces the spectator to recognize (both seriously and humorously) the interdependence between individual freedom and its opposite, but also to acknowledge the weaknesses of both. In other words, this sophism or double argument used by *Ella* to proclaim her independence and individuality –"Would you limit my freedom, asking me to act like a free woman when I'm so free that I don't need to act as if I were?"–underlines the paradoxical nature of the messengers and the message(s). *El suplicio* focuses on clichés and issues of power regarding the antagonistic relationship between women and men to portray a dramatic world whose inhabitants' social behavior (as messengers) and social beliefs (their messages) are characterized as meaningless. Berman's caricaturization of *machista* attitudes is evident throughout the play, and the audience easily recognizes that part of the message is to ridicule the traditional power structures monopolized by men.

Nevertheless, the play's understanding of the role of woman in a transformed society is not free from sarcasm and criticism. In this maze of contradictory affirmations and double arguments and negations, the play humorously problematizes the fact that women can be *subject* to the idea of total freedom. Being "subject to freedom" is one of the common inversions of the already inverted structures that *El suplicio* clearly enjoys revealing. In a parallel sarcastic way, *El suplicio*'s attempt to equate feminism with the search for and enjoyment of freedom is questioned when the audience confronts the possibility that, precisely because women can exercise their freedom, some might choose not to abide by feminists's standards of political and social behavior. The stylized and conscious instability of Berman's theatrical world is thus created by several elements: a bitter and a comic view of society (men and women in traditional and inverted roles); a vision of literature as an inadequate source of change but an instrument of communication nevertheless; and a concept of theatre as a grotesque reproduction of the extraliterary world as well as a site for experimentation and transgression. Framed within the language of farce, *El suplicio* offers a kaleidoscopic view of multiple coexisting realities, as well as the negation of those same realities.

Analyzed in the context of the entire play, the aforementioned sophisms stress the ambiguity of farce as a means of theatrical communication, of feminism as a catalyst for desired social change, and of pleasure as a source of enjoyment.[18] To add one more sophism to this overloaded baggage of contradictions, Berman's unquestionably feminist discourse is full of questions about its own questionable identity. *El suplicio del placer*, particularly its first segment, dramatizes the struggle for power between the sexes and turns problematical the notion of role-reversal.[19] The inversion of roles has been considered by critics to be one of the traditional devices of farce; however, in an environment of uncertainty and aggression, this canonical view of farce is also dismantled. If anything at all is practiced in *El suplicio del placer*, it is the more aggressive attempt to openly question sexual and social roles and identities, not the substitution of one voice for another.

Nonetheless, inversion continues to surface with different masks and in different patterns. For example, the uncertainty of both *Ella* and *Él*'s sexual identity is exacerbated by the role-reversal that takes place between the two characters, but this time the spectator does not witness a simple switch. As *Ella* is describing to *Él* what he has forgotten about his affair the night before, she reenacts the role of *Él*, and he the role of the brunette; in other words, that of a woman (I: 168-69). It is in this context of doubt that he again makes insinuations about her preference for women and demands from her an assurance that she loves him because he is a man. But *Ella*'s refusal to make such a statement stresses the environment of uncertainty, and the issue of an ambiguous sexuality and identity

---

[18] Among other well-known suspect reasonings that lead to paradoxical conclusions, such as *Ella*'s diatribe on freedom, is Don Quixote's fascination with Feliciano de Silva's intricate reasoning in his novels of chivalry: "The reason of the unreason that afflicts my reason, in such a manner weakens my reason, that I with reason lament me of your comeliness" (Cervantes, Part One, I: 58).

[19] Role-reversal has frequently been acknowledged as a key device in the development and success of farce. Walter Stanley Schutz, who summarizes the emphasis critics have given to this device in farce, defines inversion in very basic terms: "as the reversal of position, order, or relationship in characters, attitudes, actions, or speech for the prime purpose of effecting laughter" (166). Schutz then quotes Henri Bergson's essay "Laughter": "Picture to yourself certain characters in a certain situation: if you reverse the situation and invert the *roles*, you obtain a comic scene" (166). Schutz mentions other critics who discuss the importance of role-reversal: "[Robert] Stephenson identifies inversion with the phrase 'antitheses (of types, accents, dialects, behaviors)'" (167); "Historian Kernodle makes the point that playwrights have often found the key to laughter in sharp contrasts and reversals" (167). Jessica Milner Davis reminds the reader of the prevalence of role-reversal in farce, particularly noting the inversion of marital roles common in medieval drama (443-44).

takes center stage.[20] Finally, *Ella* confesses why she likes him so much: ". . . Me encantas... Porque no puedes comportarte como una persona independiente. Porque eres débil. Inseguro. Porque me necesitas para saber si eres o no un hombre" (I: 175) [I like you a lot.... Because you can't act like an independent person. Because you're weak. Insecure. Because you need me to know if you're a man or not].

Most of the information is now on the table, and in the midst of this confusion it is possible to uncover at least some of the layers: *Ella*, who seems to be attracted by women, is attracted to the "moustacheless" *Él* precisely because of his "feminine" characteristics: his weakness, his dependence on her, his insecurity. Therefore, from a stereotypical point of view, to be with him is, in some subtle way, to be with another woman without actually being with one. On the other hand, he likes her more with the moustache, recognizes how irresistible she is to other women when she wears it, and identifies with their attraction (as women): "¿Has visto cómo te miran las mujeres cuando llevas el bigote? ¿Cómo te sonríen? . . . Eres irresistible con el bigote y lo sabes. Y lo disfrutas" (I: 173) [Have you noticed how women look at you with the moustache? How they smile at you? . . . You are irresistible with the moustache and you know it. And you enjoy it]. At a primary level, roles have been switched and traditional expectations of a woman's and a man's behavior have been turned upside down. But the inversions have not yet ended: ironically, they are dismantled by subsequent inversions.[21]

What, then, is the explanation for *Ella*'s wanting to be with a womanlike man or *Él*'s desire to be with a manlike woman? What are the implications of talking about "feminine" characteristics such as weakness and insecurity and "masculine" ones such as individu-

---

[20] Costantino underlines the ambiguity of the information that the reader/spectator is receiving in the first segment of the play regarding the sexual identity of the characters (247).

[21] Michel Foucault's theories on sexuality and power are relevant to our reading of *El suplicio del placer*. Regarding the notion of inversion in Foucault, Judith Butler points out that "[Foucault's] theoretical practice is, in a sense, marked by a series of inversions: in the shift to modern power, an inversion is performed; in the relation of sex and sexuality, another inversion is performed. And with respect to the category of the 'invert,' yet another inversion is performed, one that might be understood to stand as a strategy of refiguration according to which the various other inversions of the text can be read" (69-70).

ality, strength, assertiveness, and determination? Is the exchange of characteristics between one sex and the other enough to alter social beliefs and taboos? [22] Can *Él* and *Ella*, even with their transgressive view of sexual identity, untangle (and free themselves from) all the perverse social layers that traditionally define the relationship between men and women? The moustache–a typical talisman of masculinity–used by *Ella* to avoid men and by *Él* to feel like one, poses questions about the characters' inability to transgress their traditional roles, to overcome the language of oppression in such a way that traditionally male or female symbols are destroyed or, at least, removed from center stage. [23]

Ironically, the possession of the moustache by either the man or the woman limits the action to a mere substitution and not an effective transgression. Therefore, the dismantling of roles seems incomplete, limited to an exchange of positions. As Nigro reminds us regarding this first segment of *El suplicio del placer*: "The 'masculine' still seduces here, the 'feminine' is seduced. Women (She as she) still suffer penis envy, and are metaphorically castrated. The

---

[22] The perception that one of farce's important contributions is to ridicule social beliefs and norms has been confronted with the notion that "the art and craft of the farceur is focused most directly toward laughter" (Schutz 186). Although Eric Bentley recognizes the dialectic in farce between gaiety and gravity and between what is on the surface and what is beneath the surface (241-42), he stresses farce's dealings with social taboos and how farce wishes "to damage the family, to desecrate the household gods" (226), adding that "outrage to family piety is certainly at the heart of farce as we know it" (227). Davis sees the benefits of farce and its psychological satisfactions "in the deliberate offence it gives to social norms" (26). Recognizing its duality as festive and as aggressive, she states that "farce is accepted as good-humoured fun, which is most satisfying precisely when it invites violation of social taboos" (Davis 27). When Albert Bermel tries to answer *Why farce?*, that is, why would an author who wants to teach, inform, or alert his audience about a particular issue, pick farce as a genre over comedy, he immediately answers: "One reason may be that farce is more bitter, more cruel, more downright unfair" (45).

[23] Among the many categories within which farce has been classified, Davis mentions the talisman-farces: "Among various types of circular farces there is one group whose structural principle is readily grasped. These are 'talisman farces', whose mathematical permutations and combinations are anchored to reality by a physical object (the 'talisman'), from which all confusion flows" (65). In the case of Berman's play it is possible to see in the moustache of the first segment, in the watch of the second, in the pistol of the third, and in the mouth of the fourth the talismans' role of inciting and confusing the action. The presence in *El suplicio del placer* of different objects that receive special attention creates in each of the one-act plays a sense of the ridiculous, of an oversimplified environment in which a single object is capable of determining and codifying the characters' behavior and absurd reality.

manly moustache stands for the penis and the penis stands for power" ("Inventions" 147). Nevertheless, Berman's text evades any type of fixity and continues to invert the standard inversion of roles. That is, "El bigote's" attempt to transgress the traditional notions of sexual identity and behavior, which at first sight seems dramatized merely by an exchange of roles and standard values, is again transgressed by the sexual ambiguities of the characters, provoking a more diffuse view of the traditional ending or solution of a play. But, ironically, the play–in its separate segments and in its entirety–demands, or at least suggests, other inversions.

Consequently, one wonders if there is an end to the labyrinth created by the constant inversions and if this process can be stopped. The recognition that the play will demand subsequent inversions sheds light on the apparent solution to this "infinite" process: Berman's choice of farce becomes the "final" transgression, where everything said, proposed, inverted, substituted, dismantled, and parodied is again transgressed. *Ella* and *Él*'s last dialogue and last kiss play with the "infinite" reversals and with that ultimate transgression represented by the use of farce:

> ÉL. Eres bella. Fría y bella como una diosa de mármol. . . .
> ....
> . . . Con el bigote eres de carne, pero aún peligrosa: ¿lo quieres?
> ELLA. No. ¿Para qué? Esta noche no habrá otra mujer que me tiente. . . .
> ....
> Pero si tú quieres quitártelo... Tal vez haya un hombre que te guste y si quieres que se te acerque tienes que quitarte el bigote.
> ÉL. No. Hoy me gustas tú más que ningún otro hombre. Eres irresistible con el bigote puesto. Póntelo.
> *Él mismo se lo pone. Le acaricia el bigote.*
> ....
> *Se besan en los labios.* (I: 178)

> [HE. You're beautiful. Cold and beautiful like a marble goddess.
> ....
> . . . With the moustache you're made of flesh, but you're still dangerous. Do you want it?

> SHE. No. What for? Tonight there's no other woman who tempts me.
>
> ....
>
> But if you want to take it off... There may be a man that you like, and if you want him to sit close to you, you have to take off your moustache.
>
> HE. No. Today there's no other man that I like as much as you. You're irresistible with the moustache on. Put it on.
> *He puts it on her. He caresses the moustache.*
>
> ....
>
> *They kiss each other on the lips.*]

In this incessant exchange and dismantling of roles, it seems elusive (and ludic) to determine the characters' position regarding sexual identity and desire. Who, after all, is kissing whom? Are *Ella* (the woman) and *Él* (the man) kissing, or is it *Ella* (the man) and *Él* (the woman) kissing? Or perhaps is *Ella* (the woman) kissing *Él* (the woman), or *Ella* (the man) kissing *Él* (also the man)? In *El suplicio del placer* the discussion of genre and gender issues is portrayed ironically by the disclosure of their contradictions and ambiguities, not their coherence and predictability. The use of farce and the relationship of this genre with women's writing and feminist ideology reveal the profound antiauthoritarianism and iconoclastic view of theatrical and social realities in Berman's play. Avoiding all forms of oppression and recognizing the capacity of farce and feminism to oppress, Berman opts for a constant inversion and questioning of farce and feminism's solutions to oppression. As antagonistic and aggressive voices, farce and feminism avoid fixity and struggle against positioning themselves in a privileged space.

More important, the difficulty of decoding "El bigote" is not only dramatized by its ambiguous ending regarding sexual roles and identity but is magnified by the second, third and forth segments of the play. Therefore, the last dialogue of "El bigote" is nothing more than a pseudoending, the mask of an absent ending that allows other voices–other *Él*s and *Ella*s–to ridicule the previous and subsequent ones. The uncertainty of "El bigote's" ending and the characters' response to sexual oppression and power struggles will become central issues in the other three segments of the play: in "Casa Chica," in "La pistola," and in "Los dientes." This discussion will then bring the analysis back to the problematics of pleasure in its various and contradictory expressions in *El suplicio del placer*.

In the second segment the audience witnesses the pseudomonologue (since the man does most of the talking) between a flashily dressed businessman and his subjugated lover, while she is getting ready to go out with him. Desperate to leave, *Él* insults *Ella* for her perpetual tardiness and, rubbing it in, reminds his lover of the Cartier watch he bought for her. But he immediately realizes that he has not only purchased an expensive watch that she is probably incapable of reading, but that he has also bought *her*: "Tú eres mía no porque me ames sino porque te compré. ¿Entendido?" (II: 180) [You are mine not because you love me but because I purchased you. Understood?]. In contrast with his aggressive and violent tone and his fast and foul speech, her answers are limited to short phrases of approval or responses to his demands: "Ya casi," "Sí mi amor," "Já, já, já," "Sí, muñeco," "¡Ay!," "¿Ya no me quieres, vidita?" [Almost ready; Yes, honey; Ha, ha, ha; Yes, darling; Ay! Don't you love me anymore, sweetie?]. But this apparent unconditional submissiveness gives *Él* more ammunition to degrade her as much as he wishes, since he believes he is in total control.

The scenario seems quite clear at this point. *Ella* plays the role of the submissive mistress or prostitute, and *Él* is the typical, caricaturesque, and violent macho who applies different standards to men's and women's behavior, who exploits women, and who categorizes them as objects of desire. Not only does he remind *Ella* that she belongs to him, but he tells her that his wife will inherit her when he dies. As expected, he is a married man, and he rants indiscriminately against his wife and his lover:

> ÉL. ... Eres igual a mi esposa. Desde hace años sabe que la engaño pero mientras no tenga que medir sus gastos, qué le importa si le soy infiel. Todas las mujeres son iguales. En lugar de corazón tienen una cartera. Pero lo que no saben ni tú ni ella es que ustedes no tienen nada. Ustedes sólo reciben. Yo soy el rico. Ustedes lo que compro. Son mi lujo: mis relojes Cartier... (II: 179)

> [HE. ... You're just like my wife. For years she's known that I cheat on her, but as long as she doesn't have to limit her expenses, what does it matter if I'm unfaithful to her. All women are the same. Instead of a heart they have a purse. But what neither you nor she knows is that you don't have anything. You only receive. I'm the one who is rich. You are my merchandise. You are my luxuries: my Cartier watches...]

But when *Él* tells his wife the most common lie of unfaithful husbands–he is staying late because of an important business meeting–she cannot help laughing, since she knows where he actually is and she does not seem to care at all (II: 182-83). This ironic laughter is magnified in Josefina Félix's production of *El suplicio del placer*, where there is a significantly interesting twist to this scene: while the husband believes his wife is silently tolerating his unfaithfulness, she appears in the background with another man. The wife's laughter makes this addition to the staging quite suitable, since it ridicules even further her oversimplified and pathetic macho husband. More significant is how this scene parallels *Él*'s brief telephone conversation with his daughter and the traditional double standards of a male-dominated society:

> ÉL. ... No, papi llega ya nochecita, así que usted póngase un besote en la manita y luego la manita con todo y el besote se la pone de mi parte en la frentecita; luego se pone la pijama, se mete a la camita y sueña con la virgencita y los... ¡¿Cómo que ya no hay vírgenes?! Mira encuincla: aunque tengas dieciocho años sigues siendo pura e inocente, ¿está claro? *(Cuelga.)* Ya no hay vírgenes, hija de su puta madre (II: 183)
>
> [HE. ... No, daddy will arrive late at night, so you put a big kiss on your little hand and then you put the little hand with the big kiss on your little forehead; then you put on your pajamas, you get into bed and you dream of the virgin and... What do you mean there are no virgins? Look, you pipsqueak: even though you're eighteen, you're still pure and innocent, is that clear? *(Hangs up)* There are no virgins anymore, you son of a bitch!

Who, then, is buying the story of an impeccable family life, faithfulness, purity, female devotion, and social harmony, among other virtues?

Ironically, as this second segment quickly progresses, *Él*'s perception of his wife changes: he compares her "saintliness" with *Ella*'s vulgarity, shows her how she should dress like his wife, and in the middle of a sexual rant (or, more accurately, rape) in which he throws his lover down onto the sofa, he praises his self-sacrificing wife and demands that society get rid of immoral and perverted women like *Ella*:

ÉL. ... Mi mujer, mi pobre, mi sabia esposa... Mi cónyuge legítima es una mujer admirable, quiero que quede asbolutamente claro eso. ¿Qué le importa si le soy infiel mientras le dé con qué mantener dignamente nuestro hogar? Toda su resignación para que yo pueda parecer decente ante la sociedad... (II: 184)

[HE. ... My wife, my poor wise wife... My legitimate spouse is an admirable woman. I want to make that absolutely clear. What does she care if I'm unfaithful as long as I give her money to keep a nice house? All that tolerance just so I can look decent in society. ...]

Just before falling between *Ella*'s legs he says: "¡Santa mujer mi esposa!" (II: 185) [My wife's a real saint!].

The grotesque exaggeration of the two characters–the sexy and dumb woman and the macho man–is too blatant to be taken seriously. But it is the contrast between laughing about the comic characterization of *Él* and *Ella* and reflecting on a society that tolerates these aberrations that creates the tension of the play and allows the issue of inversion and transgression of roles to surface again, although in a different light.

The disparity between actions and words and between expectations and actions is clear, particularly in regard to *Él* and his family. His supposed power over others and his naiveté about his wife's and daughter's sexual behavior and values are completely illusory; that which is initially perceived as his control over things and people is nothing but a fragile and caricaturesque mask.[24] The writer and critic Rosario Castellanos pointedly criticizes the traditional role of women in society, and her comments make Berman's play even more ironically humorous in regard to the conduct of the wife and the daughter in "La Casa Chica": "The purity of a lineage depended on the behavior of the wife or the daughter, and even the most insignificant whim or the slightest suspicion that honor had not been well kept were punishable by death" ("La participación" 24).

In this second segment of *El suplicio del placer*, the wife is no saint, the daughter is no virgin, the man is no happy guy enjoying

---

[24] In Bermel's discussion of Molière's *Les Fourberies de Scapin*, his suggestion that the spectator of farce delights in seeing the authoritative figure degraded applies pertinently to the second segment of *El suplicio* (22).

his freedom and his mistress, and even *Ella* may not be as ignorant as portrayed, since she may be exploiting him as much as he believes he is exploiting her and others.[25] Regarding this recognition of women's multiple masks and their reasons for using them, Castellanos again reminds us:

> Women have been accused of hypocrisy, and the accusation is not unfounded. But hypocrisy is the response given to the oppressors by the oppressed, it is the weak's reply to the strong, that of the subordinate to his master. Hypocrisy is the consequence of a situation; it is a conditioned response–like the change of color in a chameleon–when there are many dangers and few options. ("La participación" 25)

Nevertheless, this situation, where men who think and act as if they are in control are actually being manipulated by women, also seems too easy a reversal. The fact is that the audience faces two interdependent struggles: on the one hand, the tension between *Él*'s caricaturesque portrayal and men's historical oppressive power and, on the other, between women's apparent acceptance of men's power (hypocrisy) and the open rejection of that power. In the case of men, the struggle seems to be between manipulation through masking and a radical unmasking of men's social *farce*. For women, the dichotomy centers on the jokes made at the expense of men but also on the recognition of the prolonged history of abuses inflicted by them. Therefore, the initial inversion (men assuming female roles and vice versa, as in the first segment) is dismantled, and the conscious lack of a straightforward view of men and women's relationship becomes emblematic of a discourse that plays with and parodies its own expectations and clichés.

If the traditional idea of pleasure is severely questioned throughout the first two segments, in the third one-act play ("La pistola") the spectator confronts the overt aggression and constant reversal of the term. This third part begins with the two characters–not by chance identified as *Él* and *Ella*–exchanging just one phrase: "No entiendo."/"No entiendo."/"No entiendo." (III: 186) [I don't understand./ I don't understand./ I don't understand.]. As

---

[25] Costantino interprets *Ella*'s silence in the second segment as her most important weapon against *Él*'s caricaturesque power (248-49).

in the rest of *El suplicio*, the contradictory games with words, concepts, and social issues reflect the play's capacity to produce a diverse spectrum of mirror images, and, once again, the possibility of determining a particular meaning, a coherent dramatic form, or a systematic construction of characters is annulled by a sophism. After arguing about their lack of understanding of past events and before reenacting these events, *Ella* says: "¿Cómo puedes no entender lo que yo no entiendo si yo no entiendo lo que no entiendo?" (III: 186) [How can you not understand what I don't understand if I don't understand what I don't understand?]. It is evident that destroying, or at least masking, a fixed meaning ironically becomes one of the most meaningful elements of the play. In other words, *El suplicio*'s problematization of meaning and farce's alleged incapacity to produce it establish a humorous interplay where the transgression of what seems meaningless unmasks its own meaninglessness–or conversely, perhaps, masks its own profound meaning.

But the serious dilemma with the events being reenacted in this third segment by *Él* (Humberto) and *Ella* (María) is that their labyrinthine and oneiric nature creates an environment of distrust between the couple; throughout the play, the various levels of reality and interpretation become entangled, mixed, confused. Humberto arrives at home with a small bag containing a pistol. He claims that he bought it to protect the household from burglars, but the effect of the gun's presence is to exacerbate María's fears and insecurities. *Ella*, who is portrayed as a weak and mentally unstable woman, speaks incoherently and constantly contradicts herself. For example, she offers Humberto the dinner she has supposedly prepared, but it becomes clear that there is no food in the house. The tension grows when both *Ella* and the audience suspect that Humberto's intention in buying the gun is to terrorize and eventually kill her. He immediately rejects this idea, but the feeling of uncertainty still permeates their dialogue:

> ELLA. No juegues, puede dispararse.
> ÉL. Qué bueno que me lo recuerdas. *(Le apunta. Ella retrocede aterrorizada... Él dispara. No está cargada. Se ríe.)* No está cargada. Carajo: antes tenías sentido del humor... *(Sonríe tristemente. Vuelve a la mesa. Saca un estuche de balitas y empieza a cargar la pistola.)* (III: 194)

[SHE. Don't fool around, it can go off.
HE. Thanks for reminding me. *(He aims the gun at her. She backs off in terror... He fires. It's not loaded. He laughs.)* It's not loaded. Damn: you used to have a sense of humor... *(Smiles sadly. Returns to the table. He takes out a box of bullets and begins to load the gun.)*]

Finally, when María goes back to the kitchen for the second time to check the windows, and when she is about to hide the pistol behind the bookshelves, she hears noises coming from the front door. She sees someone through the window, screams, and shoots three times. Not surprisingly, Humberto, who had left through the bedroom window to come to the living room to pick up the gun, is the one severely wounded. Ironically, they have what seems to be a long conversation for a wounded man where he accepts his inevitable death and finally retreats to the bedroom to die. But while María is cleaning the blood stains from the carpet (a strange act for someone who has just shot her husband), Humberto returns with no signs of injury. When *Ella* reacts with surprise and joy to his healthy condition, the entire scene of the attempted murder is manipulated and framed by Humberto as another of María's nightmares, making her believe that everything–including the presence of the pistol in the house–was only a bad dream:

ELLA. Te disparaba con la pistola que trajiste a casa.
ÉL. ¿Yo traía una pistola a casa? Qué sueño.
ELLA. ¿No trajiste una pistola a casa? Una pistola de bajo calibre en un paquete forrado de... ¿cómo se dice?, de... (III: 202)

[SHE. I was shooting at you with the gun you brought home.
HE. I brought a gun home? What a dream!
SHE. Didn't you bring a gun home? A small caliber gun in a package wrapped in... what's it called?, in...]

Humberto, who deliberately wants to confuse María and to intensify her fears, and who ultimately persuades her that she has just had a dream, secretly loads the pistol and hides it again. Although she is becoming increasingly suspicious and desperate, she nevertheless embraces him and returns with him to the bedroom.

Is Humberto going to kill María sooner or later? Is it going to be by shooting her with a gun or by terrorizing her psychologically? Is the latter method a less accountable type of murder and therefore more suitable for a husband trying to get rid of his wife with impunity? Ironically, if one returns to the beginning of this third segment, "La pistola" can be framed as a game where both characters are merely interrupting the dullness of their lives and the emptiness of their relationship. Are *Él* and *Ella*, then, just playing with the notion of reality and, consequently, characterizing the roles of a fictional Humberto and a fictional María? Or maybe of a fictional *Él* and a fictional *Ella*? The initial appearance of the two characters (mostly addressed to the reader and director) describes a married couple that considers their relationship a long-standing one, while the action begins with *Ella* and *Él* back-to-back, walking in different directions as in the preliminaries of a duel or a game (I: 186). In his prologue to *El suplicio*, Hugo Argüelles suggests that playing is the only viable way for the characters to survive a long and tedious relationship: "All this is taking place with a couple–a married couple–who . . . have become bored. And so (without planning it) they both look for a more exciting way of staying together (and surviving)" (213). Understood from this particular perspective, what was initially considered an act of torture on Humberto's part becomes a pseudoludic dramatization of the emptiness in the relationship between men and women. What was initially quite clear is now confusing. Or should I say "inverted"? But the confusion that the spectator is now experiencing has been expressed already in the initial dialogue between *Ella* and *Él*: "No entiendo."/"No entiendo" (III: 186).

I am not suggesting that *El suplicio del placer* is impossible to understand but that it constantly underscores the lack of a fixed interpretation of reality–assuming there is such a thing. Ronald Burgess, in his study of the new dramaturgy of Mexico reminds the reader that the original title of *El suplicio del placer* was *El jardín de las delicias* and offers both circumstantial and thematic explanations for Berman's habit of changing the titles of her works: "The unstable texts behind the unstable titles offer examples of unstable historical realities, and therefore combine present and past instability" (81).[26]

---

[26] Other titles by Berman that have also changed are: *Esta no es una obra de teatro* to *Un actor se repara*, *Bill* to *Yankee*, *Un buen trabajador del piolet* to *Rompecabezas*, and *Anatema*, first to *Herejía* and later to *En el nombre de Dios* (see Burgess 81).

Finally, the fourth segment titled "Los dientes" presents the problems experienced by a dental patient–Ms. Berman–who has a huge mouth and whose identity is persistently confused. Thus, identity and power, both artistic and sexual, become the central conflict as the Nurse and Dentist torture the already suffering Ms. Berman, while they also express their complex sexuality: the Nurse recalls her lesbian relationship with the patient, and the doctor suffers because his wife–who is also his sister–is having an affair with another dentist. At the end, both the Nurse and the Dentist are sucked in by the huge mouth, that is, by Ms. Berman. Clearly, what seems most fascinating of this fourth segment is the presence of a character embodied by a mouth and named Berman, who happens to be an artist and who characterizes the "absent other" evoked in the previous segments but who has been kept out of sight. One should remember that in the title page of the 1985 edition, the reader is confronted with this notion of the "absent other": "Para ser representadas, estas obras requieren de un mínimo de dos actores y un máximo de seis. En cada una se trata de un ÉL, una ELLA, y un OTRO ausente" (266) [In order to be performed, these plays require a minimum of two actors and maximum of six. Each of them deals with a HE, a SHE and an OTHER who is absent]. The inclusion of "Los dientes" in the 1994 edition explores, from our standpoint, the presence of another voice/mouth–the author–who ends up swallowing the healthcare-providers-*cum*-torturers, along with their particular sexual stories and histories. Just as power, sexual identity, and pleasure were key concepts in the analysis of the three segments of the 1985 edition, they continue to play a key role in the interpretation of "Los dientes."

As stated in the introduction to this study, the critics of farce have long debated the "intentions" of this genre and its place and prestige (or lack thereof) in relation to other literary forms, particularly comedy.[27] Robert Williams's statement is, in this case, among the most enlightening:

> The very substance of farce–its *telos*, if there is one–is disruption of our phenomenal world by sudden joltings, outrageous turns,

---

[27] It is important to compare Carlson's critical position regarding comedy's identity, which questions the need to celebrate joyously life as the staple of this genre (168), with farce's iconoclastic caricaturization of this celebration.

even as it gives the illusion of being involved in sane, coherent representation. Or, as Derrida might say, farce is always in a state of tension, always an interplay between form and formlessness, restraint and freedom, control and chaos. The essential dynamic of farce is its genuine playfulness, manifest in its indeterminate nature, its seemingly perverse refusal to offer glib certainties.... [F]arce plays not only with us but with its own game. (65)

Sabina Berman's use of farce becomes the channel of a debate over purpose and meaning, since both the genre she utilizes and the male/female relationships she portrays are characterized by their elusive and transgressive nature. That is, even though there is an overt attempt in *El suplicio* to ridicule traditional male domination (purpose), the play moves through farcical means to question, invert, play with, and parody its own antitraditional stands (meaning). The role occupied by the initial inversion and subsequent transgressions of situations and of the characters' typical behavior amplifies this debate between purpose and meaning by evading categorical answers to the questions posed. Nevertheless, this debate is only one of the unifying elements of the four one-act plays, since to argue that it is *the* central issue would contradict the persistent desire of *El suplicio* to contradict itself *ad infinitum*. The problematics of genre and gender in Berman's play move beyond those two complex entities to confront and shed light upon their similar preoccupations and uncertainties.

It is significant that in Rosario Castellanos's essay "Woman and Her Image," the feminist writer recognizes the maze of contradictions into which women have, on occasion, placed themselves and others. Regarding the latter, Castellanos says: "In our case, man converts whatever is feminine into a receptacle of contradictory moods and places it at a distance from which we are shown a figure that, although varying in form, is monotonous in meaning" (237). What Berman wisely does with this statement is invert it, contradict it, and eventually transgress not Castellanos's denunciation itself but men's attempt to convert "whatever is feminine into a receptacle of contradictory moods." Ironically, and by a double contradiction–that is, by contradicting men's notion of the feminine as contradictory–Berman is exercising her right to contradict men and to proclaim women's right to avoid fixing themselves in a restrictive and intolerant mode.

The exploration and use of the genre of farce by a female and feminist playwright such as Berman invites us to revisit the feminist Mexican writer, Rosario Castellanos, who chose in several instances this problematic means of artistic communication.[28] The thematic, generic, but also ideological coincidences between Castellanos's 1975 *El eterno femenino*, subtitled "Farsa," and Berman's *El suplicio del placer* invite general comparisons between these two feminist Mexican writers and their complex works. In her essay "Inventions and Transgressions: A Fractured Narrative on Feminist Theatre in Mexico," Kirsten Nigro has already proposed the link between these two plays with a third play by Carmen Boullosa, *Propusieron a María* [*They Proposed Mary*, 1987]. Nigro states:

> All three [plays] have as a clearly feminist strategy the transgression of patriarchal boundaries–social, sexual, and artistic–which have isolated Mexican women within confining, if not asphyxiating, spaces. In each instance, these transgressions are both destructive, in that they break down barriers, and constructive, in the way that they refocus, redefine fundamental issues concerning women's subjectivity–how women experience themselves; concerning their representation–how others, especially men, construct them; and concerning their self-representation–how they construct themselves. ("Inventions" 138)

Similarly, Amalia Gladhart examines in *The Leper in Blue: Coercive Performance and the Contemporary Latin American Theatre* how Castellanos's *El eterno femenino*, Berman's first act of *El suplicio del placer*, and Susana Torres Molina's *...Y a otra cosa mariposa* (1981) "depict, in differing ways, relations between gender and perfor-

---

[28] Castellanos's first experiment with theatre, *Tablero de damas*, has also been studied from the point of view of farce. In "'Tablero de Damas' and 'Álbum de Familia': Farces on Women Writers," Kathleen O'Quinn states that "'Tablero de damas' actually deals with the farcical environment for writing prevalent in Mexico, interpreted through the particular experience of women writers" (100). In "Rosario Castellanos, Image and Idea," Mary Seale Vásquez comments on Castellanos's relationship with contemporary playwrights, particularly the fact that they encouraged her to explore this genre. At the end of *El eterno femenino* the reader/spectator will again encounter a satirical tone regarding the "female literary sub-culture of Mexico," as he/she listens to a group of women discussing nothing but Castellanos's *El eterno femenino*. Bockus-Aponte also reminds us of Castellanos's other experiments with theatre: the one-act dramatic poems *Judith*, *Salomé*, and *Eva*, *Vocación de Sor Juana* in two acts, and *La creciente* in three acts (57).

mance, including the performances demanded in accord with a presumably given gender and the construction of gender through–and as–performance" (112).

It is possible to expand further this dialogue between *El eterno femenino* and *El suplicio del placer* by connecting Nigro's and Gladhart's arguments to my own. In my view, these plays' keen understanding of oppressive social patterns regarding women, and also their critical self-awareness regarding their socio-artistic "solutions" to women's marginalization, reveal their unwillingness to accept a simple reversal of roles in which there is a mere substitution of one oppressive voice for another. In other words, I contend that Castellanos's and Berman's dramatic experiments rely on their awareness and rejection of all authoritative power (even their own).

Another justification for the comparative approach between Castellanos's and Berman's plays is what Naomi Lindstrom identifies in Castellanos's criticism, teaching, and creative writing as her pioneering "incorporation of sex role analysis into literary commentary" (66). Lindstrom states that Castellanos "is especially interested in finding in fiction the accurate reflection of the harmful effects of socially-imposed sex role distinctions" (68). In the case of *El suplicio del placer*, Berman thoroughly explores sex role inequalities and, through farce, lays out a parodic and transgressive view of these inequalities. Although in different historical moments and at times with different tools (Castellanos channeled her ideological positions not only through fiction and poetry but also through journalistic writing), both Mexican authors engage in sex-role analysis, and in the cases of *El eterno femenino* and *El suplicio*, they both have recourse to farce as a way to parody the absurdity of defining, determining, and limiting the roles of women and of men.[29]

Castellanos's influence on Spanish American feminist thought, through her journalistic essays, her direct and systematic denunciation of the controlled role of woman in Mexican society, and her literary works, has been openly acknowledged and carefully studied.[30]

---

[29] See Gladhart for the distinction between questioning the roles assigned to women in Castellanos's *El eterno femenino* and the more overt questioning of gender categories in *El suplicio del placer* (111-12).

[30] Maureen Ahern states in the "Introduction" to *A Rosario Castellanos Reader* that "in tune with her roots, ahead of her time, laughing at herself, Rosario Castellanos in her lucidity has become mirror and model for several generations of writers throughout Latin America" (xv). Stressing this influence in the rest of Latin

But equally worthy of study is *why* and *how* she deals with issues of gender in Mexico in a humorous manner and a cutting tone, and what type of parallel strategy Berman adopts in *El suplicio del placer*. The use of farce by both dramatists to denounce traditional values signals a deliberate strategy not only to address the social problems that afflict women but also to display their rhetorical power and their privileged position to discuss these problems. Both Castellanos and Berman acknowledge in their plays the double-edged and ironic "finality" of their discourses and their recourse to farce as a way to stress the unbalanced and grotesque aspects of men's and women's social, political, sexual, and artistic relations.[31]

This ironic and double-edged use of farce when confronted with societal issues has been accurately expressed by Castellanos when she looks for a means to combat the old bad habits seen in the bizarre relationship between the macho man and the self-sacrificing woman:

America, Ahern adds, "However, her second collection of essays, *Mujer que sabe latín*, which analyzes women's issues and women writers, was avidly read by women all over Latin America, particularly the younger generation of feminists and writers, when it was published in 1971" (39). Among other studies dealing with Castellanos' significant literary contributions, see Maureen Ahern and Mary Seale Vásquez, eds., *Homenaje a Rosario Castellanos* (1980), a collection of essays devoted to Castellanos's poetry, theatre, fiction, and journalistic essays; see also Kirsten Nigro, "Rosario Castellanos' Debunking of the *Eternal Feminine*," and "Para narrar la narrativa del teatro femenino–El paradigma mexicano;" Barbara Bockus-Aponte, "Estrategias dramáticas del feminismo en *El eterno femenino* de Rosario Castellanos;" Sandra Cypess, "From Colonial Constructs to Feminist Figures: Re/visions by Mexican Women Dramatists;" Mónica Szurmuk, "Lo femenino en *El eterno femenino* de Rosario Castellanos;" Carl Good, "Testimonio especular, testimonio sublime en *El eterno femenino* de Rosario Castellanos;" and Sharon Sieber, "The Deconstruction of Gender as Archetype in Rosario Castellanos' *El eterno femenino*."

[31] It is pertinent to mention here Linda Hutcheon's understanding of irony and the different ways in which her understanding of it "as a discursive strategy operating at the level of language (verbal) or form (musical, visual, textual)" (10), can be linked to our understanding of Spanish American farce. Referring to the use of irony, Hutcheon poses similar quandaries as we do here regarding the use of farce in the Spanish American context: "Why should anyone want to use this strange mode of discourse [irony] where you say something you don't actually mean and expect people to understand not only what you actually do mean but also your attitude toward it?" (2). Hutcheon's quick reply is "to look at what might be called the 'scene' of irony: that is, to treat it not as an isolated trope to be analyzed by formalist means but as a political issue, in the broadest sense of the word. The 'scene' of irony involves relations of power based in relations of communication. It unavoidably involves touchy issues such as exclusion and inclusion, intervention and evasion" (2). She later adds: "the 'scene' of irony is a social and political scene" (4).

Against this I would suggest the following campaign: not to attack customs with the fiery sword of indignation nor with the pitiful exhibition of tears, but by denouncing their ridiculous, obsolete, tasteless, and imbecile aspects. I guarantee you that we have an inexhaustible source of laughter. And we need to laugh because laughter is the most immediate form of liberation from that which oppresses us, of distancing us from that which imprisons us! ("La participación" 39)

The complicated plot of *El eterno femenino* contrasts with the relative brevity of *El suplicio*, but in both cases the fragmentary construction of the plays and the displacement of the characters create a dismembered theatrical reality. Kirsten Nigro, in her discussion of *El eterno femenino*, underlines the feminist attempt to destabilize the apparently natural order–represented by the male-dominant discourse–with the purpose of unmasking the ideological weaknesses of this so-called "order" ("Para narrar" 237).

El eterno femenino is a three-act play–each act subdivided into various segments–that takes place in a beauty parlor and focuses on Lupita's hallucinatory nightmares as she sits under the salon's hair dryer. Lupita, who will be getting married that afternoon, needs to have her hair done. But what she does not know is that she has been secretly chosen on the spur of the moment by the owner of the salon and by a salesman to test a new electronic device. The advanced technology implanted in the hair dryer stimulates dreaming and, therefore, it avoids the danger of women thinking while waiting for their hair to dry. Even more grotesque is the fact that the owner and the salesman choose from the catalogue of dreams the most adequate one for Lupita's situation as someone who is about to begin a new life: "What Does the Future Hold for Me?" (*The Eternal Feminine* I: 277-78). [32] Lupita's future turns out to be a typical woman's nightmare: she has to deal with an old-fashioned mother, an unfaithful husband, and nagging children; and finally, the play alternates among Lupita the murderer, Lupita the fat old woman, Lupita the conservative mother, Lupita the cynical happy widow, and Lupita the brainwashed consumer.

---

[32] Textual quotes are indicated by number of act and page, and are taken from Diane E. Marting and Betty Tyree Osiek's translation of *El eterno femenino* (*The Eternal Feminine*) in *A Rosario Castellanos Reader*, 273-362.

In the subsequent acts, she continues to dream, first encountering well-known women–Eve in a circus tent, and Malinche, Sor Juana, Josefa Ortiz de Domínguez, la Emperatriz Carlota, Rosario de la Peña, and Adelita, in a wax museum–who are eager to tell their own personal stories, not the ones that have been officially circulated. Next, while trying on a variety of wigs to cover her messy hair, Lupita is transformed into different and recognizable female types: "the old maid, the streetwalker, the other woman of the *casa chica*, the postiche intellectual, the trendy liberated woman" (Nigro, "Debunking" 91). Not surprisingly, Castellanos herself indicates in the initial stage directions the exaggerated and farcical nature of the play: "Exaggeration is advisable, in the same way in which caricaturists use it, who with a few lines make the models who inspired their figures recognizable to the public. As should be clear from the beginning, the text is a farce, which in certain moments becomes sentimental, intellectual, or grotesque" (*The Eternal Feminine* 273).[33]

Lupita is finally thrown out of the hair salon, and the play ends with two *corridos* or Mexican ballads that summarize the stigmatized history of woman and all the ridiculous things for which they have been blamed. Regarding this complicated and twisted plot, Nigro concludes: "*El eterno femenino* is anything but the average well-made play of dramatic realism. The characters are totally unconvincing and the story line is preposterous, to say the least. The play is also built of a multitude of episodes or cartoon-like frames that are strung together with no regard to the traditional three unities" ("Debunking" 91-92).[34] In other words, the elements of exag-

---

[33] While discussing the technical difficulties of *El eterno femenino*, Kirsten Nigro questions its success as farce: "[S]he makes it problematical for a director to build up and maintain the rapid-fire pace so vital to farce. This rhythm is just not built into the play itself, largely because the stage directions, such as Castellanos gives them, demand far too many set changes that are not always immediately negotiated with the necessary ease" ("Debunking" 99). Nevertheless, *El eterno femenino* itself–as we will show later–voices and also parodies its technical problems (see III: 351). Regarding the use of humor in Castellanos's play, see Juan José Pulido Jiménez, "El humor satírico en *El eterno femenino*, de Rosario Castellanos," and Pamela J. McNab, "Humor in Castellanos's *El eterno femenino*: The Fractured Female Image."

[34] In another of her essays, Nigro underlines Castellanos's attempts to destabilize the male-dominant and apparently stable (narrative) order as creating "a story line that is so unbelievable and so constantly interrupted that it loses authority, the latter understood in the sense of displaying logic and coherence" ("Inventions" 141).

geration, caricaturization, fragmentation, and parody in *El eterno femenino* offer an unconventional way to examine and denounce the extremely serious problem of women's social and psychological subordination to men, without necessarily imposing solutions.

More important for this study is the possibility of recognizing that the characterization of woman in *El eterno femenino* parallels the four types found in *El suplicio del placer*: the liberated/sophisticated/(bisexual) woman of the first segment, the prostitute or woman-object and the "virginal" wife of the second segment, the insecure, neurotic, tortured, and suffering woman of the third, and the authorial/intellectual type of the fourth segment. This typification of women enhances the plays' farcical elements, and, in their respective contexts, women become recognizable emblems of codified and framed objects. It is not until we get to "Los dientes" that we encounter the representation, although still of a typified woman embodied in a mouth, of an authorial and powerful voice/mouth whose name is Berman and who ends up swallowing everyone. Although this gesture in the dentist's office could be interpreted as a powerful act, the image of the woman represented by a mouth is a partial one. Just as at the end of the third act of *El eterno femenino* a group of "intellectual" women discuss mainly the failures of a play entitled *El eterno femenino* and the social and psychological instability of its author–a woman named Rosario Castellanos, Berman, while giving certain strength to her own authorial figure, also creates a caricatured and fragmented view of herself. The parallel in Castellanos's play between women's everyday reality and their nightmares is transformed by Berman into an ambiguous game, particularly dramatized at the beginning of the third segment, "La pistola." *Él* and *Ella* are looking for means of entertainment, but very soon the spectators and the characters lose track of the rules of the game and are pushed into the confusion of multiple and falsified realities. The struggle dramatized by both Castellanos and Berman between sameness and difference, between the whole and its parts, between full characterization and typification represents women's search for artistic and political expression and women's recognition that a unified voice is not necessarily a desirable goal. In other words, the unstable realities portrayed by *El eterno femenino* and by *El suplicio* attack the authoritarian nature not only of a society that sanctions male supremacy but of theatrical and literary forms that mask their own authoritative instincts.

Farce, therefore, becomes for Castellanos and Berman an efficient instrument in the struggle against social and artistic oppression, as they simultaneously denounce their own partial, privileged, and powerful position. This awareness is humorously exemplified in Castellanos's text when Lupita-academician-lecturer and the Ladies are criticizing the play *El eterno femenino* for ridiculing the values of Mexican woman and are accusing the author, Castellanos, of incompetence, bitterness, and mediocrity in dealing with women's issues and with theatrical techniques and codes (*The Eternal Feminine* III: 350-51). Taking a playful, metatheatrical, and ironic stand, Castellanos identifies, through Lupita and the Ladies, some of the "antidramatic" characteristics of her own play:

> LUPITA. Let's not consider it from the critical point of view, because we'd have to condemn the arbitrariness of its progression, the unrealistic situations, the utter inconsistency of its characters. Those are technical problems of the dramatic structure, which do not concern us, neither do the hodgepodge of genres or the abuse of untheatrical tactics, nor, above all, the language, which, when it isn't vulgar, tries to be ingenuous or lyrical and doesn't reach the level of anything but pretentiousness. (III: 351)

Ironically, the critical and technical viewpoints that do not interest the Ladies are nevertheless commented on in detail, thus signaling their important role in the interpretation and understanding of the play. Reflecting on this scene, Nigro states: "These would-be drama critics are judging *El eterno femenino* by the standards of the conventional theatre and this makes nonsense of their critical evaluation" ("Debunking" 92). Maureen Ahern, for her part, stresses how Castellanos and her play gain in stature by turning ironic humor on herself and her work: "In fact, this autocriticism constitutes a productive dramatic strategy because it is an effective way of defusing hostility by anticipating the attacks that she knew this play would arouse in Mexican social circles" (*A Rosario Castellanos Reader* 55). The irony is that this supposed unmasking and artistic role-reversal (the characters ridiculing the author) are still framed within the context of denunciation of both male and female attitudes and of artistic rigidity. In this way, Castellanos–and in many aspects Berman–establishes a tension between what is fictional and what appears factual, what is internal criticism and what is external, what is personal and what is collective, what is humorous and what is a bitter attack.

Most important, the use of farce by Castellanos and Berman in a Mexican and Spanish American context reflects the struggle of multiple and even contradictory voices that demand to be heard. But the difference between the type of farce described in this study and a theatre that overtly denounces the social and political injustices of the authors' present reality resides in the former's bitter game with itself and with that which is being denounced. In other words, both Castellanos's and Berman's plays are constantly transgressing the limits of their farcical discourse; they are questioning farce's traditional scheme of role-reversal by using it repeatedly, until its most basic structures are destroyed. Inverting the codified language as well as the most traditional social forms seems not to be enough for *El eterno femenino* and for *El suplicio del placer*. On the one hand, by revealing their internal antagonism, the two plays are ridiculing their capacity to offer (or their interest in offering) tangible solutions to societal problems, and, on the other, they are undermining their capacity to make an audience laugh by openly debunking the *status quo*. As Jessica Milner Davis suggests: "There are nevertheless some farces which are so devoted to hostile joking that they seem to come close to losing their joyousness" (27).

The ordering of the one-act plays in *El suplicio del placer* attests to the play's risk of losing its joyousness. By the time the spectator reaches the fourth segment where pain and torture have moved from the psychological to the physical realm, the pain of pleasure has become more tangible, and laughs are scarcer than in the first two parts.[35] The game, if indeed it is one, between the characters (re)creates an environment of psychological torture and death, which questions the most basic notion of pleasure and its relationship to enjoyment and desire. But as dramatized in the title, pleasure and pain go hand in hand, and in the case of women in traditionally male-dominated societies, what is pleasurable for men becomes torment (*suplicio*) for women. That is, woman, frequently

---

[35] Berman's visit to the dentist will not bring any relief to her tooth pain but, on the contrary, will create more discomfort, anxiety, and physical pain to the patient. Even worst, it will require an act of aggression and survival from the part of Berman the patient as "she" (a mouth) swallows her torturers.

stripped of individuality, becomes the object of desire and the source of pleasure for men, while her own desires are subject to the will and whims of others.

Even in the first one-act play ("El bigote"), the two characters are not similar in what produces pleasure for them, and it is not even certain that they openly acknowledge their implied sexual preferences. In other words, *El suplicio del placer* confronts in its thematic, generic, and structural aspects a transgression, a contradiction, a paradox. The struggle against fixation ultimately represents a struggle for survival, since the most powerful social and artistic forces aim for a "stability" that will inevitably become oppressive and will attempt to silence any deviation from it.

This connection between power, pleasure, and sexuality has been thoroughly discussed by, among others, Michel Foucault in *The History of Sexuality: An Introduction* (vol. 1) (in the original *La volonté de savoir* [The will to knowledge]) (1976), and *The Use of Pleasure* (vol. 2) (1984).[36] It seems obvious from the perspective of my analysis of *El suplicio del placer* that Foucault's theoretical and historical discussions of power, sexuality, knowledge, repression, and pleasure in the Western tradition are thematized, played with, parodied, turned upside down, and even "applied" in Berman's play. The seriousness of Foucault's contribution to the history of sexuality contrasts with *El suplicio*'s dramatization of this history through farce. In the context of this enigmatic relationship between

---

[36] Alan Sheridan has summarized Foucault's central postulates and the importance of his *History of Sexuality* in the following terms: "Yet when *La volonté de savoir* appeared in 1976 even those accustomed to Foucault's reversals of the received wisdom were taken aback.... What he is asking us to consider in this book is a similar thesis: that the relation of power to sex is not essentially repressive, that it is rather productive of an ever-proliferating discourse on sexuality" (165-66). On his part, Ross Chambers synthesizes Foucault's ideas in the following way: "But the classic statement of the ubiquity of power was, of course in Michel Foucault's work of the seventies, notably *Surveiller et punir* (1975) and the first volume, entitled *La Volonté de Savoir*, of his *Histoire de la Sexualité*. There Foucault insists that in the modern social formation, power is diffuse–not localized, but available in different situations and in different degrees to different people–and that it is not 'repressive' so much as it is enabling" (xiv). Finally, John McGowan looks for similarities between Derrida's works and Foucault's, from *Madness and Civilization* to the beginning of *The History of Sexuality*: "Like Derrida, Foucault suggests that humanism and reason have functioned in the West as definitive, exclusionary terms, and that a society's or an epoch's identity is formed vis à vis what it forcefully excludes.... The included and the excluded, the same and its other, are revealed as dependent on one another within the larger dynamics of the constitution of identities within a social whole that privileges some identities over others" (121).

theory and practice, between the rewriting of the history of sexuality and the parodic theatricalization of some elements of this history, that Berman's text questions both the traditional and nontraditional structures of oppression.

Is it possible, then, to speak of a deconstructive dialogue between the Foucaldian conception of the history of sexuality as interpreted by the West and a farcical representation of that history seen by a *mestizo* culture (Mexican, Spanish American) that recognizes the syncretism of first-world and third-world discourses, of Western and non-Western traditions in their understanding of sexuality? If so, the problematization of sexual pleasure in Berman's play is portrayed not only through the marginalization of women within an already marginalized theatrical form–that is, farce–but also through the supremacy of a discourse whose historical origins date from the ancient world. The triple sense of oppression dramatized and parodied in *El suplicio* (male supremacy, Western supremacy, and farce as a disparaged genre) transgresses the traditional link between sexual identity and Western cultural and political powers and allows the rewriting and re-presentation of new and unfixed relationships between sexes.

Even as it is recognized that the primary stages of the history of sexuality, power, and pleasure are the history of *male* sexuality, *male* power, and *male* pleasure, from a feminist Spanish American viewpoint, Foucault's analysis of these discourses is useful since it proposes an alternative reading of sex, sexuality, identity, power, and pleasure, and it underscores the profound contradictions within which they have been framed. Regarding Foucault's contribution to Western thought, Susan Hekman states:

> Foucault challenges the basic underpinnings of Western philosophy, particularly the modernist tradition that has held sway since the Enlightenment. He counters the definitions of truth, knowledge, power, and the subject that ground that tradition. His work transforms the tradition by questioning its fundamental goal: the will to truth. (1)

More specifically, Foucault's summary of the goals of his project in *The History of Sexuality* stresses society's contradictions when dealing with many of the aforementioned issues: "Briefly, my aim is to examine the case of a society which has been loudly castigating itself for its hypocrisy for more than a century, which speaks verbosely of its own silence, takes great pains to relate in detail the things it does not say, denounces the powers it exercises, and promises to liberate itself from the very laws that have made it function" (8).

Foucault's discussion of the steady proliferation of discourses concerning sex responds to his questioning of the "repressive hypothesis," which states that power has acted upon sex in an essentially repressive way (see *The History*, 1: 6-7; Sheridan 167). He had denounced earlier that "what sustains our eagerness to speak of sex in terms of repression is doubtless this opportunity . . . to pronounce a discourse that combines the fervor of knowledge, the determination to change the laws, and the longing for the *garden of earthly delights*" (*The History*, 1: 7, my emphasis). For Foucault, the possibility of unifying these three elements reflects people's illusory desire to dream of a New City (see *The History*, 1: 7-8), that is, to create a new future where sex is not defined in its relationship to repression. Nevertheless, this multiplication of discourses concerning sex has extended to the field of power itself: "an institutional incitement to speak about it, and to do so more and more; a determination on the part of the agencies of power to hear it spoken about, and to cause *it* to speak through explicit articulation and endlessly accumulated detail" (Foucault, *The History*, vol. 1, 18). But this discursive explosion, this verbal striptease, is parodied in *El suplicio* through the play's urge to speak about sex and to represent it in a fragmented and inconclusive manner.[37]

Ultimately, the notion of sexual and social repression and the exercise of power in *El suplicio del placer* are far more than theoretical issues. The repression experienced by both female and male characters under different and contradictory circumstances and the characters' ambiguous relationship to power represent the history imposed on marginal beings, a history written by others and with

---

[37] In the fourth segment, "Los dientes," sex is openly characterized through a more explicit discourse on lesbianism and incest. The nurse says that she recognizes the patient (Sandra) as her ex-lover: "Te digo que tan luego que te vi, te reconocí, te sentí, me sentí, me acordé... Tantas veces que tu boca estuvo dentro de mi boca, que mi boca estuvo dentro de la tuya, que tu boca estuvo en mi otra boca, que..." ("Let me tell you that as soon as I saw you I recognized you, I felt you, I felt myself, I remembered... So many times that your mouth was inside my mouth, that my mouth was inside yours, that your mouth was in my other mouth, that..." (IV: 216).

languages and ideologies determined by circles outside the dramatized space. Ironically, the traditional discourse on oppression, frequently reduced to the role played by the oppressors and the oppressed, is also part of a larger structure that has been imposed from the outside. For that reason, Berman's *El suplicio* has recourse to farce as a reaction against the most codified and simplified means of criticism and aggression.

As part of Foucault's description of the role played by repression in the understanding of sex, he questions the idealized notion of linking "enlightenment, liberation, and manifold pleasures" (*The History*, 1: 7), identifying the pleasures as the "garden of earthly delights." It is significant that the first title of *El suplicio del placer* was *El jardín de las delicias* [Garden of delights], which happens to be the title of the best-known painting of the fifteenth-century Dutch master Hieronymus Bosch. But beyond this "coincidence" in title, what becomes particularly telling is the sexual content of Bosch's three-paneled painting. H. W. Janson offers a brief summary and interpretation of the painting:

> The left panel is the *Garden of Eden*, a dreamlike landscape with exotic animals; in the foreground, the Lord introduces Adam to the newly created Eve. The right panel . . . is a nightmare landscape of blazing ruins and fantastic tortures. It is surely Hell, the *Garden of Satan*. But what of the center, the *Garden of Earthly Delights*? Here . . . nude men and women innocently parade on the backs of beasts, sit on giant birds, eat colorful giant fruits, and play in a stream; a few make love. Every bird, fruit, animal, and diversion is a symbol of temptation, of an earthly pleasure. The artist is telling us that we are the prisoners of our earthly appetites. . . . Bosch, then, is a stern moralist, and this work is a visual sermon. We are meant to find it, not a true garden of delights, but a rebuke and a warning. (152-53)

Beyond the suggestive contradiction between title and content–"we are meant to find it, not a true garden of delights, but a rebuke and a warning"–Janson's final comment recasts the supposed theme of the three panels as the "vice of lust," which sheds light on *El suplicio*'s structural and thematic link with the painting: "This panorama of our sinfulness, however, although born of deepest pessimism, develops so much poetic charm and sensuous appeal as it unfolds that we tend to admire it for what the artist meant to condemn" (153). The conscious or unconscious double transgression in Bosch's painting, where the title evokes the delights of a garden but the panels portray the excesses of vice, is again inverted by the suggestion that the observer inevitably ends up admiring "what the artist meant to condemn." In the case of Berman's play, both the garden and the traditional notion of pleasure have been transgressed: the garden (men/women relationship) turns out to be (a caricaturization of) hell, and pleasure becomes a tortuous reality. By the same token, what was initially perceived as a clear denunciation in *El suplicio* of the unjust gender structures of society becomes an ambiguous unmasking of multiple and unfixed realities wherein everything seems subject to inversion and parody. Therefore, the change of title stresses the desired instability of the play and incites the tug-of-war between what is and what is not suggested, inverted, or dramatized. Ultimately both titles, *El jardín de las delicias* and *El suplicio del placer*, evoke grotesque portrayals of excesses; they both suggest a reversal and a negation of what they are, and seem to be, at a superficial level.

It is necessary to return here to the title of Castellanos's play, since the phrase "the eternal feminine" poses parallel issues regarding notions of reversal, negation, and the problematics of authority. Castellanos does not miss the opportunity to offer her reader/spectator the source of this phrase. In the third act of the *El eterno femenino*, Lupita, in her impersonation of an intellectual, states as she attacks a play being staged at the capital: "It's called *The Eternal Feminine*. Let's not pay any attention to the title's lack of originality; it's merely a commonplace, plagiarized literally from Goethe" (III: 351).[38] Disregarding Lupita's suggestion not to pay attention to this title, we encounter the last verses of Goethe's *Faust: A Tragedy* (1832), which contrasts in tone and purpose with the *El eterno femenino: Farsa*, but which, nonetheless, poses similar complex angles regarding issues of interpretation and authority:

---

[38] Although it would be inappropriate to contradict Gladhart's statement, and suggest in turn that *El eterno femenino* is a "theory play" that reads as "a male canonical text," as Gayle Austin does in her play "Resisting the Birth Mark" with Nathaniel Hawthorne's short story "The Birthmark" (see Gladhart 129), it is important to acknowledge Castellanos's tense dialogue with a male canonical text such as Goethe's *Faust*, not only through the title of her play, but also through the historical construct of women as pure and as vehicles of salvation.

CHORUS MYSTICUS. All transitory
Things represent;
Inadequates here
Become event,
Ineffables here,
Accomplishment;
The Eternal Feminine
Draws us onward. (413)[39]

Hans Eichner begins his essay "The Eternal Feminine: An Aspect of Goethe's Ethics" by underscoring the level of difficulty of interpreting the last two lines in Goethe's famous play: "In his well-known book on Goethe, Emil Staiger declares that an insurmountable sense of awe makes it impossible for him to attempt an interpretation of the final two lines of *Faust*. Other commentators have been less reticent, but the implications of these lines seem to be inexhaustible" (615). It is clear that Castellanos's play thrives on this complexity by using Goethe's phrase in a very ironic way, by evoking not only the notion of the feminine held by a German author at end of the eighteenth-century–"the ideal of purity is seen as eternally feminine, the ideal of significant action as masculine" (Eichner 617)–but also the equally complex notions portrayed by modern feminism. Nigro states: "The play's very title [*The Eternal Feminine*] places it squarely within the debate still going on between essentialist and materialist feminists, a debate of far-reaching consequences, for whether women are seen as eternal and unchanging, or as shaped by and shapers of their everyday experiences makes a great difference both to the specifics of women's lived reality and to the political project that would improve or modify it" ("Inventions" 140). Us-

---

[39] Hans Eichner offers the context in which the lines are placed: "At the age of one hundred, Faust has died. In the final scene of the play ... we are looking into a steep valley covered with dense forests and populated by hermits. Hovering above the valley, a group of angels is carrying Faust's soul towards heaven, and above them there is a 'choir of penitent women'. Three of the penitents are identified, not without a touch of whimsy: they are the magna peccatrix who anointed Christ in the house of the Pharisee; the Samaritan woman who was told by Christ that she had had five husbands and now lived in sin with a sixth man; and the Egyptian Mary of the Acta Sanctorum. The penitents, whose sins have long been forgiven, plead with the Virgin Mary on behalf of Gretchen, who is accepted by the Virgin and told to rise with her to higher spheres: Faust would feel her presence there and follow. A saint identified as Doctor Marianus prays to Mary, and then the famous final lines are intoned by the Chorus mysticus" (615-16).

ing such a historically charged title, accompanied by the subtitle *Farce*, Castellanos seems to be posing both serious and parodic questions regarding "the eternal" in relation to "the feminine." What, then, is the meaning of a play whose title evokes Faust following Gretchen and the Virgin Mary to higher spheres, when what we actually encounter is Lupita seeing, through a new electronic device, how her future as a married woman and mother will make her experience hell? Who would then be willing to follow Lupita to this *inferno*? Not surprisingly, from the serpent's point of view in one of the stanzas of the first *corrido* at the end of Castellanos's *El eterno femenino*, women should all follow Lupita right down to hell, since this would allow them a "new view of Paradise": "'Si la comes, averiguas/ lo que va del bien al mal,/ lo que debes preferir,/ lo que debes rechazar,/ y la tomada de pelo/ que te están queriendo dar'" (198) ["'If you eat it you will know/ how far from bad to good,/ what you ought to like,/ and what you never should,/ and how they will deceive you,/ if they think they ever could" (359)].

It could be said that Rosario Castellanos's provocative and literary title, along with Berman's artistic and sexual evocations of delights, vices, and pleasures in *El suplicio del placer* are openly exposing their own ambiguous and unfixed artistic and social realities (and those of others–Goethe and Bosch?). Castellanos and Berman do this even as they parody their authority and privileged position regarding the interpretation of those realities and of history.[40]

In the case of *El suplicio del placer*, this play's grotesque caricaturization of men and women's relationships, given the history of sexuality in the West, can be at times hilarious and at times pathetic, but by the end of the play the vestiges of joy have almost completely disappeared, and a sense of contradiction and lack of closure permeates the "closing" of the play. For the characters, the traditional notion of sexual pleasure has gone sober, has become a real *suplicio*, and for the reader or spectator the so-called "pleasure of the text" (written or representational) has become a burden.

In a systematically contradictory way, *El suplicio* seems to shed

---

[40] We should not miss this opportunity to offer Eichner's final analysis of Goethe's last two lines: "The Eternal Feminine in the last lines no doubt refers to divine forgiveness, and, in a halfhearted way, it must also refer to Gretchen, who precedes Faust in his ascent to higher regions; but most meaningfully, it refers to the ideal of purity that must inspire, though it must not inhibit, even the man of action, and that, to Goethe, always appeared in feminine guise" (624).

both light and darkness over the dialectic of sexuality and power, over the dialectic's connection to male/female relationships, and finally over their respective sense of pleasure. In Berman's play, it is evident that pleasure means different things in different contexts; its meanings for male and for female characters are different. In "El bigote," for example, the mere ambiguity of *Él* and *Ella*'s sexual identity requires a reinterpretation of pleasure from the viewpoint of what Foucault calls "peripheral," that is, unorthodox sexual behavior (*The History*, vol. 1, 39).[41] In the second segment man's sexual and psychological pleasures are fulfilled mostly at the expense of woman, but in consonance with the ambiguities of the rest of *El suplicio*, even this traditional hierarchical pattern where men enact their power is drastically shaken by parody. The woman of this second segment succeeds in defying male pleasures mostly through manipulative silence, while *Él*'s verbal aggression and pseudopower create an environment far removed from the joys of sexual desire to which men are accustomed. The third one-act play dramatizes the debunking of pleasure through the emptiness and torture of married life.[42] Finally, in the fourth segment the Nurse and Dentist are performing an extremely painful and absurd "medical" procedure: they are draining the mouth of the patient with a sword and a vacuum cleaner, to which the mouth/patient suddenly responds by swallowing the Dentist. As the Nurse is searching for her partner, and orders the mouth to close, it not only refuses to do so, but ends up also swallowing the Nurse (IV: 216-17). Presumably, the mouth remains open and the perpetrators of pain and torture are gone. But has the cause of the pain actually been discovered and eliminated? Should we con-

---

[41] For Foucault, what comes under scrutiny during the discursive explosion of the eighteenth and nineteenth centuries is "the sexuality of children, mad men and women and criminals; the sensuality of those who did not like the opposite sex; reveries, obsessions, petty manias, or great transports of rage. It was time for all these figures, scarcely noticed in the past, to step forward and speak, to make the difficult confession of what they were. No doubt they were condemned all the same; but they were listened to; and if regular sexuality happened to be questioned once again, it was through a reflux movement, originating in these peripheral sexualities" (*The History* 38-39).

[42] Foucault reminds his reader that up to the end of the eighteenth century, the three major explicit codes that governed sexual practices—canonical law, the Christian pastoral, and civil law—were all centered in matrimonial relations: "The marriage relation was the most intense focus of constraints; it was spoken of more than anything else; more than any other relation, it was required to give a detailed accounting of itself. It was under constant surveillance...." (*The History* 37).

clude then that instead of eliminating the source or sources of the pain (the Dentist and the Nurse), the swallowing of the torturers will perpetuate the pain? If the mouth remains open, should we expect other things to happen, other painful segments to be inserted into the play, or into the mouth? Has the mouth/patient/author been able to end the excruciating pain created throughout *El suplicio del placer*?

In addition to *El suplicio*'s structural and ideological complexity, it is the play's obsession with multiple forms of sexuality and power, and with the ambiguity of the notion of pleasure, that actually triggers and enhances the pleasure of Berman's text. But even this notion of the pleasure of the text can be subjected to the same political polarization and inversions identified in the discussion of sexual pleasures. Can or should the spectator of *El suplicio*, under these circumstances, empathize with and "enjoy" the dramatization of gender issues, specifically the marginalization of women, when they are framed within a farcical structure? Should the idea of the pleasure of the text be avoided, or is it something that transcends even the political and social implications of a text? As Roland Barthes has suggested, the idea of pleasure has frequently been simplified by both the ideology of the right and that of the left: the former by championing it and the latter by disdaining it:

> On the right, with the same movement, everything abstract, boring, political, is shoved over to the left and pleasure is kept for oneself.... And on the left, because of morality... one suspects and disdains any "residue of hedonism." On the right, pleasure is championed *against* intellectuality, the clerisy: the old reactionary myth of heart against head, sensation against reasoning, (warm) "life" against (cold) "abstraction".... On the left, knowledge, method, commitment, combat, are drawn up against "mere delectation".... (22-23)

How can, then, either sexual or textual pleasure be measured or defined? What are the implications in *El suplicio del placer* of connecting these two forms of pleasure? In whose terms can pleasure be defined? One wonders if the emphasis on the problematics and ambiguity of pleasure call into question the significance of Berman's feminist agenda, which at a primary level would be to expose and ridicule the traditional power structures monopolized by men. Is this not what farce is already doing, that is, questioning every attempt to establish a fixed and authoritative voice? What, then, are the implications of this double affirmation? Does it constitute a negation? Barthes's response to the dilemma of the pleasure of the text is expressed in the following terms: "Pleasure, however, is not an *element* of the text, it is not a naïve residue; it does not depend on a logic of understanding and on sensation; it is a drift, something both *revolutionary and asocial*, and it cannot be taken over by any collectivity, any mentality, any ideolect" (23, my emphasis). Berman, on her part, portrays sexual pleasure in *El suplicio* in similar terms, undermining the traditional notion of sex as a source of joy and desire. Despite *El suplicio*'s rejection of a fixed and stable notion of reality and its antagonism toward powerful voices, I close this discussion with Barthes's view of the pleasure of the text, which underlines the text's multifaceted construction and its contradictory representation:

> A text on pleasure cannot be anything but *short* (as we say: *is that all? It's a bit short*); since pleasure can only be spoken through the indirection of a demand (I have a *right* to pleasure), we cannot get beyond an abridged, two-tense dialectics: the tense of *doxa*, opinion, and the tense of *paradoxa*, dispute. A third term is missing, besides pleasure and its censure. This term is postponed to later, and so long as we cling to the very name of "pleasure," every text on pleasure will be nothing but dilatory; it will be an introduction to what will never be written. Like those productions of contemporary art which exhaust their necessity as soon as they have been seen (since to see them is immediately to understand to what destructive purpose they are exhibited: they no longer contain any contemplative or delectative duration), such an introduction can only repeat itself–without ever introducing anything. (18)

Barthes's dialectic between the tenses of *doxa* (opinion) and *paradoxa* (dispute) becomes central to *El suplicio*'s conception of pleasure, since it establishes a dynamic fluctuation between what is codified as traditional and its necessary inversion. That Berman's play seems never to lose sight of the forthcoming and endless inversions reveals its awareness of the elusiveness of its own discourse and the paradoxes of its implicit solutions. In other words, Berman seems to be dealing with what Barthes calls "the missing term"

–that which recognizes the contradictions and limitations of the concept of pleasure and at the same time faces the possibility of writing about it.

Ultimately, Sabina Berman's *El suplicio del placer* establishes a complex dialectic and an implicit parallelism between Spanish American farce as an ambiguous and multifaceted genre that constantly avoids fixation and the oppressed role of women in a male-dominated society. It also presents pleasure as undefinable, contradictory, and interwoven with the forces of sexual and textual power. That is, the fragmented structure of *El suplicio del placer* reflects the ambiguity, subjectivity, and contradiction that farce, the discourse of women's issues, and the notion of pleasure all share.

CHAPTER 3

TRANSCRIPTION, TRANSGRESSION AND POWER IN VARGAS LLOSA'S *KATHIE Y EL HIPOPÓTAMO*

> Así se inició el reino de la máscara, el imperio de la mentira. Desde entonces la corrupción del lenguaje, la infección semántica, se convirtió en nuestra enfermedad endémica; la mentira se volvió constitucional, consubstancial.
>
> Octavio Paz, *Los hijos del limo*

> It is evident how much men love to deceive and be deceived, since rhetoric, that powerful instrument of error and deceit, has its established professors, is publicly taught and has always been had in great reputation....
>
> John Locke, *An Essay Concerning Human Understanding*

SINCE the publication and performance in 1981 of Mario Vargas Llosa's play *La señorita de Tacna*, the popular Peruvian novelist has again taken up the dramatic genre cultivated in his youth (*La huida del Inca*), publishing four more pieces over a decade: *Kathie y el hipopótamo* (1983) [*Kathie and the Hippopotamus*], *La Chunga* (1986) [*The Chunga*], *El loco de los balcones* (1993) [*The Madman of the Balconies*], and *Ojos bonitos, cuadros feos* (1996) [*Pretty Eyes, Ugly Paintings*].[1] From this study's perspective, the fact that a distinguished novelist has written dramatic works is not central to our discussion. Nevertheless, it is important to acknowledge that critics have wondered, as Lucrecio Pérez Blanco has in his comments on Vargas Llosa's incursion into drama, if the audience and the reading public have been attracted to these writers' theatrical productions mainly out of sympathy (or curiosity) for the author

---

[1] There is scarce information about Vargas Llosa's first play (also his first literary text) *La huida del Inca* (The escape of the Inca). In a 1986 interview conducted by Carlos Espinosa Domínguez, Vargas Llosa indicated that *La huida del Inca* premiered in July 1952 in the Teatro Variedades (57). One of the most prestigious and prolific Latin American writers, and a major figure of the Latin American literary *Boom*, Vargas Llosa was born in Arequipa, Peru in 1936. I will comment on several of his narrative works throughout this chapter.

(201), and not predominantly out of appreciation for the plays themselves. Could this be the case with plays written by well-known Spanish American novelists of the twentieth century, such as Alejo Carpentier's *La rebambaramba* (1927) or *Manita en el suelo* (1931), Julio Cortázar's *Los reyes* (1949), Carlos Fuentes' *Orquídeas a la luz de la luna* (1982), Severo Sarduy's *Para la voz* (collection of plays), Manuel Puig's *Bajo un manto de estrellas* (1982), or Gabriel García Márquez's *Diatriba de amor contra un hombre sentado* (1993)? [2]

Although this issue of distinguished novelists who have written dramatic works is not part of our main argument, in the "Introduction" to this book we briefly contextualized this issue as part of the discussion on theatre's marginality within Spanish American literature in general and farce's lack of prestige within Spanish American theatre in particular. The point here is that this tension between genres and regions that occupy the center and those that occupy the margins, and even the tension between pre-text (prologue) and text can be expanded to include the issue of well-known novelists who have made incursions–with either modest results or great success–into theatre, since it brings to the surface aspects of positionality and prestige, of hierarchy and power, of authority. [3] Are we paying attention to *Kathie y el hipopótamo* because of the signature that accompanies this play? That is, are we subjecting the valorization of Vargas Llosa's dramatic production to its intertextual relationship with the very prestigious narrative work written by its author? Or are we rather enhancing our understanding of Vargas Llosa's theatre through intertextual dialogue with his novels? [4]

---

[2] With regard to authors such as Griselda Gambaro, Elena Garro, and Vicente Leñero, who are well-known writers of both theatre and narrative, it would be inadequate to argue that the audience is attracted to their theatrical productions on the basis of their reputation as novelists.

[3] Even Vargas Llosa, when asked in an interview if it was easy for him to adapt to the reality of theatre as the product of collective work and not as exclusively dependent, as in the case of narrative, on his own imagination and capabilities, the Peruvian writer responded addressing issues of positionality and authority: "Since writing my first play, I discovered that, unlike the novelist, who can be sovereign in his creation, the playwright must be modest and must accept that what he does is only one piece within the machinery of the spectacle. I also learned . . . that one provides a sort of raw material on the basis of which a performance is staged with the collaboration, the imagination, and the inventiveness of the director, the actors, the scenographers, the technicians (Santos 118-19).

[4] In the case of *La señorita de Tacna*, Gerdes believes that "The intertextual relationship between this play and Vargas Llosa's previous works . . . goes far toward

Beyond the possible responses to these questions, our interest lies in how Spanish American farce, in particular *Kathie y el hipopótamo*, has confronted, in creative and iconoclastic ways, issues of dominance and hierarchy on many levels: narrative means of communication vs. theatrical discourses, text vs. performance, author vs. scriptwriter, man vs. woman, upper class vs. lower class, among other parodied polarizations. In other words, *Kathie*'s farcical identity is reafirmed by displacing the authoritative and hierarchical forces of both traditional theatre and of literature as a whole, ironically placing marginality at the center.⁵

On examining the criticism of Mario Vargas Llosa's theatre, we encounter unfavorable judgments aimed at his dramatic production. Pérez Blanco identifies the Peruvian writer's theatre as his new and unfortunate obsession and protests that spectators of the new Vargas Llosa cannot help feeling more than a little cheated: "[There is] neither weeping nor laughter . . . [only a] monotonous reencounter with the known. Dramatic movement is patently absent" (207). Carlos Espinosa Domínguez prefaces his interview with Vargas Llosa–centered on his theatre–with the following comments about the plays' "mixed bag" critical reception: "Critics have seen not inconsiderable merits in both plays [*La señorita de Tacna* and *Kathie*]; but they also point out the lack of dialectical grasp, of stage sense, and of what the Greeks called dramatic joy" (57). Another critic who questions the theatrical identity of *La señorita de Tacna* is Peter Standish:

---

understanding the complexities involved in writing fiction. The narrative world of the play is virtually built on the fictitious realities of Vargas Llosa's previous novels" (161).

⁵ *Kathie y el hipopótamo* was first staged in April 1983 in Caracas, Venezuela, as part of the VI Festival Internacional de Teatro (Sixth International Theatre Festival) with the well-known Argentine actress Norma Aleandro in the role of Kathie Kennety (see *Kathie* 23). In the doctoral dissertation "Sex, Sin, and Storytelling: Eroticism in the Theatre of Mario Vargas Llosa," Kenneth W. McCoy offers as an appendix information regarding the staging of *Kathie y el hipopótamo*, indicating the year, the theatrical organization that produced it, and the place of production from 1983 until 1993 (200-01). Textual citations are based on the Seix Barral 1983 edition, immediately followed by the pagination of the English translation placed in brackets. Translations of these citations are by Kerry McKenney and Anthony Oliver-Smith from *Kathie and the Hippopotamus*. I have sometimes added to or otherwise modified these translations in the interest of exactitude. I indicate these changes within the translation in brackets.

> The ending of the play is weak. More generally, the self-analytical style of Belisario, so unnaturally voicing his thoughts, is flat and undramatic; instead of providing a counterpoint to the inner action, it counteracts its drive and deprives the play of life. This undramatic quality is found elsewhere, not least in the very real staging difficulties the play poses with its shifting levels of reality and time. (135)

Standish's and other critics' understandable misgivings about a characteristically narrative and shamelessly self-reflexive theatre, as is the case of Vargas Llosa's dramatic production, focus on the negative view of these so-called "antimimetic," "antidramatic," and narrative elements, and emphasize the intertextual exchange between Vargas Llosa's more recognized narrative work and his plays. For example, Gerdes states about *La señorita* and *Kathie*:

> The curious mixture of narrative and dramatic elements in the two texts makes the experience of reading them as important as viewing the stage production of the plays.... [I]t is possible to consider these plays as discussions in dialogue form of abstract questions rather than as dramas of concrete action. In essence, Vargas Llosa has merged concepts of "literature" and "drama" in these works. (155)[6]

---

[6] Raymond Leslie Williams, in chapter 7 of his book on Vargas Llosa, also examines his dramaturgy in the context of his novels. In the case of *Kathie y el hipopótamo* one of the two protagonists, Santiago Zavala, is a character from the novel *Conversación en La Catedral* (1969) [*Conversation in The Cathedral*], who is married to Ana, in both the novel and the play. Regarding this double literary reality, Jacqueline E. Bixler points out: "The fact that both Santiago and Ana are characters lifted from an earlier fiction serves to highlight their fictional status within the present drama" ("Vargas Llosa's *Kathie y el hipopótamo*" 261). Frank Dauster underscores the connection between *Kathie* and *La tía Julia y el escribidor* (1977) [*Aunt Julia and the Scriptwriter*]: "[I]n the background of *Kathie* ... appears, if only in passing, the monstrous Pedro Camacho" ("Bridging" 9). Peter Standish, in "A Novelist's Theatre," also stresses the link between Vargas Llosa's novels and his theatre: "When the first of these appeared (*La señorita de Tacna*, 1981) it was to be metafictional, highlighting the role of the storyteller and the status of (his) story. It appears, then, that Vargas Llosa was writing a novelist's theatre; in asserting this, I am suggesting, too, that his novelistic techniques are still visible in his theatre" (133). For José Monleón, Vargas Llosa's great adventure and the real "interest" of his theatrical proposal is that his is a nontheatre done through theatre, a theatre of a nature different from the already established one (125). Sara Castro-Klarén, in her chapter devoted to *Historia de Mayta* (1984) [*The Real Life of Alejandro Mayta*] and *El hablador* (1987) [*The Storyteller*], makes general comments on Vargas Llosa's *La señorita de Tacna* and on *Kathie*, focusing on issues of authorship, authority, and writing (190-93). Vargas

As part of a larger discussion on the interconnections between genres, critics such as Frank Dauster and John W. Kronik have examined this dialogue as it pertains to the increasing relationship between narrative and theatrical discourse in Spanish American theatre. In "Bridging the Quantum Gap: Considerations on the Novelist as Playwright," Dauster examines the close dialogue between the narrative texts and the theatre production of well-known novelists of the *Boom* in Spanish America. Dauster traces some of the prevalent issues that surface in this interaction between genres and the writers' challenges (or failures) to deal with them. For example, the statement that "theatre is not exclusively a verbal medium" (Dauster, "Bridging" 6), underscores the intervention of other "voices" in theatre such as those of the director, actor, costume designer, or lighting technician. But more important to our discussion is that this plurality of systems of communication highlights the weaknesses of the excessive use of verbal language in many plays written by novelists and underscores the unnecessary attempt to describe verbally what is visibly happening on stage. Also, as Dauster reminds us in the case of writers like the Argentine Roberto Arlt and the Mexican Carlos Fuentes, this excessive verbosity calls our attention to endings that seem too abstract, intricate, and metaphorical to actually work on stage ("Bridging" 8).[7] For Dauster, the plays written by well-known *Boom* writers demonstrate how the authors maintain in their theatrical works the principal concerns of their novels –"the question of identity, the interrelationships between society and the individual personality, the relativ-

---

Llosa himself stresses the links between his novels and his theatrical production: "I think that there is a relationship between my novels and my plays. In the latter I have tried to play with simultaneity and parallel planes, to create a specific atmosphere, to give a signifying function to the links between past and present, and all of this is also in my novels" (Espinosa Domínguez 58).

[7] Dauster offers an explicit example of how the technical and thematic links between Fuentes's novels and his plays frequently result in less than adequate dramatic works: "*Todos los gatos son pardos* is clearly related to *La muerte de Artemio Cruz*, *La región más transparente* or the massive later novels in the way in which Fuentes manages large casts and the essentially essayist focus. The problem is that the technical virtuosity of a novel like *Artemio Cruz* is not visible, perhaps not even possible, in *Todos los gatos*, with the result that the play is much more straightforward, bordering on a dramatized essay" ("Bridging" 8). In contrast to this view of Fuentes's plays, Dauster stresses Vargas Llosa's success in avoiding some of these problems: "Vargas Llosa never falls victim to the temptation to attempt to bring to the stage the enormous casts of characters and the sweeping social panoramas of the novels" ("Bridging" 10).

ity of individuality and indeed of verifiable reality"–and how they attempt "to recreate in theatrical terms the complex techniques of the novels" ("Bridging" 14), sometimes successfully and sometimes not.

In "Invasions from Outer Space: Narration and the Dramatic Art in Spanish America," John W. Kronik traces with lucidity both the historical and artistic implications of the complex relationship between narrative and dramatic genre and argues that in recent years narrative has become within Latin American theatre "a highly active option" (25).[8] Kronik's examination of texts such as Sánchez's *Quíntuples* and *La pasión según Antígona Pérez*, René Marqués's *Los soles truncos*, Osvaldo Dragún's *Historias para ser contadas* (1957), and Emilio Carballido's *Yo también hablo de la rosa* (1966) uncovers the technical and philosophical implications of the presence of narration in theatre: issues of artistic identity, authority, self-consciousness, irony, aggression, liberation, memory vs. enactment, fusion and confusion of rules and spaces, and others. For Kronik, the prevailing presence of narration in theatre "records a lingering feature of drama that this century's iconoclastic drive towards experimentation has energized" (27).

Although Dauster correctly stresses that Vargas Llosa does not abandon in his plays the technical characteristics of his novels, Vargas Llosa does rely on narrative discourse, as in *Kathie y el hipopótamo*'s prologue, "El teatro como ficción" ["The Theatre as Fiction"], and conveys an uncertainty about theatre's power to communicate in its own terms, that is, with its virtues and limitations. It is a truism to say that theatre can speak for itself, as *Kathie y el hipopótamo* does, but still we encounter in the prologue to this play a Vargas Llosa too eager to "narrate" to his reading audience the nature, meanings, and complexities of what will follow, that is, the intricacies of the dramatic action. Vargas Llosa's very explicit prologue describes the ideas that will dominate the play, which in his own words, aim at "las relaciones entre la vida y la ficción" (12) ["the relationship between life and fiction" (97)]. Therefore, it could be argued that the link between Vargas Llosa's prologue and

---

[8] Kronik states: "Even if drama's narrative essence becomes a matter for critical debate, the deliberate unfurling of narration is obvious even to the most casual observer of the Latin American theatre of the past three decades or so" (32). It would be necessary to connect this trend, in a direct and systematic way, to the strength and popularity of performance theory after the 1960s.

his play ironically embodies the relationship between reality and fiction (which itself emblematizes other relations such as outside and inside, text and performance) and the problematics of textual and theatrical authority, anticipating *Kathie*'s concern with the boundaries of genre, art, language, communication, and power.

The apparent redundancy of Vargas Llosa's prologue in *Kathie y el hipopótamo* should not surprise anyone. He presents similar proposals to his reading audience in the prologue to *La señorita de Tacna* entitled "Las mentiras verdaderas" ("True lies"). In *La Chunga* (1986), he again uses the recourse of the prologue as a pre-text to anticipate and reflect theoretically on the nature of theatre. [9] But more important, as Kronik reminds us in his discussion of the use of the prologue in overtly narrative plays like *Quíntuples*, the audience is confronted with issues of authority and control, with the dilemmas of presence and absence, with the masking and unmasking of authorial or artistic power. [10] One wonders then if the presence of the prologue changes the identity of the play. And if so, how is this inclusion an attempt on the part of the author to maintain control of his creation? Who has the last word: the author, or the director and actors as interpreters and performers of the text? Or should we place the authority and final word in the hands of the audience, themselves interpreters of others' interpretations?

This intense dialectic between prologue and drama, or rather, between pre-text and text in *Kathie y el hipopótamo*, points to Vargas Llosa's insistence on theorizing in his prologues about the act of

---

[9] See Standish for important reflections on the use of the prologue in Vargas Llosa's plays. I agree with many of Standish's statements regarding Vargas Llosa's (ab)use of prologues, but their presence can be interpreted, and even justified, as part of his works' long-standing concern for both the role of the author and of authority in literature and as emblematic of the complex relationship between reality and fiction.

[10] Speaking about the "Prólogo para ser contado" in Dragún's *Historias para ser contadas*, Kronik establishes a difference between a play were the prologue is identified with the author and the case of *Historias*, where "the narrated prologue, an internal segment of the dramatic structure, carries no indication as to its speaker (one actor? a group of actors? the director?)" (38-39). Kronik ends his paragraph with the following assessment of the prologue in *Historias*, which contrasts with Vargas Llosa's narrative insertion as an authoritative and controlling voice in "El teatro como ficción": "When the prologue [in *Historias*] has finished exalting art and establishing the importance of telling stories, the show can go on" (39). The difference between the two plays is that, in the case of *Kathie y el hipopótamo*, the show will go on stage with neither the benefits nor the perils of Vargas Llosa's prologue.

theorizing in his plays, the latter being a feature easily recognized in his dramatic production.[11] The irony of this dialogic process between prologue and play in *Kathie* is the a priori description of a system or work that announces not only its fictional character but also its conflictive relationship with the extra-literary. To some extent, the prologue's eagerness to clarify what the piece is about, hinders the examination of a fictive world through fiction and poses an obstacle to confirming the system's autonomy by staging the dismantling of the system. Even more ironic, regardless of the authoritative voice of the prologue, *Kathie y el hipopótamo* does not become a text held subordinate to its pre-text but is a piece that, through its metatheatrical nature and farcical character, comments on a discourse that it finds redundant, while at the same time distancing itself from that discourse. Ultimately, the fact that the prologue can be addressed only to a reader and not to the theatre audience stresses its ironic displacement and actually brings to the surface the problematics of language and communication so adequately developed in *Kathie y el hipopótamo*. It is precisely from a linguistic and communicative perspective that we will examine in this chapter *Kathie*'s farcical identity as it confronts and dramatizes the problematics of meaning, marginality, and authority through the lives of two marginalized character-authors, Kathie Kennety and Santiago Zavala.

Vargas Llosa's *Kathie y el hipopótamo: Comedia en dos actos* stages the wealthy patron Kathie Kennety as she dictates to Santiago Zavala, with an exaggerated colloquial language and from her Parisian-style bohemian loft in Peru, her adventures in Black Africa

---

[11] Regarding *La señorita de Tacna* and *Kathie y el hipopótamo*, Dauster states: "Both plays deal with two of the author's most obsessive ideas: the nature of individual identity and the relationship between life and creation, between reality and illusion" (9). Dick Gerdes points out in his chapter "*La señorita de Tacna* and *Kathie y el hipopótamo*: Storytelling and Dramatized Art" that in both plays the primary concern is "the task of fully comprehending the process of creating fiction" (155), and he adds: "Despite the different approaches, both plays communicate the same idea: there is no reality other than the one created by fiction" (167). For Monleón, Vargas Llosa's theatre attempts to question the traditions of theatre; it attempts to go beyond the traditional expectations of a spectator who is able to understand and judge the characters' behaviors: "Vargas Llosa . . . aims to create a feeling of uncertainty, to play with times and spaces without the slightest continuity, to turn the stage not into a mirror of visible reality, but into the immaterial realm of the imagination" (124).

and the Arab world. A marginalized and unsuccessful writer, Santiago, in turn, dictates his new version into a tape recorder and then transforms Kathie's "autobiographical" narration and supposed experiences into literary material:

> KATHIE. Había montones de estrellas. Sentía no sé qué, solita en ese lugar, a esas horas, en medio de tanta tumba egipcia.
> SANTIAGO. Deambulo entre sepulcros piramidales y colosos faraónicos, bajo el firmamento nocturno, sinfín de estrellas que flotan sobre El Cairo en un mar azulino de tonalidades opalescentes. (I: 28)
>
> [KATHIE. There were lots of stars. I felt... oh, I don't know... kind of small and alone in that place, you know, at that time of night and in the middle of all those Egyptian tombs.
> SANTIAGO. I wander around the colossal pyramids and by the statues of mighty pharaohs that seem to sleep under the nocturnal firmament, its infinity of stars floating above Cairo in an azure sea of opalescent tones. (I: 101)] [12]

Throughout *Kathie y el hipopótamo*, the audience is confronted, both in humorous and sober ways, with the complex interweaving of multiple spaces, temporal planes, histories, identities, personalities, and relationships that are characterized mainly, although not exclusively, by Kathie and Santiago. [13] Beginning with the uncertainty of the characters' "real" names and their willingness to be identified with others (like Mark Griffin or Víctor Hugo in the case of Santiago), followed by the characters' capacity to impersonate other people, we recognize how these constant changes underscore the game of identities in spatial and chronological terms and how the play overtly portrays the multiple levels of reality and fiction. When Santiago Zavala asks Kathie how her name was born, she answers:

---

[12] Rosemary Geisdorfer Feal says about this linguistic transformation: "Santiago Zavala transforms Kathie's simple speech into formulas derived from subliterature, from the romance novels with their typical affectation" (140).

[13] Gastón Fernández de la Torriente indicates about the multiple planes in *Kathie*: "The reader and/or the audience is transported–by means of the magic tricks of the stage, which counterpose different spatial and temporal planes, as well as subjectivities–to an imaginary dimension in which time flows freely in its atemporality, and space is a place in the memory or the imagination of the protagonists" (111).

Si usara el mío, nadie tomaría en serio mi libro. Los nombres peruanos no parecen de escritores. Kathie Kennety, en cambio, sí: es extranjero, musical, cosmopolita. (*Lo mira reflexionando*.) Tampoco Santiago Zavala suena bien, para un artista. ¿Por qué no lo cambiamos? . . . ¡Ya sé! ¡Mark! ¡Mark Griffin! ¿Lo puedo llamar así? Entre nosotros, aquí, en la buhardilla. ¿No le importa?" (I: 35-36)

["Well, I thought that if I used my own name, no one would take my book seriously. You know, Peruvian names just don't sound right for writers. On the other hand, Kathie Kennety does. It's foreign, musical, cosmopolitan. (*She looks at him reflecting*.) You know, Santiago Zavala doesn't sound right for a writer either. Why don't we change it? . . . I know! Mark! Mark Griffin! What do you think? Can I call you that? Just between the two of us, up here in the loft? Would you mind?" (I: 104)]

At certain instances and as part of the multiplicity of histories and identities, Santiago becomes Kathie's former suitor, also named Víctor (I: 42 [106]); Kathie represents Adèle, Santiago's student and lover (I: 64 [113-14]); and Kathie's husband, Juan, and Santiago's wife, Ana, take the part of Kathie's children (II: 89 [122]). At other moments, Kathie travels, not to distant countries, but rather to her youth and intimate past with her immature husband Johnny Rompeolas [the surfer], while Santiago reveals–truthfully or not–his intellectual and sexual experiences and frustrations.

At the end of the play, the final exchanges between Kathie and Santiago (or Mark Griffin, as Kathie calls him) unmask the reality of the literary and vital game in which the characters have placed themselves. Both Kathie and Santiago reveal, in a direct way, the intimate need to protect that space and time that they dedicate to (re)creating, fantasizing, inventing, lying, remembering, and rewriting their real or fictionalized experiences. As Jacqueline Bixler has pointed out, it is within this mirrorlike structure that we encounter in *Kathie y el hipopótamo* two characters who participate in their own dramatization while at the same time possessing complete self-consciousness: "These characters, a middle-aged woman from the upper crust of Lima society and a junior journalist named Santiago Zavala, are at once fictional creations and creators of fiction, in the outer dramatic frame as well as the metaplays that evolve therein" ("Vargas Llosa's *Kathie*" 255). Both

Kathie and Santiago not only acknowledge their mediocrity outside of the loft but recognize the need to create worlds or texts that supplant the necessities that life outside does not provide, and, ultimately, they realize that they have to protect the radical transformation they experience upon penetrating into the new space. Kathie acknowledges:

> KATHIE. Cuando subo la escalerita de esta azotea, abajo se quedan San Isidro, Lima, el Perú, y le juro que entro de verdad en una buhardilla de París, en la que sólo se respira arte, cultura, fantasía. Allá abajo se queda la señora llena de compromisos, la esposa del banquero.... Usted es parte de este pedacito de mi vida que hace llevadero el resto. Usted me ayuda a que mi sueño se haga realidad, a que mi realidad se haga sueño.... (II: 140)

> [KATHIE. See, when I come up here, I seem to be able to leave San Isidro, Lima, Peru, behind and I swear I'm really in a Paris loft where there is only culture and fantasy. I can actually forget being a banker's wife.... You make my dreams real and my reality a dream.... (II: 139-40)]

Meanwhile and in a parallel fashion, Santiago also believes that when he enters the loft he leaves behind his life as a mediocre, insignificant professor and becomes an excellent prose writer, intellectual, creator, dreamer, and inventor (II: 142 [140]). When Santiago works in this private room he experiences loves he has never had and Greek tragedies that he never hoped to experience; he travels not only through the Far East and Africa but to other places as well (II: 142 [140]). Not surprisingly, the audience's attention is drawn to the loft by the exaggerated feelings and actions linked to Kathie and Santiago's invented realities. The representation of the marriage of Kathie with Johnny the surfer, the infidelity of both, the "true" love between Víctor and Kathie, Santiago's pseudosocialist discourse, his desire to incarnate Víctor Hugo's sexuality and creative capacity, and Johnny's suicide provoked by Kathie's unfaithfulness, are all events imprisoned within the enclosed space of the Parisian loft whose world answers to the psychological, existential, and linguistic imperatives of the world of creation. In other words, sexual desires, scenes of jealousy, intrigue, murder, social inequality, greed, class and power struggles, ambition and fame, all reach hyperbolic dimensions inside the loft and stress the theatrical and fictional identity of this particular world. At a primary level, then, the characters' capacity to transform their respective realities into more exuberant ones is framed within a ludic environment, and the play could be perceived as a straightforward reflection on the dichotomy between the world inside the loft and the one outside it.

But the play turns out to be more problematic than initially perceived, since it goes beyond this dichotomy between inside and outside as it stresses the human need to create and cross boundaries –physical, existential, moral, artistic, linguistic–underscoring in the process the ambiguities of multiple and contradictory worlds. As would be expected, the separation of spaces and times in the lives of the already ambiguous characters has also become part of an illusion, and the audiences of *Kathie y el hipopótamo* recognize the uncertainty regarding the truthfulness or fictionality of the characters' narrations, versions, and representations. If at any moment the audience believed that they could distinguish what belonged to Kathie and to Santiago's *fictional* constructions (that is, to the Parisian loft) from what belonged to their supposed *real* worlds ("down there"), by the end of the play the only transparent truth is that the two characters' existences are shaped by the interdependence of various real and fictional languages.[14] Like the snake that bites its own tail, Kathie and Santiago not only cling to the imaginative nature of art as a new and more seductive reality, but they also end up unmasking its contradictions and inconsistencies, and providing glimpses of what could be their respective realities outside the loft. That is, they express their awareness of the contradictory and interdependent nature of the doubly creative activity that they are executing. In schematic and simplistic terms, Kathie and Santiago simultaneously construct and undo the fictional nature of reality and the truthful nature of fiction. The characters themselves acknowledge

---

[14] As part of the line of thought where the audience cannot distinguish anymore between fantasy and reality, Gerdes observes: "The distinction between truth and lie has been erased, and the destructive truths are exchanged for pious lies so that some of the characters may continue to live" (166). Standish, for his part, points out: "The spectator of *Kathie* . . . is not asked to believe in the truth of any story enacted on stage, any theatrical illusion, but only in the palliative power of the fiction. . . . [T]he fundamental concerns [of *Kathie*] are human, not a matter of how a story comes into being but of what its value is for our existence" (137).

without subtleties the interdependence between fiction and reality–an interdependence that we will later question.

In Vargas Llosa's explicit prefaces to the play he insists on representing human experience as both objective and subjective, real and unreal (*Kathie* 22 [98]), which simultaneously establishes and erases the focus on opposite structures. He emphasizes how the individual speaks and acts but also dreams and creates, and how he/she represents history and reason as well as fantasy and desire (*Kathie* 22 [98-99]). Vargas Llosa highlights the interdependence rather than the distance between polarized structures like reality and fiction or life and art, revealing a "new truth" with theatrical, linguistic, and existential connotations. Yet, within the frame of farce this apparently new truth also lives in continual danger of being substituted. In other words, the irony of this goal of interdependence in the context of farce is that by parodying oral and written communication–the narration of the story and its transcription, and the creative process itself–*Kathie y el hipopótamo* "transcribes" and transgresses its characters' inner realities as well as fiction itself. Even the notion of interdependence that was initially perceived as part of a "more problematic level," becomes in *Kathie* too obvious, too schematic, too simplistic. Nevertheless, the explicitness of the characters' statements and views of the coexistence of opposite forces turns out to be misleading given that the structures of communication have been portrayed throughout Vargas Llosa's play not as direct and transparent, but as metaphoric, ironic, and double-edged.

The farcical dimensions in *Kathie y el hipopótamo*–mainly the clash between the ludic nature of reality and fiction's capacity to reflect on and parody life–are portrayed through the transgression of the play's structures of communication, particularly as they characterize representational-theatrical language and textual-literary discourse. *Kathie*'s complex understanding of language and communication is underscored by its diverse manifestations: language in the form of informal, oral communication; in its written form, with literary or poetic overtones; in its physical and theatrical expressions; as a vehicle of seduction; as an expression of the inner self; in its rhetorical dimensions; and language as a misleading mask. But more important is to recognize that in *Kathie* these contradictory manifestations interact with each other in the context of farce, itself an aggressive and transgressive theatrical language.[15]

Ironically, *Kathie* not only critically examines multiple means of communication but it also reflects on what farce is attempting to communicate, if anything at all, in this play. The spectator focuses, then, not so much on the farcical aspects of what is being communicated as on the farcical aspects of communication itself. Vargas Llosa's use of a marginal and supposedly meaningless genre such as farce as a strategy to unmask artistic hierarchies along with sociopolitical ones, questions traditional communication as well as the power and authority linked to the act of communication.[16]

When Vargas Llosa talks about the farcical nature of *Kathie y el hipopótamo*, he clarifies that this play "no es una farsa por la forma exterior de la representación sino por su contexto secreto, la invisible raíz de lo que se dice y se hace en el escenario" (21) ["is not a farce on a surface level, but in its subtext, the invisible root of what is said and done on the stage" (98)]. In other words, communication, both linguistic and physical, overshadows what Vargas Llosa considers the external elements of farce, bringing to the surface the hidden and invisible aspects of this traditionally explicit genre.[17] It

---

[15] It is appropriate to anticipate that for Gerdes and Holzapfel, language in *Kathie* is "heavily dependent on both hyperbole and sexual euphemism" (24), to which they add: "Highly rhetorical language and bawdy euphemisms mesh to give recourse to desire as well as to create a deformed bourgeois perspective on society" (24).

[16] The emphasis on the multiplicities of histories and identities in *Kathie* opens the door to the multiplicity of critical approaches with which critics have examined the play. Óscar Rivera-Rodas, for example, divides *Kathie y el hipopótamo*'s action into two basic levels–the fictional and metafictional–and then proceeds to describe in detail the coexistence of various temporal, spatial, and narrative structures in the play. Gerdes and Holzapfel suggest that not only in *Kathie* but also in *La señorita de Tacna* and *La Chunga*, Vargas Llosa uses "the melodrama of events and the melodrama of presentation to obtain unusual aesthetic effects and a specific intellectual message" (18), and they end their essay counterpointing this use of melodrama with the author's recourse to irony (26). Specifically regarding *Kathie*, Gerdes and Holzapfel observe: "*Kathie y el hipopótamo* . . . uses innovatively a 'thwarted escape' plot as a basis for an absurdist play about the crisis of the capitalist family and modern escapism" (18).

[17] In what could be considered the play's stage directions entitled "Decorado, vestuario, efectos" (19-22) ["Set Design, Costume and Effects," 97-99], Vargas Llosa acknowledges that laughter does not come to *Kathie* through the excesses of words and gesture–as it would be the case in buffo comedy–but that the purpose is to lead the audience to accept, through humor, suspense, and melodrama, the prevailing confusion of separate levels or expressions of reality: "the visible and the invisible, the real and the dreamed, the present and the past" (21 [98]).

is within this communicative framework that *Kathie y el hipopótamo* "plays" with the notion of meaning–placing it, replacing it, displacing it–as a way to question the identity of verbal, written, and theatrical communication.[18]

The abundance of metaphors and metaphorical language in *Kathie* dramatizes the problematics of communication in artistic and personal terms, underscoring the tension between what is said and what is not said, between the explicit and what is implied. The play also portrays this linguistic tension through a ludic interpretation of the act of "translating" from one oral form (Kathie's) to another (Santiago's) and eventually transforming oral communication into written language. But most significant is that the recourse to rhetorical expressions as powerful as metaphor and to a linguistic operation as important as the act of translation are framed within another rhetorical device, irony, which emphasizes the contradictions of the communicative process, particularly the play's reflection on the conflict between reality and fiction.

Because of *Kathie y el hipopótamo*'s focus on language, the audience of Vargas Llosa's play cannot but laugh at the persistent incongruities between oral and written discourses (what Kathie dictates, what Santiago records, and the written version). The contrast between these forms of communication calls attention to issues of authority and the fragility and clichés of the codes and conventions of oral and written language: excessive informality vs. exaggerated poetization; spontaneity vs. calculated embellishment; the direct vs. the mediated; the natural vs. the artificial; past vs. present; primary vs. secondary, and other polarized elements. But what can be more ironic in the context of the play's incongruities than recognizing the dual identity of theatre itself in its oral and written dimensions, that is, as both textual and representational?

---

[18] See the introduction to this book, in the section entitled "The Urge to Define," for a summary of comments by critics who denounce what they consider to be the erroneous definitions of farce offered by dictionaries and encyclopedias. See Hurrell, Davis, Freedman, Williams, and McDonald, among others. It is particularly meaningful that Gerdes and Holzapfel examine Vargas Llosa's plays in the light of melodrama and the melodramatic, and that they begin their essay by confronting the stigmas of this genre, as we have attempted to do with farce: "Melodrama and melodramatic are terms charged with pejorative overtones. Throughout much of the 20th century, literary critics have used them to indicate supercilious effects such as exaggeration, sentimentality, pretense and hysterics..." (17).

In the context of the play's obsession with the dialectics between reality and fiction, the audience is confronted with the quandaries of which of these languages–Kathie's spontaneous and informal oral expression, Santiago's dictation into a tape recorder of a poetic version of Kathie's narration, or the expected written version–transmits a deeper sense of truthfulness ("reality") and which is more closely linked to false constructions and lies ("fiction"). We may ask whether oral communication is more authentic, for example, than the written word and how orality and textuality interact in *Kathie y el hipopótamo*.[19] Should we relate these dichotomies with the also conflictive issues in *Kathie* between love and sexuality, life and death, authority and subordination, theatre and narrative? This issue of authorial representation in Vargas Llosa's play must be explained since it involves two complementary figures who represent different angles of artistic creation in general and literary writing in particular. One wonders if it is feasible to characterize the authorial figure within the loft and clearly distinguish between the person who lives and orally narrates those experiences (Kathie) and the person who "translates" that oral narration into a new language and into writing (Santiago). What would it imply if Kathie's autobiographical discourse were itself an invention, and what does Santiago's insistence on his subordination to Kathie's realities and fictions mean?

The issue of authority in *Kathie y el hipopótamo* takes us back to the discussion of the tense relationship between narrative genre and theatre. What *Kathie y el hipopótamo* does as a farcical play is not only emphasizing its marginal position within the context of literary creation but also stressing its conflictive interaction with narrative discourse as a mechanism for portraying and consequently questioning this genre's authoritative, powerful position. To some extent, this relationship between narrative and theatre is reflected in Kathie's creation of a Parisian loft which, on the one hand, becomes a haven where she and Santiago can enjoy the "freedom" to explore their selves and respective literary ambitions but, on the other, becomes a space where the audience recognizes the struggle between textuality and performance, between the prevalence and authority

---

[19] The supposed link between orality and authenticity will be taken up later in a brief commentary on the narrative and communicative elements of Vargas Llosa's novel *El hablador*.

of narration and writing, or of representation and acting. In a way, the creation of the Parisian loft in *Kathie* emblematizes the geographical and cultural trajectory of many Spanish American writers since the nineteenth century who frequently traveled to France to experience the epitome of high culture and art: in the past, mainly narrators and poets–Sarmiento, Echeverría, Darío, Asunción Silva–and more recently, the well-known narrative writers of the *Boom* and *post-Boom* period–Cortázar, García Márquez, Carlos Fuentes, Vargas Llosa himself, Bryce Echenique, and Sarduy. Significantly, *Kathie y el hipopótamo* confronts in a reflexive and parodic way the position it occupies *vis-à-vis* the authoritative and prestigious narrative discourses. As part of the dialectics between theatre and narrative, Vargas Llosa's play ironically portrays as a cliché this tradition of the French literary experience of Spanish American novelists.[20]

Why this emphasis on writers of narrative, on their creative space, and, in the case of a theatre piece, on textuality? Should one argue that the text narrated and written by Kathie and Santiago takes center stage in Vargas Llosa's play? Or should one say that what actually prevails is the theatrical representation of this narration and writing, and of the real and fictional lives of those who write? It is clear that there is a tension between the characters' narration and writing of a text and the theatricalization of this writing. It is also obvious that theatre becomes the mechanism for dramatizing the decentralization of narrative authority–be it of the author, the text, or the reader. Quite characteristically of farce, it also struggles against theatre's own authority–be it of the author, the director, the technical team, or the audience, among other voices.

Vargas Llosa's farcical portrayal of the life of a writer in Paris is connected to the caricaturization of narrative discourse and textuality. This portrayal can be interpreted as part of *Kathie y el hipopótamo*'s critique of Spanish American narrative traditions, particularly to the *Boom* and *post-Boom* literature–to which Vargas Llosa's novels belong– and is explicitly related to issues of artistic and political authority. Literary traditions in Spanish America such as the dictator novel, documentary narrative, feminist writing, testimonial novel, autobiographical writing, and detective fiction, to mention the

---

[20] For a serious examination of Spanish American writers' view and understanding of Paris as cultural center, see Cristóbal Pera, *Modernistas en París: El mito de París en la prosa modernista hispanoamericana*.

most prevalent during the 1970s and 1980s, overtly deal with the dynamics of power and authority and appear in a consciously fragmentary and parodic way in Vargas Llosa's play. *Kathie*'s farcical relationship with some of these literary traditions, particularly the "literature of dictatorship," addresses the complex relation between writing and authority in Spanish American literature.[21]

In *Kathie y el hipopótamo*, temporal, spatial, and linguistic transgressions are not limited to revealing the artificiality of theatrical discourse but also point to the rhetoric of writing through ironic humor. In *La señorita de Tacna* we see how the presence of the writer on stage dramatizes the narrative and creative acts, which over the course of the play becomes a test of memory.[22] In the case of *Kathie y el hipopótamo*, the presence on stage of both the one who dictates and the one who transcribes or writes forces the audience to focus on the humorous displacement of the literal and tangible by the metaphorical and abstract, which includes the loss of the referent in the very lives of the characters and in the language they use. That is, the dismantling of the literal underscores the complex role played by the use of metaphor, translation, and irony as rhetorical and linguistic structures that, beyond their recognizable differences, share the function of substituting, of displacing one concept or object with another. But more importantly, this act of substitution so prevalent in *Kathie* reveals its farcical and playful nature in the fusion and confusion of those same structures: in the ironic use and abuse of metaphorical language, in the literal and metaphorical act of translation, and in the ironic dimensions of the excesses of irony. In other words, it is possible to identify in *Kathie y el hipopótamo* the farcical dimensions that simultaneously emphasize the construction of structures of communication and meaning

---

[21] "The Dictatorship of Rhetoric/The Rhetoric of Dictatorship," a chapter in Roberto González Echevarría's 1985 book *The Voice of the Masters: Writing and Authority in Modern Latin American Literature*, will serve as point of departure in the discussion of writing and authority.

[22] See Eva Golluscio de Montoya's "Los cuentos de *La señorita de Tacna*," Sharon Magnarelli's "Mario Vargas Llosa's *La señorita de Tacna*: Autobiography and/as Theater," and Meléndez's "Creación y autocreación en *La señorita de Tacna* de Mario Vargas Llosa," to mention just a few articles that address the characterization of the writer on stage. The presence of the writer on stage in *Kathie* and its implications regarding the issues of authority, power, and hierarchy, will be discussed in more detail later.

and also their displacement. Within the context of Spanish American theatre, farce is engaged in a double task of constructing and deconstructing (and vice versa): on the one hand, deconstructing its generic language and conventions and, on the other, constructing its own pseudocomic, self-conscious, and deconstructive version of the genre.

To begin with, the use of metaphors throughout *Kathie* is emblematic of farce's game with the power and authority of language and meaning, and with their possible displacement. The discrepancy between what is said and what is written or transcribed, between the narrated and the acted, between true and false statements reveals the substitution of certain communicative codes through the use of rhetorical conventions. For example, the role played by metaphor–that is, the action of substituting one word for the meaning of another under the premise of certain similarities (cf. de Man, *Allegories* 146)–distorts the relationship, itself arbitrary, between the signifier and the signified. More recent philosophical criticism has discarded the positivist interpretation of metaphor as "frivolous and inessential, if not dangerous and logically perverse," incapable of possessing or transmitting meaning, lacking an absolute connection with the event or even with the signified (Cohen 3). Still, we recognize that the linguistic and rhetorical structures in *Kathie* become instruments that seek to deceive the spectator and to distort a reality that is in itself uncertain and questionable. This emphasis on the deceitfulness of rhetorical language makes it pertinent to quote here what both Ted Cohen in "Metaphor and the Cultivation of Intimacy" (2-3) and Paul de Man in "The Epistemology of Metaphor" (13) cited from the third book, chapter 10, of *An Essay Concerning Human Understanding* by seventeenth-century English philosopher John Locke:

> Since wit and fancy find easier entertainment in the world than dry truth and real knowledge, *figurative speeches* and allusion in language will hardly be admitted as an imperfection or abuse of it. . . . If we would speak of things as they are, we must allow that all the art of rhetoric, besides order and clearness, all the artificial and figurative application of words eloquence hath invented, are for nothing else but to insinuate wrong ideas, move the passions, and thereby mislead the judgment, and so indeed are perfect cheats. . . . Only I cannot but observe how little the preservation and improvement of truth and knowledge is the care and

concern of mankind; since the arts of fallacy are endowed and preferred. It is evident how much men love to deceive and be deceived, since rhetoric, that powerful instrument of error and deceit, has its established professors, is publicly taught and has always been had in great reputation. (285; my emphasis)

Vargas Llosa's persistent use of metaphorical discourse as a vehicle for blurring the world outside the loft and the world inside it underscores both the power and the deceitful nature of language and its playful (in)capacity to communicate. Who is Kathie's husband after all, and what is he like? Is he Johnny, the surfer-philanderer who kills himself, or rather a respected banker who, according to his wife, "es un alma de Dios, el hombre más bueno del mundo..." (II: 138) ["is the sweetest soul in the world" (II: 139)]?

Second, as part of this sleight of hand that substitutes Kathie's prosaic language for Santiago's pseudopoetic rendition, the act of translation that seeks to express in one "language" something originally said in another, also problematizes the ties between signifier and signified. But in the context of *Kathie y el hipopótamo* the concept of translation acquires a farcical angle (and ironically a "wider meaning"), since it is not really one language but rather one linguistic expression being replaced by another. Are we dealing, then, with a metaphor that seeks to cover, or rather to reveal, the nature of both the translation and what was translated, of the "imitation" as well as the "original"? As part of the continual dramatic and linguistic transgression, the act of substituting the language and narrative style of Kathie Kennety for a stereotypically literary vocabulary and prose inverts, in Borgean terms, "la superstición de la inferioridad de las traducciones" (239) ["the superstition about the inferiority of translations" (69)].[23] At first glance and quite ironically, Santiago's stylized version suggests that spontaneous language (Kathie's

---

[23] In "The Homeric versions," Borges reiterates the transcendence of the act of translation in the aesthetic task and examines the multiple English versions of *The Odyssey*: "Which of these many translations is faithful?.... I repeat: none or all of them" (74). The impossibility of differentiating "what belongs to the author from what belongs to the language" (Borges 240) results in the parallel difficulty of deciphering whether the translations correspond faithfully to Homer's imagination or to his purposes or intentions (243). For an insightful analysis of *Cien años de soledad* that benefits from the theories offered by Benjamin, Derrida, and Borges, see Aníbal González's "Translation and Genealogy: *One Hundred Years of Solitude*."

"original" version) is actually inferior to deliberately aesthetic language and that it is permissible to transgress the facts if this transgression creates a "poetic" version:

> KATHIE. Había unos turistas. El perfumero nos explicó en un *inglés zarrapastroso* que la tienda era viejísima y nos hizo probar unas muestras. No me quitaba los ojos de encima, hasta ponerme nerviosa.
> SANTIAGO. El perfumero es alto, delgado, de ojos negros y dentadura blanquísima. Su mirada no se aparta de mí mientras nos explica, *en francés, la lengua de la seducción,* que la perfumería es tan antigua como las más remotas mezquitas egipcias.... Nos hace aspirar elixires cuya fragancia dura años en la piel. Y, mientras habla, sus ojos–obscenos, voraces, lujuriosos–siguen fijos en mí. (II: 42; my emphasis)

> [KATHIE. Some tourists were in the shop. The perfumist explained *in really awful English* that the shop was very old. He had us try some samples of perfume. The entire time, he never took his eyes off me. It made me nervous.
> SANTIAGO. The perfumist is tall, slim, with black eyes and flashing white teeth. His eyes never stray from me while he explains to us *in exquisite and seductive French* that the shop was as old as the most ancient Egyptian mosques.... He offered us elixirs whose fragrance lasts for years on the skin. And while he speaks, his sensual gaze consumes me with unbridled lust. (II: 106, my emphasis)]

It is ironic that, in this particular example, Santiago chooses not only to substitute the adjective "zarrapastroso" for "la lengua de la seducción" but also to replace a language traditionally associated with the crudely commercial (English) for the epitome of refinement and the exotic (French). Clearly, we are confronted here with the codes and clichés of both the literary and nonliterary vocabulary of a particular language, and also with the codes and clichés of a particular language and its capacity–or lack of it–to communicate in what is traditionally considered literary terms. In this case, the apparent hegemony of one language over another language, of a certain vocabulary over another vocabulary, of a style over another style is clearly related in *Kathie* as to issues of authority, hierarchy, and power.

In theorizing about the role played by the translator, Walter Benjamin observes that the dialectic character of both languages –the original and that of the translation–cancels the supremacy of one over the other and reaffirms the translator's work as that which brings to the surface (liberates) from the translated language a pure language that underlies it, one that is imprisoned in a certain text and that needs to be liberated while re-creating the text: "Translation thus ultimately serves the purpose of expressing the central reciprocal relationship between languages" (72). In *Kathie*, the clash of one language that is absurdly prosaic with another that is laughably poetic not only unmasks their interdependence, but also parodies the insufficiency of creating an infinite and nontranscendental cycle. Ironically, in this world of the Parisian loft the action, or rather, the infinite re-creation of the multiple actions, appears subordinate to language; but it is a language that deliberately reveals its imprecise and unfaithful character. At any rate, what Kathie and Santiago achieve as creator and re-creator, respectively, of Kathie's adventures is the imitation and falsification of the world of writing and fiction, thus "translating" Kathie's real or imaginary trips to the Far East and Black Africa into a new textual and linguistic reality.

Not surprisingly, the contradictory relationships between different languages and means of communication represented in the act of translation are connected to another rhetorical structure in *Kathie*: ironic speech wherein, according to Kierkegaard, the opposite of that which is meant is said. In Vargas Llosa's play, this third means of communicative strategy reveals the function of transgression and substitution alluded to earlier. The distance between the concept and the enunciation is not restricted in *Kathie* to linguistic issues but extends to physical, psychological, and artistic ones, including the ambiguous relationship between the world inside and outside the loft, between interior and exterior action, between the real and the fictional. At a primary level, the characters are confronted with their contradictory realities and dreams, and their real and fictional lives consist of reconciling them. What the force of irony achieves is the transgression of the play's overt preoccupation with these structures of opposition, creating additional levels of contradiction in which these structures themselves are questioned.

Moving a step further in this schism between what is said and what is meant, we are confronted with the role played by dramatic irony, which specifically depends on the reader's or spectator's knowledge of something about the character's situation that the character does not know (Booth 255). The staging of the act of writing in *Kathie y el hipopótamo* is one of the key elements that helps to reveal, before the spectator's eyes, the work's various levels of fiction. In Vargas Llosa's play, the characters themselves, also creators, are conscious of this dichotomy of worlds, of the artifice of life and of art. Initially, Santiago makes fun of the invention of this loft and of this absurd game:

> SANTIAGO. ... Claro que la creía una señora rica y chiflada jugando a un juego carísimo. Me reía y creía venir aquí cada día, ese par de horas, por los soles que me pagaba. Pero ya no es verdad. La verdad es que desde hace tiempo el juego también me gusta y que estas dos horitas, de mentiras que se vuelven verdades, de verdades que son mentiras, también me ayudan a soportar mejor las demás horas del día. (II: 141)

> [SANTIAGO. ... I thought of you as an eccentric rich lady playing a very expensive game. I had a good laugh and came out here a couple of hours every day for the money. But I don't think so anymore. The truth is that for a while now I've been enjoying this game too. I enjoy these two hours of lies that become truth and truths that become lies, and it helps me to get through the rest of the day too. (II: 140)]

Nevertheless, what Kathie and Santiago do not seem to suspect is that the protection and privacy offered to them by the loft have been compromised by the theatrical "fourth wall" through which the audience observes their lives and fantasies. Ironically, the desire that they both express not to meet their respective partners, and therefore not to destroy the illusion they have created inside the loft becomes the counterpoint of a linguistic and theatrical discourse that brazenly exposes its defining mechanisms, destroying, in this way, the characters' desire for privacy and isolation. In another twist, both discourses–the private and the public, or theatrical– share in the examination of the intrinsic, of that which demands an introspective glance.

D. C. Muecke takes the idea of dramatic irony one step further in attributing to it an inherent character and suggesting that the nonliterary elements are equally capable of offering the spectator additional information not possessed by the character: "In many plays the audience will already know what the outcome will be from the prologue or the program notes or the title or previous performances or from earlier versions in literature or legend or from history" (70-71). The initial commentaries on the prologue to *Kathie y el hipopótamo* reflect the plurality of relationships developed by the text with other structures inside or outside the play that may or may not pertain to the literary activity. This link between what is internal and what is external to the work is evident at both the thematic level–the pleasure that Kathie and Santiago feel about the act of self-alienation–and the formal level, where the artificial nature of the dramatic work becomes evident. Vargas Llosa's prologue to *Kathie y el hipopótamo*, which establishes a tense relationship with the piece itself, generates a structure that is constantly subjected to self-examination and displacement.

As part of this separation between the concept and the enunciation, the three rhetorical and linguistic operations that we have been focusing on–the metaphorical plane, the act of translating words or lives, and the evident dose of irony–generate a plurality of readings and writings that problematize the dialogue between fiction and reality, and also the means used to justify this dialogue. If we accept what Kierkegaard points out in the sense that the irony of the rhetorical figure cancels itself (265), we can suppose that the act of implicit substitution in the three structures mentioned is at the same time replaced by a word that makes reference to another meaning, by a word in another "language," or by the inverse of the named.

As we move from an abstract to a more concrete sphere, it is possible to identify at the beginning of the second act of *Kathie y el hipopótamo* a characteristic example of the linguistic and rhetorical games that the audience constantly encounters in this play. During a night in Black Africa, an unidentifiable noise awakens Kathie, who soon discovers that the din comes from a "love duel" between two male hippopotamuses fighting over a female. At that point the spectator is confronted directly with the title of the play and recognizes the parallels among the multiple love triangles re-created in the loft: Kathie, Johnny, Víctor (Hugo), Bepo Torres, Abel, Santiago, Adèle, Mark, etc. Jacqueline Bixler correctly explains the contradictory relationship between the hippo's sexual capacity and its gastronomic fragility and "translates" it to represent similar situations in the lives of the drama's characters. Moving a step further, she adds: "The image of the hippo . . . not only bridges the outer play and the plays within, but also serves as a *dramatic metaphor* for pretension and deception as they relate to this play in particular and to the theatre in general" (Bixler 260; my emphasis). Also reflecting on the play's title, Gerdes stresses "the special use of euphemistic language that deflects and disguises the true nature of the characters' problems" (164).

It is also possible to recognize that the grotesque and comic title, even with its metaphorical implications, points to what could be considered the more overt aspects of the play: its elements of exaggeration, of extreme feelings and sensations, of several and caricaturized love triangles, of contrasts or lack of contrasts between strength and power. It is even possible to argue that the awkwardness of Vargas Llosa's title is one more mechanism through which the play problematizes artistic communication and places itself in contrast to the prestige and sophistication of literary discourse –most ironically, to the literariness, sophistication, and prestige of Vargas Llosa's own narrative texts. To some extent, then, *Kathie y el hipopótamo*'s obsession with the interdependence between reality and fiction is both represented and parodied in what is considered literary, poetic, and delicate on the one hand, and grotesque, brutal, and exaggerated on the other: that is, between a sublime love relationship and "an insatiable sexual voracity" (II: 89) [122]; between the delicate throat of a hippopotamus capable of eating only little birds and butterflies and its "cataclysmic potency" during sexual intercourse (II: 88-89) [122].

As we return to the critical disjunction between the person who contributes the ideas and the one who writes them down, between the one who has lived and coarsely narrated the experience and the one who stylizes it, we are confronted with these problematics of authorship, authority, and centrality. The issue of who occupies center stage in *Kathie y el hipopótamo*, that is, who, if anyone, possesses the authorial power in literal and metaphorical terms, who has the "last" word in the process of narrating and writing, underscores the image of the writer on stage, which inevitably suggests questions of power and of authorial representation. Michael Boyd describes this trope in narrative discourse when he points out that in order to insist on the notion of the text as process, as activity, it has been necessary to stage an actor's representation of this part –that is, the role of the writer who, while writing, assumes all of the functions previously ascribed to his invention (147). In *Kathie y el hipopótamo* the creative voice inside the text has been broken down into two figures: the woman who dictates and the translator/transcriber. The particularity of this breakdown is that in the context of traditional narrative discourse, it distorts the standard triangle among author, text, and reader, and in the case of dramatic discourse it adds another level of complexity to the already plural nature of theatre's structures of communication where the author, willingly or not, shares the creative power with directors, actors, the technical team, and the audience. Even more ironically, Vargas Llosa's play shows its capacity to multiply even further the two main narrative and theatrical voices of communication by placing on stage a tape recorder and typewriter that will aid the characters-cum-writers in the literaturization of their respective dreams and desires. To some extent both machines parody the dichotomy between oral and written languages and dramatize the linguistic transgressions so prevalent in the play, since they are artificial mechanisms and stage props that seek to reproduce the voices of the characters-authors and of their respective narrative and theatrical texts.

The rhetoric of power, authorship, and authority in the context of theatre extends to the dynamic participation and sometimes tense relationship between creators, actors, and spectators. What is of particular significance regarding this relationship is that beyond Kathie's and Santiago's traditional roles as characters of Vargas Llosa's play, they are also creators who re-create themselves as actors-characters and even as spectators of various dramas destined to be represented though never lived. However, this representation seems to exclude the broader notion of a theatrical audience, for it seeks the pleasure of the game neither on a public stage nor in real life but in the privacy of the inner realm (psychological and physical, that is, mental creations inside a loft) and in the desire and possibility of writing.

Regarding Kathie's role as writer, her difficulty to transform into "poetic" language her inner world–her desires, her pleasures–demonstrates the problematics of self-expression and of the content of her communication. Her need to call upon the services of a secretary (Santiago Zavala) questions the sense of authority of the person who dictates while placing in doubt the authority of language itself.[24] That is, by stressing the contrast between Kathie's unsophisticated narration and Santiago's literary version (although it is obvious that his is a pseudoversion of literature), the play establishes a comic hierarchy within language, attempting to legitimize one over the other (the poetic over the prosaic) but, ironically, deconstructing both expressions. Kathie's inability or unwillingness to write, and her preference to *dictate* her experiences to Santiago and let him turn them into literary language, allows us to connect, in a farcical way, this issue of literary authority and power with the well-known (and serious) literature of the dictatorship in Spanish America. In "The Dictatorship of Rhetoric/The Rhetoric of Dictatorship," Roberto González Echevarría briefly identifies the antecedents and "origins" of the dictator and the dictator-book:

> The most clearly indigenous thematic tradition in Latin American literature, the dictator and the dictator-book, can be traced as far back as Bernal Díaz del Castillo's and Francisco López de Gómara's accounts of Cortés's conquest of Mexico. . . . The modern tradition, which has its origins in Sarmiento's *Facundo* (1845), has produced masterpieces such as Valle-Inclán's *Tirano Banderas* (1925), Asturias's *El señor presidente* (1946), Carpentier's *The Kingdom of this World* (1949), and Rulfo's *Pedro Páramo* (1955). What could be called the postmodern tradition consists essentially of three novels that appeared in 1974: Carpentier's *Reasons of State* . . ., García Márquez's *The Autumn of the Patriarch* . . ., and Roa Bastos's *Yo el Supremo*. . . . (65)[25]

As part of the relationship between power, writing, and authority in Latin American literature, González Echevarría states that his interest in novels focusing on dictators is not "the emergence and evolution of the dictator in history" (65), but rather the tendency of these texts to "deal more abstractly with authority figures and with

---

[24] In the prologue, Vargas Llosa clarifies: "Para ella es un pasatiempo; para él, un trabajo" (9) ["For her, it's an amusement, a pastime; for him, it's a job" (95)], and later Santiago offers another note elucidating several hierarchical schemes: "Estoy trabajando para usted, dése cuenta. La veo como a mi jefe" (I: 36) ["You have to remember that I'm working for you. I see you as my boss" (I: 104)].

[25] Vargas Llosa's novel *La fiesta del chivo* (2000) is an excellent example not only of the "nature and ways of contemporary political power" but also of the power that constitutes a literary text and the role of the figure of the author in its relationship with the dictator (see González Echevarría 65).

the question of authority" (65). After briefly tracing the antecedents of these novels and naming the ones that he considers influential in the contemporary history of Latin American literature (we need to remember that this essay is from 1985), González Echevarría focuses on their literary aspects: "The revival that the dictator-novel is enjoying in these works is an inquiry not only into the nature and ways of contemporary political power, but also into the power, the energy that constitutes a literary text, particularly a novel, and the function within it of the figure of the author" (65).

Can we argue, then, that as part of its discussion of issues of power and authority, as well as of literary identity, *Kathie y el hipopótamo* is ironically linked to such Spanish American dictator novels as *El otoño del patriarca*, *El recurso del método*, and *Yo el supremo* (the ones alluded to by González Echevarría)? Is *Kathie* attempting to parody the centrality of these novels within the Spanish American literary tradition or, rather, as González Echevarría suggests, to highlight their own authority and authoritative characters through the intertextual dialogue that these novels themselves question? What is significant is that, although the dialogue in *Kathie y el hipopótamo* between the voice of the female dictator and that of her secretary explicitly recalls the Spanish American discourse of history, politics, and ideology as portrayed in dictator novels, *Kathie*'s farcical conversation with these discourses stresses its own complex understanding of the role of the author inside and outside the multiple levels of the play as it searches for nonauthoritative and decentralized systems of communication.

Of particular interest to our study of *Kathie y el hipopótamo* are González Echevarría's examination of the contrast between the power of the dictator-author and that of the secretary-writer in dictator novels (76-77), and Vargas Llosa's transgressions and games with the paternalistic and *macho* nature of the figure of the dictator as it is described by the Cuban critic (66). But as we will see, these two aspects are closely connected in *Kathie*, and the already-formulated question in the early pages of this chapter of who has the final authority among author, director, or audience in the case of theatre takes new form in literal and metaphorical terms in the relationship between Kathie the dictator (-author?) and Santiago the secretary (-writer?). Who has the last word: the person who lives or even invents an experience and orally narrates it, or the person who transforms that narration into a new text? Kathie herself wonders to whom the book belongs: "¿Lo estoy escribiendo realmente? ¿O lo está escribiendo usted?" (II: 137) ["Am I really writing it? Or are you writing it?" (II: 138)].

As we compare the power of the dictator-author and that of the secretary-writer, it is relevant to mention that González Echevarría's assessment of the postmodern novel in general–"from Proust and James on" (69)–and the Latin American dictator-novel in particular, stresses how the figure of the author goes through a weakening process and how, as a result, his power vanishes: "The great figure of the author has been replaced by the uncertain figure of the writer" (70). In a more detailed fashion, he states:

> The postmodern novel, even going as far back as Flaubert, holds a mirror, so to speak, up to that image of the author-dictator, of the author-rhetor, and reveals instead a weak and fragmented *scriptor*, who is the secretary of a voice no longer enthroned, no longer his or hers. The Latin American dictator-novel undergoes and reflects a similar process. (González Echevarría 70)

In the case of Vargas Llosa's *Kathie*, we recognize the farcical and labyrinthine angles of this conflict between the lost power of the author (Kathie probably never possessed it) and the weak stature of the secretary-writer, where both end up in marginal positions: Kathie's partial control is limited to the loft, and Santiago's dreams of becoming a great writer are diminished by his subordination to Kathie as an employee: "Estoy trabajando para usted, dése cuenta. La veo como a mi jefe" (I: 36) ["You have to remember that I'm working for you. I see you as my boss" (I: 104)]. It is clear then that when Kathie wonders who actually owns the book on the travels to Black Africa and Yellow Asia, Santiago's response confirms what González Echevarría identifies in the postmodern novel as the fragmented, weak position of the author replaced by an uncertain and diminished figure of the writer (see 70): "Yo soy el amanuense de la historia, el que pone los puntos y las comas y uno que otro adjetivo. El libro es suyo, de principio a fin" (II: 137) ["I am just the one who puts in the periods and commas and chooses one adjective over another. The book is yours from beginning to end" (II: 138)].

The significance of Kathie and Santiago's weakness as both author and writer is that it is precisely their disperse and unsophisticated "authority" that unites the two characters inside and outside the loft and that allows Vargas Llosa's play to question the structures of power and communication inside and outside the realm of literature. As stated in the introduction to this book, marginality is at the center of farce, and in this study its central position has had the purpose of creating an environment of tension and transgression between Spanish American farce and other theatrical expressions, between Spanish American theatre and other literary genres (particularly the novel), and between Spanish America and other regions and cultures (particularly the West). Therefore, what we see in *Kathie*'s farcical identity and in its focus on the dialectics between reality and illusion is the play's persistent transgression of basically everything that represents traditional authority, its persistent questioning of both physical and literary boundaries, its comic refusal to be kept on the margins of literary discourse, but also its refusal to occupy center stage, and ultimately its willingness to question different and contradictory forms of communication, including its own.

The second issue that is of great significance in the dialogue between *Kathie y el hipopótamo* and Spanish American dictator novels is how the traditional male relationship between dictator-author and his secretary-writer, as described by González Echevarría, is partially transformed in Vargas Llosa's play by placing a woman in the position of the one who dictates ("the dictator"), and preserving the male figure as the so-called secretary or transcriber.[26] If the purpose of *Kathie y el hipopótamo* is partly to establish a farcical intertextual dialogue with other genres and literary traditions, such as the novels of dictatorship, as a mechanism for dismantling authority and power, this displacement of the male figure for a female character–just as García Márquez does in "Los funerales de la Mamá Grande" ["Big Mama's Funeral"]–may be interpreted as a transgres-

---

[26] González Echevarría emphasizes the male aspects of dictatorship and links them to literary tradition: "The dictator, Primer Magistrado, Comandante en Jefe, Supremo, el Hombre, is a paternal figure who in turn embodies yet another figure, the *macho*" ("The Dictatorship" 66). Although in traditional terms the figure of the dictator is predominantly linked to men, we can underscore García Márquez's "Mamá Grande's Funeral," whose main character is a brutal, tyrannical woman. But as González Echevarría reminds us, "García Márquez's aggression against Mamá Grande is the traditional joke at the wake. As with old José Arcadio, the violence of laughter, of ridicule, is a weapon; from central, ominously powerful sources, both are turned into clowns whose only center is the ring of a textual circus" ("Big Mama's Wake" 56-57).

sive attempt to ridicule male supremacy in social, political, cultural, and authorial terms. That is, this aspect of the play may be seen as a straightforward attempt to question the traditional male authority so clearly portrayed in novels of dictatorship and so parodically performed by Johnny rompeolas and Mark Griffin in *Kathie*. What at first view seems a displacement of a male voice by a female one subsequently becomes the displacement of feminine discourse, since the latter is characterized as coarse and nonpoetic and is again substituted by a masculine voice. Ironically, Kathie's desire to generate a text that belongs to the literary tradition is parodied by the fact that its literariness appears as the property of Santiago, the one who transforms it.

But again, Vargas Llosa's play refuses to stand still and, in another turn of the screw, portrays Santiago's voice as diminished and weak, stresses the *pseudo*literariness of his text, and caricatures his compliance with his role as translator/amanuensis and not as author.[27] The displacement of feminine discourse is again transgressed when the force that supposedly displaced it (a male voice) turns out to be incapable of preserving its authority. Ultimately, what is meaningful in Kathie's and Santiago's failure to produce literary texts of their own is not only that literary authority becomes a persistently diminished concept but that, as a consequence, the main characters' relationship and their respective fictional worlds inside the loft are strengthened by this "failure":

> KATHIE. ... Me alegro haberle dado confianza desde el primer momento. Mi intuición no me engañó. Muchas gracias, Mark.
> SANTIAGO. Soy yo el que le da las gracias. Cuando subo a esta buhardilla, también empiezo otra vida. Abajo se queda el periodista de *La Crónica* que escribe mediocres artículos por un sueldo todavía más mediocre (II: 142)

---

[27] As part of this constant inversion of structures, where Kathie seems incapable of creating a language and a text that fits within a schematic literary tradition, it is significant to remember that she once developed another expression of her pseudoliterary discourse in her love letters to Víctor (although whether they belong to the world outside or inside the loft is ambiguous): "Contigo medito, de rodillas sobre losas heladas, frente a esa calavera que nos contempla como diciendo 'Los espero'. Contigo lloro por las maldades que han convertido al mundo en un charco de pus" (I: 48) ["With you I pray. I kneel on frigid flagstones and face the mask of death, that skull that stares at us as if to say 'I'm waiting for you.' I weep for the evils that have made our world a mire of corruption" (I: 108)].

[KATHIE. ... I'm really glad I trusted you from the beginning. My intuition didn't betray me. Thank you, Mark.
SANTIAGO. I'm the one who should thank you. When I come here I get to play out a secret life too. I guess I can be just a little more than *The Chronicle* reporter writing mediocre articles for an even more mediocre salary. (II: 140)]

It is this stronger relationship that allows Kathie and Santiago to recognize the double nature of their existence, that allows them to continue creating worlds that supplant the necessities which life outside the loft does not provide, and that encourages these two characters to *create* their own harmonious and nonauthoritative reality—even if it is just another illusion.

Kathie y el hipopótamo's focus on the complex figure of the fictional author/writer on stage and his/her authority or lack of it invite a discussion of what González Echevarría calls the author's "parodic self-portrait." Should we include Vargas Llosa, the Peruvian writer, as part of our discussion of Kathie and Santiago's struggles as creators? What are the possible relationships among the three of them? What elements of Vargas Llosa's extensive narrative writing are parodic in *Kathie*? What are the ironic implications of Vargas Llosa's creation of Kathie, a character-author who focuses on (fictional) autobiographical writing, when many of his own novels have an autobiographical component (see Dauster, "Vargas Llosa" 90)? Should we look into the Peruvian writer's narrative production for a complex understanding of his role as creator, but to *Kathie* as an instrument for ridiculing his artistic authority? Although this is not the place to engage in an in-depth discussion of Vargas Llosa's novels, it is still pertinent to recognize his interest (should we say obsession?) in including himself, or his image as author, or the image of an author, within his texts: *La ciudad y los perros* (1963) [*The Time of the Hero*], *La tía Julia y el escribidor*, *La guerra del fin del mundo* (1981) [*The War of the End of the World*] *Historia de Mayta*, *El hablador*, *La fiesta del chivo* (2000) [*The Feast of the Goat: A Novel*], with the clear image of the dictator, Trujillo, and his secretary, Balaguer.

Vargas Llosa's 1987 *El hablador*, although it takes the identity of a documentary text rather than a dictator novel, also explores the problematics of language, communication, and authority (specifically the inclusion of various authorial voices) in Spanish American literature and reality. Not surprisingly, the Peruvian writer revisits his well-developed technique of alternating narrative voices, successfully accomplished in *La casa verde* (1966), *Conversación en La Catedral*, and *La tía Julia y el escribidor*, among others, where one of the narrators responsible for some of the chapters has been commonly identified with Vargas Llosa himself. That is, on the one hand, we hear in *El hablador* the voice of the character-author who relates his stories and memories after stumbling across a photographic exhibit on the Machiguenga Indians from the Amazon while in Florence and whom most critics and readers have linked to Vargas Llosa. On the other hand, we hear the voice of the speaker (compiler and transmitter of Machiguengan history) strangely incarnated in the figure of the Jewish Mascarita, an old friend of the other narrator. This duality of voices and problematization of authority not only bring to the surface issues of positionality (inside/outside, center/periphery, Western and non-Western cultures) but emphasize the complexity of communication and language between the narrative forces inside the text and their respective social, political, and linguistic relationship with the reader. Who has the power over the communicative capacities of the story and of the text? In a short review of this novel, Rubén Ríos correctly maintains with regard to language in *El hablador*:

> Mascarita, like Flaubert's Felicité, also has a parrot. He too is a simple hearted soul who ends up distrusting the perverse and prostituted language of the colonizers and decides to adopt the free and pure discourse of the Machiguengas. His parrot is a reflection of his poetic solipsism, of his flight from the world of society's deceitful messages and of his surrender to the primitive language of the Indians. Like the sounds the parrot makes, the Machiguengas supposedly speak a more spontaneous tongue, perhaps because it has not been contaminated by the reflexiveness of Western man. (14-15)

In a parallel manner, Kathie's "spontaneous" language and Santiago's "literary" one in *Kathie y el hipopótamo* are mechanisms that bring to the surface the dichotomies between oral and written language, text and performance, reality and fiction, inside and outside the loft, the discourse of man and that of woman. But more important, while the play underscores these polarized structures, the dichotomies themselves are questioned and parodied. To some extent, then, Vargas Llosa seems to be exploring in *Kathie* issues already prevalent in his novels, such as the problematics of literary language and communication. But the particularity of this play is that by using farce as an alternative means of communication, the inconsistencies of those prevalent issues are exposed and caricatured. For example, in *El hablador* there is a philosophical problematization of cultural, social, and economic power between the two narrators/authors, while in *Kathie* the comical overtones and straightforwardness of the two main voices dilute not the philosophical issues themselves but their centrality and authoritative dimensions. That is, in *El hablador* and in many of Vargas Llosa's other novels, the reader encounters authorial figures who take center stage, making the creative process an important element of the narration. Although some of the same elements regarding authority are present in *Kathie y el hipopótamo*, they are perceived more strongly in the context of celebrating the weakness of the author-writer than in the context of their centrality, that is, in the light of a subdued, marginal, and farcical view of authorship and authority.[28] The figure of the powerful political dictator so characteristic of Spanish American reality and fiction is transformed in Vargas Llosa's play into a weakened, nonpolitical, and nonliterary woman dictator–that is, a woman who dictates her experiences to Santiago, who, in turn, will transform her story into pseudoliterary language. In a way, this new figure redefines the social, political, and literary implications of the author/dictator analogy by showing it to be a mainly literary and rhetorical construct. Furthermore, this new figure of the dictator ironically lacks the power to bring about not only effective social change but even change at the personal level.

As we recognize *Kathie y el hipopótamo*'s concerns with the concepts of reality and fiction within life and literature, it is inevitable that we come to contrast these concerns with other manifestations

---

[28] Feal proposes a link between Juan's sexual triumphs on his surfboard with the successes of the writer: "Might the surfboard not be a symbol of literature in the modern world, in which famous writers are seen as stars who are adored by an audience that also demands of them a certain type of behavior?" (141). But she also suggests that the play dismantles this connection: "This glorification of the champion is contradicted by his degradation–which he brings upon himself, of course–when Kathie informs him that she has cheated on him with his friends and even with his brother Abel" (141).

of this dichotomy in Vargas Llosa's historical and autobiographical novels. Is *Kathie* more fictional than *La guerra del fin del mundo*, which is based on the historical events of Canudos, or than *La tía Julia y el escribidor*, about which the real life Aunt Julia, Julia Urquidi Illanes, wrote a book entitled *Lo que Varguitas no dijo* [What Varguitas didn't Say] (1983)? Although these questions are rhetorical, it is clear that *Kathie* parodies its complex relationship with "real fictional texts" written by its creator, whose authority has been persistently questioned. Ultimately, in *Kathie y el hipopótamo* the tension between the multiple levels of expression seeks to stage the questioning of the communicative vehicle, of that which is communicated, and of those who have the "power" or authority to communicate.

Finally, the game of contradictions–evident in phrases such as "los recuerdos falsos" or the tautological character of "inventar mentiras," which we encounter in the prologue to *Kathie y el hipopótamo* and in the play itself–recognizes the *aporia* of a discourse/language that constantly transgresses its referent and authority. We have seen that *Kathie y el hipopótamo* simultaneously incorporates and parodies narrative discourse as well as the writing/creative process. The play also establishes a complex intertextual dialogue with various narrative traditions, to which some of Vargas Llosa's novels belong. Nevertheless, refusing to conform to a singular project, *Kathie*, as is characteristic of Spanish American farce, has not only problematized the authoritative aspects and central position of narrative discourse, but has consistently parodied its theatrical identity and rejected any attempt to be placed at the center of artistic discourse. We are confronted, then, with a play that parodies its apparent meaninglessness as a strategy to question the audiences' understanding of the position that farce occupies within the realm of theatre, the position that theatre occupies in its relationship with other genres, and the position occupied by Spanish American literature, culture, and society *vis-à-vis* Western tradition.

Although communication is at the center of *Kathie y el hipopótamo*, of particular interest are the farcical aspects of this communication in various forms: in its verbal and literary dimensions, and in its oral and written forms, as narration and representation. Playing with the notions of language and of meaning–placing it, replacing it, displacing it–becomes one of the most meaningful and farcical aspects of *Kathie* and allows us to see how, through farce, Spanish

American playwrights unmask oppressive forces in political and artistic terms. A key example of the play's focus on the intricacies and contradictions of literary language and communication is the questioning in *Kathie* of these structures when, at a certain point, Kathie Kennety demands that a fragment that has been already "translated" and recorded by Santiago be erased from "her" text (I: 29 [102]). The strange act of getting rid of language and of memories, of eliminating a specific moment in time, becomes more ironic when these memories are the product of something that probably has never existed, that is, when the very act of remembering and of freeing oneself from those memories is an act of the imagination. It is not a matter of distorted memory or erroneous documentation of the facts, but rather a conscious manipulation and parodization of language through rhetorical figures (metaphor and irony), through a transgressive notion of translation, and through games with time and space, reality and fiction. A farcical spoof of narrative and theatrical forms of communication, *Kathie y el hipopótamo* also denounces their complicity with mechanisms of authority and power.

CHAPTER 4

POPULAR CULTURE AND CLASSICAL TRADITIONS: FARCE
AND INCEST IN *QUÍNTUPLES* BY LUIS RAFAEL SÁNCHEZ

> ... Farce is by its nature popular.
> Albert Bermel, *Farce*

> Incestuous propagation leads to formless duplications, sinister repetitions, a dark mixture of unnamable things. In short, the incestuous creature exposes the community to the same danger as do twins.
> René Girard, *Violence and the Sacred*

> Puerto Rican theatre, which is accustomed to plays that end with women setting themselves on fire, machines swallowing the protagonist, or crazed prostitutes on their way to the madhouse, does not possess an extensive tradition of farce, parody, or humor.
> Rubén Ríos, "Del teatro ambulante al libro"

HUMOR, masks, aggression, mockery, excessive histrionism or simple excess, violence, laughter, and madness are expressions that have been associated with the genre of farce at various stages in its development, and throughout this book. The plurality of semantic levels in farce, the diversity of elements it comprises, and its resistance to definition (as is true of all genres) accentuate the diverse perspectives from which farce can be examined.[1] Farce's inclusiveness and expansiveness incite us to analyze a dramatic form whose essence consists, in part, of the subversion of familial social rituals (sometimes uncovering the underlying structure of life through ritual and other times subverting ritual or putting an unexpected end to it) (Bermel 8). Even more so, the diversity and openness of farce triggers one's interest in exploring this genre's capacity to parody it-

---

[1] Scholars who center their work on farce confront the hazards of defining this genre. Most strikingly, what W. Stanley Schutz called "the long-standing but erroneous belief that farce is inferior drama" (131) has led to contemptuous definitions of farce.

self, to dismantle its own rituals or structures, and to play with multiple identities and discourses. This capacity of farce has already been seen in the examination of Sabina Berman's *El suplicio del placer*. By the end of Berman's play, neither farce nor female/feminist writing occupied a fixed position, nor did the aggressive discourses of farce and women's exploration of this discourse offer a constructive alternative for the "destruction" of a traditional literary and social order. *El suplicio*'s awareness of the elusiveness of its farcical discourse and the paradoxes of its implicit solutions was persistently underscored throughout our analysis.

Quíntuples (1984) by the Puerto Rican writer Luis Rafael Sánchez (1936), deals with elusive realities and discourses: on the one hand, the problematization of a familial and sociohistorical order and, on the other, the breakdown of literary and theatrical structures and expectations.[2] From one perspective, the purpose of this chapter is to explore how the elements that epitomize farce (humor, masks, mockery, aggression, violence, excess) experience in Sánchez's *Quíntuples* a process of transformation through hyperbolization, parodization, and inversion. But more importantly, the goal is to examine how these processes allow one to see farce's refusal to fit within a singular artistic and thematic frame. Humor,

---

[2] The playwright, novelist, short story writer, essayist, and university professor Luis Rafael Sánchez is considered one of the most important Puerto Rican writers of the second half of the twentieth century and a central figure in the renovation of Puerto Rican drama and narrative. His first plays appeared in 1960, *Los ángeles se han fatigado* and *Farsa del amor compradito*, followed by *La hiel nuestra de cada día* (1961), *O casi el alma* (1965), *La pasión según Antígona Pérez* (1968), and *Parábola del Andarín* (1979, unpublished). *Quíntuples* has been highly acclaimed and was considered by critics the best play of 1984 (Burgos 53). Sánchez's anthology of short stories, *En cuerpo de camisa* (1966), signals what Efraín Barradas has called "the birth of a new art of story telling in Puerto Rico" (xvii), and his first novel *La guaracha del Macho Camacho* (1976) [*Macho Camacho's Beat*], is considered an important text of the post-*Boom* for its carnivalesque use of language, its playful eroticism, and its understanding of Puerto Rico's cultural reality. Regarding *La importancia de llamarse Daniel Santos* (1988), Sánchez's second novel, Aníbal González emphasizes its essayistic element as it "reflects on the relation between mass culture, society, and literature in Latin America" ("Puerto Rico" 579). He is also the author of three books of essays: *La guagua aérea* (1994) and *No llores por nosotros, Puerto Rico* (1997) and *Devórame otra vez* (2004). The most recent bibliographical compilation of Sánchez's works can be found in John Perivolaris' *Puerto Rican Cultural Identity and the Work of Luis Rafael Sánchez* (2000). Regarding *Quíntuples*, I refer the reader to essays by Emmanueli Huertas, Kronik, Morell, Perivolaris, and to my own essay published in *Latin American Theatre Review*, which served as the basis of this chapter.

for example, reveals its violent side, even as it becomes a victim of violence; mockery faces the threat of being deconstruct, and in turn attempts to mock and deconstruct any possible threats; and hyperbolization lead to the masking and unmasking of what is literal and what is metaphorical, what is real and what is not. The masking of reality through farce–or at least of certain social, political, existential, and artistic realities–and the unmasking of farce by the referential traits of dramatic discourse expose the reflexive aspects of the apparently senseless language traditionally linked to the genre. It will be shown that *Quíntuples* performs a complex game of identity and power that simultaneously touches on the artistic, the social and the political, and that the acrobatic, iconoclastic, humorous, and contradictory stands are necessary as means to play with and escape from the authoritative dimensions of these same powerful forces. *Quíntuples*'s humorous and farcical exploration of artistic and theatrical issues–in conjunction with its pseudoserious sociopolitical statements–reveal the play's attempt to reformulate in a parodic manner its artistic and historical identity as farce.

From another perspective, the generic and structural complexity of *Quíntuples*–a farce composed of six monologues and acted by two performers who represent all the members of the dysfunctional Morrison family–invites spectators to examine the play's use of elements of contemporary popular culture and its abundant references to the classical world and to high culture. The play's humorous and iconoclastic dimensions–mostly achieved through strategies identified with icons of contemporary popular culture– interact with artistic and social conventions linked to mythical and literary traditions of the classical past.

The quintuplets and their father's persistent allusion to celebrities (Elizabeth Taylor, Libertad Lamarque, Toña la Negra), to writers of romance novels and of mystery narratives (Corín Tellado and Agatha Christie), to cartoon and circus characters (Super Ratón, Mandrake el Mago, Besos de Fuego, La Princesa Come Fuego de Catay), and to playful children's stories ("el cuento del Gallo Pelón"), as well as the importance of orality and improvisation in this play, characterize the inclusive nature of farce and of a culture (Puerto Rican) with humorous and popular roots. Humor, as a "quality that appeals to a sense of the ludicrous or absurdly incongruous" (*Webster's* 552), appears in *Quíntuples* through family relationships that emphasize elements of difference, disjunction, fragmentation, aggression, the grotesque, and exaggeration. Not surprisingly, John Fiske reminds us that "Popular culture is often excessive, and is frequently criticized by those who do not understand it for being 'sensational.' Excessiveness, sensationalism, and exaggeration are stylistic devices of contradiction, and . . . the contradictory is characteristic of popular culture" (328). Contradiction is at the heart of *Quíntuples*, not as a strategy of evasion but rather as a device for unmasking the play's artistic, communicative identity and the complex identity of the world that surrounds the characters. If, as Fiske proposes, "Popular culture is the culture of the here and now, not of the always and forever" (334), then to emphasize, as *Quíntuples* does, figures in the popular arena and to underscore orality and improvisation, bring to the fore a tense relationship with notions of transcendence, textuality, coherency, moderation, and unity, which are traits linked to high culture and classical traditions. For Fiske, "popular culture is more a culture of process than of products" (323), a notion that inevitably leads to the last scene of *Quíntuples*, where the two actors who had performed the roles of the six members of the Morrison family remove their makeup on stage and acknowledge their incapacity to continue performing.

This emphasis on humorous elements, on the language and icons of popular culture, and on the impulse of mass media in *Quíntuples* are aspects that have been studied in considerable detail in other works by Sánchez–particularly in regard to *La guaracha del Macho Camacho*. These aspects have also led interpreters of the play to deal with contrasting languages, opposing philosophical views, with what is normative and what is not, with the role of industrialization and technology as they pertain to literature, and with the level of communication between artistic objects and their audience in Sánchez's literary production. Sánchez himself has masterfully condensed the opposing languages and perspectives that can come together through humor:

> Humor is still a serious business: fruitful in the pages of Aristophanes, who is ruthless to the point of cruelty; revealing in the pages of Molière, who fought against moral hypocrisy; incendiary in the pages of Valle-Inclán, who was always angered by the duplicities of his accidental tribe. Therefore, one needs to turn to humor when one wishes to attack sanctimoniousness and falsehood, to corrode an oppressive composure. One needs to turn to

a pitiless, accusatory, and incendiary humor; to a humor that is committed to settling scores and readjusting whatever is disproportionate. ("Cinco problemas" 164-65)[3]

Nevertheless, there is another side to the recognition and celebration of elements of humor and of popular culture in *Quíntuples*. What seems to make this play such an explosive, joyful, and profound text is not exclusively Sánchez's appeal to elements of the mass media and his complex and politically charged use of humor, but the play's capacity to interject into the discourse of popular culture, and within a popular genre such as farce, the images and codes of classical tradition and high culture. These images and codes include, among others, the historical codification of the discourse of genre (the implicit allusion to the origins of theatre through the use of farce); the presence of characters named Dafne, Ifigenio, Carlota, and even Mandrake; and, particularly, the allusion through incest to dramatic characters such as Oedipus, with their vast cultural and literary implications. More specifically, the use of monologue in *Quíntuples* emphasizes its dual identity as a communicative structure linked to both ancient Greek tragedy and postmodern performance.[4] What is underscored in Sánchez's play is the farcical nature of this interaction of "opposing" discourses and the examination of what is being dismantled, reversed, or parodied as a consequence of this explosive encounter of the popular and the classical.

---

[3] Humor in Sánchez's literature can be identified as far back as 1960 in his *Farsa del amor compradito*, in many of his short stories in *En cuerpo de camisa*, in his two internationally recognized novels, and in his prolific essay production with titles such as "La generación o sea," "Hacia una poética de lo soez," "La guagua aérea," "En busca del tiempo bailado," among many others. Critics have examined Sánchez's humor in its many manifestations: Luce López-Baralt, Efraín Barradas and Gloria Waldman. See also Alvin Joaquín Figueroa, Carmen Vázquez Arce, and John Perivolaris. Another text devoted exclusively to the study of Sánchez's theatre is *El teatro de Luis Rafael Sánchez* by Eliseo Colón Zayas.

[4] The possible conflict created by describing the six characters' speeches as monologues, and Sánchez's suggestion of calling them "dialogues for one voice," will be discussed later. Describing in his "Prólogo a la representación" ["Prologue to the Representation"] the audience's participation and their dual role as attendees to a Conference on Family Affairs and a play, Sánchez adds: "Dichos envolvimiento y dinámica agilizan los ritmos narrativos de los monólogos que se convierten, entonces, en diálogos para una voz" (xiv) ["The aforementioned involvement and dynamism give movement to the narrative rhythm of the monologues, which then turn themselves into dialogues for one voice"].

Within this amalgam of actions, themes, and conflicts, family relationships constitute the principal nucleus of the contradictions presented in the play. The theme of love, which is considered an essential component of family rhetoric, highlights the physical and verbal discourses of the participants as well as the forms of love that each of them reveals or hides: promiscuity, polygamy, masturbation, homosexuality, pregnancy, unfaithfulness, and above all, incest. The differences in the love experienced by the characters are obvious and clash with traditional structures, that is, with basic expectations about a family of children who, because of their quintuplicity, should be closely linked physically and psychologically, particularly in view of their shared gestation. The theme of incest in *Quíntuples* establishes a literal and metaphorical relationship with farce and with the play's principal means of communication and discourse. Among those discourses we recognize the role played by monologue and the emphasis on and problematics of improvisation.

In the midst of contradictory identities and discourses, *Quíntuples* does not allow us to ignore its national identity and, as a consequence, that of the author. Although the complex political and social reality of Puerto Rico (the birthplace of the quintuplets) will not be discussed extensively, the fact that the audience knows where they are from forces the interpreter to deal with the complexities of Puerto Rican history and political reality. Connections will be established between the employment of humor and farce in *Quíntuples* and the Puerto Rican national identity as it relates to artistic and political independence (from the family, from colonial powers).[5] Regarding *Quíntuples*'s strategic recourse to humor in the context of Puerto Rico's social and historical reality, Sánchez's own trenchant words resonate:

> *It is better to laugh than to write with tears*, said Rabelais. Rather than a predictable discourse on colonialism and its well-known miseries, rather than an attack on the newfangled intellectual

---

[5] For an examination of *Quíntuples* as representative of Puerto Rican identity, see Perivolaris's first chapter, "'¡El cuento no es el cuento! ¡El cuento es quien lo cuenta!': Terms of Identity in *Quíntuples* (1985)." Perivolaris states: "I would wish my major contribution to Sánchez scholarship to be a vigorous reflection on how, in a coarse vernacular laced with learned Spanish wordplay, Sánchez *humorously* explores both the complexities of the vexing issue of Puerto Rican identity and the related difficulty of proposing any project of independence within a Puerto Rican context" (16; my emphasis).

colonialism proposed by the annexationists, the rotten Puerto Rican situation begs for, cries out for, a writing with mocking, surly, and uncouth overtones. The *esperpento*, the mocking masquerade, the tragicomedy, the political skit, all allow one to propose a theory of laughter as consciousness raising, as a ceremony of collective justice. ("Cinco problemas" 164-65)

Luis Rafael Sánchez's play deals with the Morrison family, made up of the Gran Divo Papá Morrison and his quintuplets–Dafne, Baby, Bianca, Mandrake, and Carlota–who have been invited to speak in the Conference on Family Affairs. Each of them proposes to hold forth on the topic of love and imagination, but they inevitably end up examining discourse as an act and themselves as those who perform at the lectern. By means of six monologues, or "dialogues for one voice," as Sánchez calls them, we gain access to the Morrison family's dysfunctional past, their present condition, and the interaction among the members of the family. Their infancy is characterized by a great deal of attention because of their rarity as quintuplets, although this attention is eventually overshadowed by political events. Later, they are forced by their father to exploit their uniqueness for economic reasons, and in their present discourses each of the quintuplets reflect their inner desire to go their own ways, to break with the family structure and with an authoritative father.[6] Regarding the unique identity of each of the characters, Jorge Martínez, in one of the first reviews of the premiere of *Quíntuples*, offers a synthesis of the various roles played by two well-known Puerto Rican actors:

---

[6] The sense of economic exploitation felt by the five siblings is evident in Bianca's description of their infant and childhood years, and it brings to the surface the political overtones of the play: "La leche Pet compró la felicidad de los quíntuples Morrison. Para ilustrar su campaña publicitaria de que los bebés más felices del universo toman leche Pet.... Mi hermano Baby Morrison fue el culpable. Lloró tanto, chilló tanto en las sesiones fotográficas que los fotógrafos de la leche Pet y los alimentos Clapp's para bebés protestaron. Los contratos fueron cancelados. Papá Morrison dijo el que no trabaja no come. Y nos puso a los quíntuples Morrison a sudar la gota gorda" (iii: 37-38) [Pet milk bought the happiness of the Morrison quintuplets.... The contracts with the two big U.S. companies were abruptly cancelled. My brother Baby Morrison was to blame. He cried so much, he squealed so much during the photo sessions that the photographers from Pet milk and Clapp's baby food protested. The contracts were cancelled. Papá Morrison said that whoever doesn't work doesn't eat. And he made us, the Morrison quintuplets, really sweat it out].

Francisco Prado runs the gamut from the imagined "shyness" of Baby Morrison, through the vain and arrogant personality of Mandrake Morrison, to the overpowering and lustful Papá. For her part, Idalia Pérez Garay breaks the ice with a ravishing Dafne, freezes us with the imperious but equivocal coldness of Bianca, and presents at the end a laughable and domineering hypochondriac, Carlota.

The ravishing Dafne, who besides aspiring to mythical status is also the Spanish voice of Mighty Mouse's girlfriend, narrates her amorous adventures and confesses her desire to abandon the family and run away with her new love, the main dwarf of the Great Antillian Circus, Besos de Fuego ["Fiery Kisses"]. This secret aspiration to abandon the family is shared by her brother Baby, but his obvious cowardice and his psychological dependency on an imaginary cat named Gallo Pelón ["Bald Rooster"] prevent him from leaving the oppressive environment of his family. Bianca's hostility and repressed sexuality contrast with the frivolity and excessive virility of her brother Mandrake el Mago ["Mandrake the Magician"], who is always drawing the audience's attention to the nature of art and performance and to his pact with the Devil. Unlike her two sisters, Carlota does not speak of love, but she presumably "incarnates" it by being pregnant, also with quintuplets. A teacher of Spanish to the end, she devotes all of her presentation to giving the audience, and some individual audience members, instructions on what to do should she begin to give birth while on stage. Finally, the figure of the Gran Divo Papá Morrison ["Big Stud Papá Morrison"], wearing a tuxedo with a fresh camellia in his buttonhole, comes onstage in his personalized wheelchair with flashing lights, loudspeaker, and minibar to discourse on imagination and its effects and on the difficulty of raising five children. The ending of the play is particularly surprising if we are expecting any type of resolution regarding either the preservation or dispersion of the Morrison family. Beyond the six playful monologues, it is the extremely brief and sober final conversation between the play's two actors–held while they remove their makeup in front of the audience–that mocks the theatrical, false, and farcical nature of this family and of what each of its members has "improvised" on the stage:

> EL ACTOR. No queremos ahondar más en la magia porque le dañamos la magia. Porque se arriesga la hermosura de su

mentira. Una mentira que es como una maroma entre ustedes, el público y nosotros, los actores.
LA ACTRIZ. Que en arte todo es premeditación y alevosía.
EL ACTOR. Una maroma sin redes.
LA ACTRIZ. Una maroma con redes no es maroma, no es riesgo.
EL ACTOR. Y el teatro es, por más que lo embelequen, una maroma audaz, un feroz riesgo.
La Actriz se acerca al Actor que interpetó a Baby Morrison, Mandrake Morrison y el Gran Divo Papá Morrison y le ofrece un poco de crema limpiadora. El Actor la acepta, con alegría y agradecimiento. La Actriz y el Actor comienzan a quitarse el maquillaje frente al público. (vi: 78-79)[7]

[THE ACTOR. We don't want to go deeper into the magic because we'll spoil the magic. Because we risk damaging the beauty of its falsehood. A falsehood that is like a somersault performed by you, the audience, and us, the actors.
THE ACTRESS. In art all is done with malice aforethought.
THE ACTOR. A somersault without nets.
THE ACTRESS. A somersault with nets is no somersault, is no risk.
THE ACTOR. And theatre, no matter how much you dress it up, is an audacious somersault, a ferocious risk.
The Actress approaches the Actor who plays Baby Morrison, Mandrake Morrison, and Big Stud Papá Morrison and offers him some cleansing cream. The Actor accepts it with joy and gratitude. The Actress and the Actor begin to remove their makeup in front of the audience.]

The sudden shift of attention from the lives of six family members who perform at a Conference on Family Affairs to the reality of two actors who are characters in Sánchez's drama forces the critic to wonder what is being unmasked by the sudden interruption of the conference and by the actors removing their makeup onstage. Is this ending part of an irreverent stand towards traditional theatre?

---

[7] Citations are based on the Ediciones del Norte, 1985. Although the play is divided into two acts and six scenes, the citations will be indicated only by scene and page number since the numbering of the scenes is not interrupted throughout the play. After the end of the third scene, the lights of the theatre are turned on while Bianca Morrison remains smoking onstage. The second act, fourth scene, begins with the entrance of Mandrake el Mago even as the lights continue to be on and the audience has not yet returned to their seats. I will offer my translation after citing the original.

Or is it the reverse? Have the quintuplets lost their authorial or authoritative roles supposedly granted to them by the use of monologue? [8] How should we view the ambiguity created at the end of the play? [9] Should we talk about this ending in terms of the *masking* of identities and of psychological or political situations or in terms of the *unmasking* of the nature of theatre and farce?

The inclusive, expansive nature of the characters and their capacity to follow contradictory paths emphasize the dual nature of the family as a unit and as individual beings. As part of this dual identity, the conference becomes a performance, but the performative character of the play also takes on the appearance of a conference. On the one hand, we encounter the rigidity of a formal address and prescribed script and, on the other, the improvisational nature of the six monologues lead the characters toward a more overt, autobiographical, and confessional discourse. [10] The audience, as the stage directions indicate, plays a dual role by attending Sánchez's *Quíntuples* and by participating in a Conference on Family Affairs.

It is clear that the simultaneous masking and unmasking of the identities of the characters/performers/actors and of the play itself question the expectations raised by farcical discourse, which in traditional terms should have a superficial meaning, if at all. Nonetheless, it has been stated throughout this study that Spanish American farce thrives on not fulfilling expectations, on departing from its discourse and traditions. As a consequence, this recognition that expectations will not be met forces us to confront the tension between overt and covert languages, explicit and implicit meanings, between the alleged shallowness of farce and its complex dimensions.

---

[8] Deborah Geis points out in *Postmodern Theatric[k]s: Monologue in Contemporary American Drama* that "the speaker of the monologue tends to take on an 'authorial' or 'authoritative' role, especially if he or she plays the part of a narrator" (12-13).

[9] It is important to underline the distinctions that critics have made between character, performer, and actor, and how these distinctions play out in Sánchez's *Quíntuples*. In terms of performance theory, the character of a traditional play is frequently portrayed as the puppet of an author in a closed and coherent work; the performer, in contrast, is conceived as an autonomous being who frequently presents the audience with autobiographical material without theatrical mediations.

[10] Johanna Emmanuelli Huertas describes the struggle between familial discourse (perceived as unconventional and sincere) and public-official discourse (linked to social hierarchies and conventions) as one of the discursive elements that will give shape to the monologues in Sánchez's play (343).

Quíntuples allows the audience to identify easily those elements that invite a discussion of the play in terms of its ludic and humorous development and its theatrical and communicative postures: the exaggerated characterization of the siblings and the father; the implicit dialogue between them and the audience carried out through the six monologues-cum-lectures; the parodic vision of the comedy of suspense that the playwright outlines in his "Prólogo a la representación;" and the falsely improvisational character that the drama insists on.[11] Thus, we recognize that Sánchez's play does not attempt to disguise either its ludic tone or its generic conflict, not even the moral and psychological pathos of the six characters played by two actors, or the play's preoccupation with the activity of theatre itself. The farcical nature of the play and its consciousness of this reality seems, then, unquestionable.

Quite strikingly, however, we discover that the "straightforwardness" of farce in Sánchez's drama can be described as mere illusion, or at least as part of a complex game. Ironically, while Sánchez places *Quíntuples* within the traditional discourse of farce, he offers what could be considered the antithesis of this discourse. The antagonism between what is said and what is done in the play, between a family that pretends to incarnate unity but actually reveals the breakdown of familial and social relations, points up the disparity of the structures that make up both the family and the farcical reality of the piece. The fact that there are six siblings/characters engaging in conversations with the audience and not with one another turns upside down the notions of family and theatrical unity as well as the expectation of onstage physical action, which is replaced with intricate and egocentric wordplay. The contradictory nature of the theatrical structures and language throughout this work is emphasized by the absence of physical movement and of onstage interaction among the characters, the presence of a lectern from which the actor-characters speak, the lack of sets and minimal play of lights, the employment of musical effects only during the intermissions, and the recourse to dialogue between character/actors only during the last moments of the play. In his "Prólogo a la representación," Sánchez contrasts these absences and the simplicity of the surroundings with the level of madness, exaggeration, and "drunkenness of emotions" represented by the characters:

---

[11] We will later allude to the dichotomy between orality and the written text, between improvising on stage and following a script written by the father.

> *Tan calculada opacidad en el escenario más la economía de la luminotecnia y los muebles y la ausencia de musicalización cuando empieza la obra contrastan con la efervescencia, el histrionismo permanente, la desgarrada intensidad que proponen los seis personajes–a ser interpretados por una actriz y un actor.* (xiii-xiv)
>
> [*The deliberate opacity of the stage, in addition to the spareness of lighting and furnishing, as well as the lack of music when the play begins are in contrast to the effervescence, the persistent histrionics, the wrenching intensity displayed by the six characters–which will be performed by one actress and one actor.*]

Quíntuples not only transgresses key traditional codes of theatre, such as physical action, movement, dialogue, and the creation and preservation of illusion. As an exemplar of farce, Sánchez's play also problematizes its supposedly showy nature and its attempt to purvey laughter through exaggerated action and movement.

As one takes this level of complexity a step further, it is of interest to underscore how *Quíntuples* shows its critical stance with respect to critical discourse. By way of action and language that exhibit their possibilities as well as their limits and limitations, one perceive the ability of farce to disarm the critic, to transcend criticism itself. As Sánchez points out, *Quíntuples*, besides having qualities of vaudeville and comedy of errors, has those of "the parody of a comedy of suspense" ("Prólogo a la representación" xv), in which the nature of the genre is defined, exemplified, and transgressed. Unquestionably, the dramatic complexity and plural nature of *Quíntuples* becomes text, textual commentary, and pretext for the theatricalization of the discourse of farce as it relates to the characters' personal and familial perils. In other words, neither the Morrison family nor farce is willing to limit itself to its traditional, expected roles: the former as a unified and loving family, and the latter as a straightforward, meaningless genre.

In a structure of dualities and obvious contradictions the use of monologue–or should we say, the absence of dialogue?–throughout most of the play is particularly revealing in terms of our perception of the six characters and of their historical context.[12] The profile

---

[12] It is pertinent here to consider Deborah Geis's statements on the dislocation of time through the use of monologue, since it sheds light not only on the six char-

that each of them offers through monologic language about who they are, where they are coming from, where they are going and how they perceive the other allows us to interpret them in isolation but also to construct a complex view of their collective identity within a historical frame. Although these characters occupy the stage by themselves, we cannot avoid comparing them with their counterparts, that is, seeing how similar to or different they are from one another.[13] As the emphasis of monologue is being examined, one is confronted with questions about its origins, and about the position it occupies in contemporary theatre. Does the use of monologue shed light on the dysfunctional nature of the Morrison family and on the complexities of the world around them?[14] One also wonders what are the possible layers of interpretation regarding the prevalence of monologue throughout the play and its disruption at the end.

Deborah R. Geis's book on the use of monologue in contemporary American drama stresses "the theatrical status of monologic language" and challenges the notion that monologue frequently becomes "the absent opposition, the implicit other to which dialogue is compared" (2). From Geis's point of view, monologue should not

---

acters' search and profiling of themselves, but on the sociopolitical space in which they grow up: "The speaker of the monologue has the ability to compress time by narrating a series of events, to suspend time entirely by offering words that do not affect the time elapsed in the play, to move either forward or backward in time . . ., and to alter time by changing our perception of the rate at which time moves during the monologue itself and/or during the onstage events that follow it" (10-11). Monologue is used in a meaningful way in other plays by Sánchez: through Ángela's insanity in *Los ángeles se han fatigado*, in Tisbe's initial speech in *La hiel nuestra de cada día*, and through direct addresses to the audience, particularly by Antígona, in *La pasión según Antígona Pérez*.

[13] Regarding the interdependence among the six characters, Emmanuelli Huertas observes: "[E]ach character responds, adds, and directly or indirectly alludes to the others, so that the audience-reader witnesses at every instance the close relationship between the characters and the familial microworld which has shaped them, and which is in itself a mirror of Puerto Rican and Latin American society" (341).

[14] Geis addresses the ancient origins of monologue as well as its most contemporary expression, that is, performative art: "The history of the monologue goes back to ancient Greek tragedy, which provides us with the earliest examples of monologic speech as well as two types of speeches that might be termed forerunners of the monologue" (15). By the end of her study, she "moves away from multi-character plays that preserve a framework of 'fiction' and toward contemporary performance artists who speak exclusively through the monologic voice in semi-autobiographical mode that can be referred to as 'autoperformance'" (4). It is clear that *Quíntuples*'s emphasis on monologue alludes both to its classical origins and its contemporary popular and iconoclastic roots.

only be defined as opposed to dialogue– "its lack of a responding 'other,' its refusal to relinquish the 'floor,' its implicit 'deviance' from interpersonal discourse" (2)–but should be examined as a theatrical and discursive tradition in its own terms. Nevertheless, in the case of Sánchez's *Quíntuples* the possible differences between underscoring the use of monologue and the absence of dialogue are subtle but pertinent. On the one hand, emphasizing monologue in *Quíntuples* can be interpreted as an attempt to create an independent and unique view of the self, of the subject. On the other hand, focusing on the absence of dialogue can be seen as a way to stress the characters' incapacity or unwillingness to communicate with others. Most importantly, in Sánchez's *Quíntuples*, the characters' speeches fulfill both functions: they tell us about the speakers' selfness, their personal stories, and their sexual preferences, as well as about the siblings' relationship (or lack of it) with one another and with their father.

But how is the concept of monologue altered in *Quíntuples* once we know that there is an audience not only attending a play but playing the part of participants at a Conference on Family Affairs? What is implied by their function as the silent half of a "dialogue for one voice"? As Geis confronts the problematics of the use of monologue, she reminds her reader of a basic fact in theatre: "the status of a play presupposes that even a speech performed in the imagined solitude of a character will always include the audience as acknowledged or implicit witnesses," and she adds that this "inevitable status of the spectator as recipients foregrounds the 'telling,' or 'narrating,' function of the monologue" (7). The irony of this statement suggests that *Quíntuples* has an audience with a dual identity and that its characters are aware they are addressing at least one of them. In the context of a conference there is no "imagined solitude" on the part of the character, and none of the quintuplets ever lose sight of the audience's presence and pseudoparticipation. On the contrary, the six characters and their respective "dialogues for one voice" reveal their need for an interlocutor, for someone to attend and listen to their presentation and/or performance. Although Geis correctly reminds us that the employment of monologue "causes us to focus our attention to the speaking subject" (10), nevertheless, what is significant about the six characters in Sánchez's play is that they consciously focus the conference-goers' attention on their respective conflicts, insecurities, and eccentricities.[15] Ultimately, the lack of onstage communication between the siblings and their father calls into question traditional family structures and values, the physical and spiritual unity and identity of the quintuplets and of their performance, and their authorial roles. It also stresses the unstable position of the audience, alternating between conference participants and playgoers.

This reflection on monologue in *Quíntuples* leads us to the meaning and effects of the dialogue at the end of the play between the two actors who performed the roles of the six characters and who then remove their makeup on stage. If we return to Geis's statement that the isolated monologue in an otherwise dialogue-based drama represents a climactic moment (8), then it is important to recognize the role played by an isolated dialogue in an otherwise monologue-based drama and to interpret the meaning of this climactic moment. It should be clear by now that unmasking the characters and revealing their identity as actors question the authorial and authoritative roles of the members of the Morrison family and the strength of their respective monologues. That is, the unique identities of the quintuplets, of their eccentric father, and of the attendants at the Conference on Family Affairs seem to melt in the face of the theatre audience, who in the midst of laughs and exaggerated histrionics, confront the sober tone of two actors who cannot go any further in their representation, in the construction of lies.

Nevertheless, this apparent unmasking frequently related to farce also masks other texts and contexts dealing with the dialectics between popular culture and classical traditions, and with a sociohistorical subtext. The last-minute change from monologue to dialogue signals the identity crises portrayed at all levels of the play: theatrical, sexual, social, linguistic, political, and historical. As a result of this move from monologue to dialogue at the end of *Quíntuples*, the audience is confronted with the complex codes and expectations of farce in particular, and of theatre in general, as well as

---

[15] Geis examines the implications of a monologuist addressing the spectators: "When a monologue seems to address the audience directly, the paradoxical position of the audience in respect to the speaker intensifies. It is possible to argue that this type of monologic utterance simultaneously includes the spectators in a more direct way than otherwise and reasserts their very powerlessness.... This indicates that the spectators have chosen to accept their role as helpless, frozen ... yet, for the duration of the monologue addressed to them, they are given a (pseudo)privileged status as the characters' confidants" (14).

with the nature of the relationship among the siblings and their father. The audience is forced to deal with the traditional values of the family structure on the one hand, and the parody of those values on the other. The audience deals with the prevalence of silence after incessant chattering, and with the referential context from which the Morrison family emerges.

More dramatically, through the particular "finale" of *Quíntuples*, the audience members are not only left in the air, in limbo, ignorant regarding the whereabouts and the paths followed by the quintuplets and their father, but are explicitly reminded that the members of the Morrison family are mere invention, that they do not exist, that their dilemmas, conflicts, and eccentricities are not real. The Actor, in what seems to be a state of exhaustion, says: "No puedo construir más peripecias de unos quíntuples inventados y del Padre también inventado que los acompaña" (vi: 77) [I can not make up more incidents for quintuplets that are themselves invented, and for their equally invented Father who accompanies them]. The liminal nature of this ending seems particularly ironic since the implicit request is that the audience subordinate their interest in the intricate lives of fictional beings and focus more on the complex, metaphorical nature of artistic discourse and on those who create and perform it: that is, on the actors, their desire to entertain, their capacity to transform themselves and become the other, their willingness to employ dialogue, their reality outside the theatre, and their symbolic nature. But the supposed subordination of the Morrison family to concerns regarding art and artistic creation can only take us back to the members's capacity as performers and entertainers, to their lives and desires outside the family structure, to the nature of their sameness and their differences, to their problematic means of communication among themselves and with the society that surrounds and contextualizes them (the sociopolitical complexity of later twentieth-century Puerto Rico).

Evidently, communication (or the lack of it) occupies a central position in Sánchez's *Quíntuples*, and the foregoing reflections on the use of monologue attest to that centrality. Regarding this issue of communication, the audience is confronted with the act of improvisation and with the characters' individual perceptions of and reaction to it. Although it is eventually revealed that Papá Morrison is in charge of writing the scripts that the quintuplets always follow, this time Dafne requests that they all improvise in this Conference on Family Affairs, since it is in this environment that familiarity should prevail (i: 6). Her father approves of Dafne's request and stresses that each of the siblings will have to cope with both the benefits and the inconveniences of improvisation. But to Papá Morrison's warning we should add that the audience also will have to cope with the transgressive nature of improvisation: Should improvisation be understood in the light of freedom of characterization and speech? Should it be perceived as a tool to liberate the actor from a restrictive and authoritative text and author? Has ad-libbing been looked at as a virtue in theatre or as a detraction from it? Does it enhance acting or does it weaken it? Should the audience praise this tool as a mechanism to see things "as they are" rather than as they seem to be, or as others (author, director) force us to see them? What is the role played by improvisation as it relates to the genre of farce? [16]

From the beginning of Sánchez's play, we are told that improvisation is a divisive element among the Morrison family. Dafne, for example, is the one who incites the use of improvisation, and her father loves the idea (i: 6). Baby Morrison dreads it and prefers to follow his dad's quite traditional text, which portrays a loving and "normal" family (ii: 22-23). Bianca, on her part, reviews the papers that she brings on stage and realizes that improvisation has tricked her into revealing the homosexual nature of her love. Significantly enough, Mandrake reminds the audience that even ad-libbing is a premeditated endeavor and explains how to improvise: "Así es cómo se improvisa, inventando las peripecias sobre la marcha, dejando que el cuento se construya a sí mismo, ajustando un nudo que amarro regularmente, reservando el buen golpe que deja aturdido a quien escucha, observa y se interesa" (iv: 45-46) [This is how you improvise: inventing complications as you go, letting the story build itself, tightening the knot I tie periodically, holding back the punch that stuns the listeners, the watchers and the curious]. Finally, Carlota combines her apparently rigid script, which details to members of the audience what to do if she goes into labor while

---

[16] Improvisation is important in the development of theatre, particularly as it pertains to the well-known *commedia dell'arte*: "[F]rom beginning to end improvisation was what determined the special quality of the Italian style and distinguished it from other stage methods" (Nicoll 25). Emmanuelli Huertas proposes that the act of improvisation in *Quíntuples* represents a constant transgression of censorship (347).

participating in this conference, with a matter-of-fact, less theatrical and improvisatory tone that frames the time that goes by until the onset of childbearing.

What is then the play's understanding of improvisation once we recognize the characters' contradictory stands toward it? It is most significant that both Mandrake and the Actress at the end of *Quíntuples* indicate that in art there is actually no improvisation–"Que en todo es premeditación y alevosía" (iii: 44, vi: 78)–that is, everything is done with malice aforethought. Sánchez himself, in the essay "Strip-tease in East Lansing," acknowledges the crucial role played by improvisation in *Quíntuples*: "Toda la pieza la sostiene la difícil empresa de *representar la improvisación*, de *fingir* los baches o lapsos en la memoria de los personajes, de *mentir* la pérdida y el reencuentro del hilo dialogístico" (142; my emphasis) [The whole play is sustained by the difficult task of *representing improvisation*, of *feigning* the holes or lapses in the characters' memories, of *simulating* the loss and recovery of the dialogistic thread]. To a high degree, improvisation in *Quíntuples* is seen as deceptive, as a trick or mask that attempts to hide issues concerned with structures and systems of communication, that wants to conceal its complex identity and its tense relationship with authorship and authority. In this regard, improvisation and its link to orality characterized by the quintuplets, establish a counterpoint with the written word, represented by Papá Morrison's scripts and by Sánchez's own play. It is most significant that the author indicates in the stage directions–in a quite authoritative but somehow humorous tone–that stage directions themselves should, under no circumstances, be offered to the audience (xiv). [17] These statements are humorous and ironic precisely because Sánchez's inflexible stage directions should never be staged. That is, unless it is in contact with the written text, the audi-

---

[17] "*De ninguna manera, bajo ningún pretexto de experimentación, distanciamiento o muestra de originalidad, deberán dichas acotaciones ofrecerse al público*" (xiv) [*Never, under any pretext of experimentation, distancing, or attempts at originality, should these stage directions be revealed to the audience.*] And later, on two different occasions in the first scene, Sánchez reiterates that stage directions should not be communicated to the audience (see i: 1; i: 17). For Perivolaris, Sánchez paternalistically attempts to limit the characters' freedom to improvise (34). More appropriately, Kronik suggests that "Sánchez, with a gesture that is at once self-effacing and self-aggrandizing, calls attention to the role of the stage direction in the conduct of the theatrical experience and of the author's relationship to the receiver of the dramatic script" (33).

ence will never know about the author's authoritative statements. In addition, time, space, and theatrical practices can always (and frequently do) challenge the written word in theatre. Regarding Sánchez's "inflexibility," Kronik wisely states: "No matter how emphatically he puts it, the author's control is limited, and short of a lawsuit, Sánchez can do nothing about it if some future director of a Brechtian or original stripe decides to project those stage directions on a screen or a placard" (33). Obviously, this marginalization of the written word in theatre is not surprising, but what seems ironic is that it becomes central when acting and improvisation are persistently thematized and, more important, when they establish an antagonistic relationship with textuality, represented either by the father's traditional script or by Sánchez's *Quíntuples*.

Ultimately, the perception of ad-libbing as a misleading discourse that feigns familiarity, spontaneity, and therefore, truthfulness, becomes evident when Dafne fails to find the other members of her family and realizes that they have gone to the bar next door to rehearse their respective improvisations. Dafne ironically states: "¡Si se improvisa no se ensaya pero mi familia es así!" (i: 9) [If one improvises one doesn't rehearse, but my family is like that!"]. This revealing aporia reflects one of the most prevalent aspects of our focus on farce in *Quíntuples*: contradiction between truthfulness and deceit. The conflicting use of monologue in the midst of a Conference on Family Affairs, as well as the disagreements among the six characters regarding improvisation, exacerbate the tensions of the play and stress farce's deceptive identity. If one asks what is this play attempting to communicate, what is its focus, it is possible to respond that one of *Quíntuples*'s concerns is the exploration of contradictions and paradoxes of communication in plural terms: communication among family members, communication in the artistic arena, and in the social, historical, and political sphere. The insertion of a brief dialogue at the end of the play, the sudden disappearance of the quintuplets from stage, and the audience's confrontation with the statement that the Morrison family is a mere construction, highlight the farcical, conflictive communicative interaction among characters, performers, actors, audience, play, and author. Ironically, the contradictory nature of artistic and social communication becomes one of the main issues that *Quíntuples* is trying to "communicate."

As part of our discussion of *Quíntuples*'s dialectics between what defines a family and what destroys it, we are confronted with the role played by the socially and symbolically charged notion of incest in relation to farce. Why insert in the analysis of farce this nonhumorous issue, and how can it be connected with the dialectics between popular culture and classical traditions in social and literary terms? The theme of incest present in *Quíntuples* allows us to explore the intricacies of the play: for instance, the development of the self in each of the quintuplets; the presence of the collective through images of family and country; and the search for sexual and political identity represented in homosexuality, hypersexuality, frigidity, colonialism, authoritarianism, and oppression. Of particular interest regarding the theme of incest is that Sánchez's focus on the dialectics between popular culture and classical traditions, together with his focus on the farcical, lead us back to one of the most important myths in Western culture–that of Oedipus–and to some of the most recognizable plots in tragic theatre, found in Sophocles' *Oedipus Rex, Oedipus at Colonnus* and *Antigone*; in Euripides' *Phoenicians*, and in Aeschylus's *Oedipus*.

Quíntuples's intertextual communication with classical theatre and mythology should not be surprising at all. Sánchez's accomplished contemporary rewritings of mythical discourses have produced a political recasting of the story of Piramus and Thisbe in *La hiel nuestra de cada día* (1962), and of Antigone in *La pasión según Antígona Pérez* (1968). He also recreates in *Quíntuples*, with obvious irony, some of the most troublesome aspects of family structures as represented in the Oedipal myth and tragedy. The clash in *Quíntuples* between a conventional view of the play's family and the suggestion of the family's incestuous origins creates a farcical atmosphere and lays bare the falsehood of the characters' actions and relationships as well as the interplay among various and even opposing cultural traditions: popular culture and literature, mass culture, religious taboos, and the classical-literary culture.[18] Regardless of their overt differences, incest and farce are grotesque and exaggerated manifestations of love and art, respectively. In the case of

---

[18] It is not capricious on the part of Sánchez to allude twice in his play to Melquíades, a character from what is considered the most important novel of the twentieth century–García Márquez's *Cien años de soledad* (1967)–which happens to deal directly with the theme of incest. Morell chooses to connect the Melquíades allusion to Mandrake (46).

Quíntuples, incest and farce aim to subvert the traditional formulae of familial and theatrical communication.

Stephen Greenblatt discusses the paradox between culture as a structure of limits and culture "as the regulator and guarantor of movement" (228). He stresses that "limits are virtually meaningless without movement; it is only through *improvisation*, experiment, and exchange that cultural boundaries can be established" (228; my emphasis). It could be argued that this paradox represents *Quíntuples*'s tension between the characters' limitations (existential, social, physical, artistic, linguistic) and their need to negotiate and (ex)change the place that each of them occupies within the family structure, within society, and as cultural symbols. In a way, the interdependence in the realm of culture between setting limits on the one hand, and mobility on the other can metaphorize *Quíntuples*'s characterization of farce as dynamic, experimental, and iconoclastic. In contrast, incest is perceived as a metaphor for passivity, lack of dialogue among characters, and lack of movement from their limiting familial milieu. In addition to the cultural realm, this metaphor can be extended to the political arena, since Puerto Rican reality has been frequently described as caught between change and passivity.

Central to this paradox, and linked to artistic and social issues, is Greenblatt's statement that for anthropologists the "crucial indices of the prevailing codes governing human mobility and constraint" (229-30) are culture's narrative (myths, folktales, and sacred stories) and culture's kinship system, which entails, among other things, its conception of family relationships, *its prohibitions of certain couplings*, and its marriage rules (229; my emphasis). From this perspective, incest–"prohibitions of certain couplings"–is a constraint imposed by culture, but culture's concern with narratives and its emphasis on a structure of improvisation counterbalance these constraints and limitations. If, as Greenblatt suggests, "art is an important agent . . . in the transmission of culture" (228), then the link between art and family relations in *Quíntuples* allows us to contextualize the dialogue between farce and incest in view of the play's characterization of culture's limits and its mobility.

In a parallel manner, Eric Bentley has pointed out in his well-known essay "Farce" this crucial relationship between farce and the family structure: "Outrage to family piety is certainly at the heart of farce as we know it" (227). This comment prompts us not only to posit a thematic link between *Quíntuples* and Bentley's view of the codes of farce and family but also invites us to link farce to the incestuous nature of the Morrison family. It is not surprising that Bentley mentions the role played in modern drama by the everyday love triangle of husband, wife, and lover. But he also points out that contemporary dramatists go beyond a mere obsession with adultery to hide their true obsession with incest, to mask their hidden interest in the father-mother-child triangle (227-28). For Bentley, it is specifically by means of farce that the audience can express or channel their most private desires and secrets, those to which they must not give voice–desires like incest, for example: "Farce in general offers a special opportunity: shielded by delicious darkness and seated in warm security, we enjoy the privilege of being totally passive while on stage our most treasured unmentionable wishes are fulfilled before our eyes by the most violently active human beings that ever sprang from the human imagination" (229).

Unlike Bentley's dramatic strategy of secret relationships among the characters, *Quíntuples* does not resort to covering up what it wishes to reveal; rather, it puts on display the device that both unites and separates the six protagonists. The problematic concept of brotherhood and sisterhood and the conflicting visions of love held by each of the members of the Morrison clan contrast with their not very transparent (but particularly ironic) participation in the Conference on Family Affairs. It is not difficult to characterize the fundamental needs–whether academic or personal–which motivate the participants to take part in the conference. One assumes immediately, if anecdotally, what these characters will contribute to the analysis of family relationships. Baby Morrison himself points out: "Yo insistí en que prefería repetir el libreto que escribió Papá Morrison sobre las grandes ilusiones de la vida en familia, sobre la urgente necesidad de amar... sobre los recuerdos de haber crecido juntos como una familia de pollitos" (ii: 23) [I insisted that I wanted read the script that Papá Morrison wrote about the great joys of family life, about the urgent need for love... about memories of growing up together like a brood of chicks]. But by improvising and not sticking to the script, he achieves results that are quite different from those he expected. One recognizes from the beginning of the play the conflict that results from "exalting" topics such as narcissism, infidelity, polygamy, homosexuality, and incest, all in front of an audience that is likely to be in search of more traditional family values. The incongruity of these topics in the context of the Conference on Family Affairs seems to disturb the harmony that should prevail in such a context, confronting the participants with highly antagonistic perceptions of fraternal and filial togetherness.

Dafne Morrison, the first character to appear onstage, is going to expound on love and its effects, but by the end of the first scene we have heard instead about love and its defects. Dafne's excessive narcissism and the fact that she has had seven husbands bring to mind the husband-wife-lover triangle mentioned by Bentley. Instead of the idealized discourse on love, the knowledge gleaned from the aberrant sense of love expressed by Dafne in her "dialogue" with the audience suggests the idea of incest. The images and language she uses constantly allude to a most unfamily-like eroticism, centered on the perception of the "self" and on an alienated view of "the other." Obsession and the confusion between self and the other invite reflection on incest not just as a relationship between relatives–Dafne calls her father Big Stud Papá Morrison–but as the character's need to turn to herself (or to someone who can mirror her) as a source of pleasure. The similarity between Dafne's narcissism and her metaphorically incestuous leanings has its root in the introspective nature of both attitudes. Dafne defines love not just by exalting her own beauty and sensuality, that is, by insisting on the uniqueness of the self, but by a constant impulse to pluralize and, finally, to deform the other. The hug that Dafne gives herself (i: 8), the confusion about the identity of one of her sudden lovers, Besos de Fuego (who turns out to be, to our "surprise," a circus dwarf), the theme of redundancy that characterizes her speeches, and the contradictory notion that sanity is achieved through disorder–all of these suggest a structure of opposites in which the familiar becomes unfamiliar or, as Shklovski and the Russian formalists would say, becomes "estranged." [19]

The antagonistic links among the members of the clan, who dramatize their contradictory unity, plurality, and unfamiliarity before the Conference on Family Affairs, are seen in a parallel way as Baby Morrison talks with himself, has difficulty deciding whether he is

---

[19] Victor Erlich observes that: "If in informative 'prose' metaphors attempt to bring themes closer to the audience, or to round out the issues, in 'poetry' they work to intensify the desired aesthetic effect. More than translating the strange into familiar terms, the poetic image 'makes strange' what is familiar, showing it in a new light, placing it in an unexpected context" (252).

himself or his brother Mandrake (ii: 23), and answers, in fact, to the same name as his father (Ifigenio) and his brother (Ifigenio Dos) (iii: 32). This defamiliarization is stressed even further by the peculiarity that the characters refer to their siblings and father using the formality of their last names (Dafne even referred to her many husbands by their full names). It is ironic that while the emphasis on the last name might be underlining their mutual and unique origin–particularly as quintuplets–this constant repetition of the last name Morrison also creates a space between them, disconnecting them from one another, and emphasizing their identity more as performers than as unified and coherent members of a family. Throughout *Quíntuples*, we perceive love's defects rather than love's effects, in just the way that Dafne's speech places us within a system of opposites in generic as well as dramatic, moral, and social terms.

Regarding the symbolism of Dafne's name and its connection with incest, it is pertinent to remember that as the mythological character of Daphne flees from Apollo–the twin brother of Artemis, and thus also the fruit of a simultaneous insemination–she asks her father to turn her into a laurel tree in order to escape Apollo's love. It is superfluous to conjecture about the existence of a more-than-paternal relationship between Daphne and her father Peneus, but doing so serves to place the mythical and dramatic planes within a certain intertextual or textually incestuous frame. Dafne Morrison insists on connecting her tumultuous (sexual) existence to a mythological and grandiose past: "¡Soy aspirante a mito!" (i: 5) [I aspire to become a myth!]. Hortensia Morell suggests about Dafne that although she models herself on the most appealing images of sexuality in popular culture (Vanessa Williams, Catherine Deneuve, Sonia Braga, Jane Fonda, María Félix) (i: 1), in her interaction with the audience she behaves like the Dafne of classical myth, that is, a woman who is only an image, who is inaccessible at the very moment one attempts to possess her (41).

It is not surprising that the three male characters in *Quíntuples* carry the male version of another mythological name–Ifigenio Uno (Papá Morrison), Ifigenio Dos (Mandrake el Mago), Ifigenio Tres (Baby Morrison). It must be remembered that the female mythological version, Iphigenia, is the daughter of Agamemnon, who has been told by the oracles that he must sacrifice his daughter so that the goddess Artemis will allow his ships to depart from Aulis and bring his men to fight against Troy. Most striking, when Iphigenia's father is willing to reverse his decision and others are willing to intervene in her favor (Achilles, for example), Iphigenia nonetheless heroically accepts death for the well-being of others.[20] What is the relationship of this powerful story of parricide, deceit, political power, honor, and divine intervention, to *Quíntuples*? What is the meaning of this change of gender from the story of a daughter who is going to be sacrificed by her father but then graciously accepts to save the honor of her country, to the self-centered male characters in Sánchez's play? In the parodic allusion to the story of Iphigenia, the theme of parricide is transgressed in *Quíntuples* through gender transformation and multiplication. (As mentioned before, there are three male Ifigenios in this play.) Sánchez is underscoring the contradictory and farcical elements of gender and sexual identity as well as playing with the most objectionable actions that can threaten family life; parricide and incest.

Among the fundamental aspects regarding the two direct allusions to the classical myths of Daphne and Iphigenia in *Quíntuples* is the relationship between father and daughter, and how Sánchez reformulates these characters and myths. On the one hand, in both Daphne's and Iphigenia's stories the two women depend on their fathers' intervention and decision to save or not to save their lives, and, on the other hand, in the case of *Quíntuples*, the complex relationship between Dafne, her sisters, and the three male Ifigenios –with their particular sexual and social issues of identity–ends up parodying the life/death struggle of the mythological characters, focusing instead on the power struggle between the siblings and the authoritative father.

This parodic allusion to the myths of Daphne and Iphigenia also sheds light on the intertextual dialogue that the play establishes with other popular and classical literary traditions, in contrast to the monologues of the members of the Morrison family. Another example of this incessant dialogue is the character of Mandrake el Mago, particularly his seductive name and complex origins. Mandrake is not only the name of the main character of a popular American comic-strip entitled "Mandrake the Magician," which used to be published in the sensationalist Puerto Rican newspaper *El Imparcial*, but it also leads us to Machiavelli's sixteenth-century

---

[20] In addition to Euripides' *Iphigenia*, Morell alludes in her essay to Racine's and Goethe's use of this myth (43).

play entitled *Mandragola* [*The Mandrake*].[21] Suffice it to say in the context of this study that Machiavelli's drama could be connected to Sánchez's play in general and to Mandrake el Mago in particular, at least in two ways. Mandrake's name (in Italian *mandragola* and in Spanish *mandrágora*) refers to a "Mediterranean herb . . . with ovate leaves, whitish and purple flowers, and a large forked root *traditionally credited with human attributes*," and, even more relevant to *Quíntuples*, the root of the mandrake was "formerly used especially to promote conception, as a cathartic or as a narcotic and soporific" (*Webster's* 692). Conception is a recurrent theme in this play: the main characters are quintuplets and one of the quintuplets is pregnant herself with quintuplets, and Mandrake el Mago's unparalleled beauty comes, or "is born," from his intimate and magical relationship with the devil. That is, it comes from a deal with Lucifer, who has given him winning dice and beauty in exchange for the bread Mandrake eats (iv: 52-53).[22] The fact that the mandrake plant has been linked to conception, to narcotic effects and, as *María Moliner* indicates, to the practices of witchcraft, sheds light on the mysterious and magical nature and origin of Sánchez's Mandrake. It also illuminates the implications of art as mysterious

---

[21] The comic strip "Mandrake the Magician" was created by the cartoonist Lee Falk in 1934 and continued to be published until a short time before he died in 1999. For more information about Mandrake the Magician as a comic-strip character, see online «http://www.kingfeatures.com/features/comics/mandrake/about.htm». Machiavelli's *Mandragola* is about Callimaco's desire to possess the beautiful, virtuous, and childless Lucrezia, wife of the Florentine lawyer Nicia Calfucci. The couple's desire for children allows Callimaco to trick them by offering to give Lucrezia a fertility potion made from the mandrake root. After setting in motion a series of farcical complications, Callimaco, the impostor doctor, enters Lucrezia's room and is accepted by her as brought by divine providence (*The Mandrake* V: 269). Pleased with the results, Lucrezia's husband, Nicia, says: "Lucrezia, thanks to this young man, we will have a staff to lean on in our old age," and later adds, "And I'm going to give them [Callimaco and Ligurio] a key to the downstairs guest room off the porch, so they can get back in whenever they feel like it, since they don't have women at home to take care of their needs" (V: 273). Callimaco ironically responds, "I accept, and I will make use of it whenever the ocassion arises" (V: 273).

[22] It is impossible to the famous verses from John Donne's poem "Song," with its theme of falsehood: "Go and catch a falling star,/ Get with child a mandrake root,/ Tell me where all past years are,/ Or who cleft the Devil's foot" (Abrams et al. *The Norton Anthology of English Literature* 1183). For Perivolaris, "Mandrake alludes to the economic, political, and ideological dimensions of creative survival in society by suggesting that the materials (language, persona) of his performance are 'lent' to him by the culture in whose processes he participates as a performer who interacts with other members (the audience) of a common public space (48).

and magical (and false?), and lays emphasis on the character's dual intertextual identity: his relationship with a canonical play of the sixteenth century and with a character of a popular American comic strip. This duality inevitably underscores the multiple Mandrakes that the audience can perceive, his various and contradictory origins, the masking and unmasking of his multifaceted identities, his attachments to and detachments from his siblings and father (is he Ifigenio II or Mandrake el Mago?), his donjuanesque profile, and his caricatured identity in the light of his father's sexual prowess.[23]

It is also possible to suggest that Machiavelli's complex employment of farce in *Mandragola* can be metaphorically connected to *Quíntuples*'s use of this genre, particularly as it pertains to both endings. In an introductory essay to the bilingual edition of Machiavelli's comedies, James B. Atkinson stresses the farcical identity of *Mandragola*: "[E]lements from farce are the second main dramatic technique that Machiavelli uses to urge his audience to scrutinize the nature of the social fabric formed at the end of the play" (21). He adds: "*The Mandrake* is not a good representative of the comic mode. Nothing is unveiled at the end. On the contrary, everything is dressed up in garments of reconciliation and resolution. Without Machiavelli's meticulous preparations for exposing deception through the elements of farce, the audience might well accept the ending at face value" (22). Masking and unmasking, dressing and undressing (characters and situations), truthfulness or deception, communication or lack of it are also major trades of the final scene of *Quíntuples*. Once more, we see in Sánchez's ending a reverse strategy, although still farcical in nature, to that used by Machiavelli. The unmasking by the actors who have been playing the roles of the members of the Morrison family challenges the audience to interpret the play at contradictory levels and to see what is being masked in the process of unmasking. The monological reality of *Quíntuples* and its connection with autobiographical discourse seem to expose the psychological and personal identities of the Morrisons. At the same time, the characters' farcical dimensions playfully mask the political and sociohistorical double entendres re-

---

[23] In a parallel manner, Perivolaris accurately discusses Papá Morrison's artistic models: his links with romantic and post-romantic fiction, with opera, and with popular musical forms: "The mixture of popular and high cultural models in Papá's improvisation indicates a *bricolage* inherent in the chosen models themselves. . ." (51).

lating to issues of colonialism, lack of independence, authoritarianism, and conflicts of cultural and national identity.

These unexpected twists and turns of the characters, their complex sexual and social identities, and their constant metamorphosis (parallel to that of the two lone actors) also emphasize the dialectic between the self and the other, which is incarnated in the figure of Bianca Morrison. The title of the third scene, "Tema y variaciones de un amor que no se atreve a decir su nombre" [Theme and variations on a love that dares not say its name] alludes to Bianca's implied homosexuality. As Bianca tries to explain her nervousness and irritability, she involuntarily uses the pronoun "she," revealing her lover's sexual identity and the secret and introspective nature of her "condition:"

> BIANCA. Ella...quiero decir...ella...una persona con quien hice de pronto amistad. Ella...es decir...la persona...se embarca mañana por la mañana y nos prometimos despedirnos esta noche.... (iii: 40)
>
> [BIANCA. She... I mean... she... a person I became friends with. She... I mean... this person... is leaving tomorrow morning and we'd agreed to say good-bye tonight....]

Before coming onstage, Bianca gets a phone call from "her," canceling the evening's plans because her trip has been moved ahead. This scene, in addition to revealing Bianca's homosexuality, unmasks the identity of her lover: "she" is La Princesa Come Fuego de Catay [The Fire-eating Princess of Cathay], who works with the Enano Besos de Fuego in the Great Antillian Circus and who took the role of Chinese princess from Dafne–whose circus name is Melao, Sensual y Bandolera [Sweet Sexy Bandit].[24] The characters'

---

[24] The image of the circus as a place where Dafne and Baby Morrison can escape to from their own complex realities poses questions regarding the nature and identity of this dynamic, exuberant and exotic space. Can one assume that the "unfamiliar" nature of Papá Morrison and his children becomes the mirror image of a caricatured vision of the circus show put on by Besos de Fuego, La Princesa Come Fuego de Catay, and the cat/lion Gallo Pelón, among others? Performance, masking, representation, and the multiplicity of identities are at the heart of both theatrical experiences portrayed in *Quíntuples*–that of the conference and that of the circus–and they problematize the multiple identities of all the characters/performers/actors that occupy both spaces: Dafne as Melao Sensual y Bandolera; Baby as liontamer; Bianca as the lover of La Princesa Come Fuego de Catay.

relationships with themselves and with others are a source of tension in their lives: tension in the relationship between the family members, with themselves, with their respective lovers or husbands, with the audience of the Conference on Family Affairs, with other powerful forces. As one encounters Bianca's obsessions, one can only wonder who is actually slapping her hand when she feels the urge to smoke. Is it she herself or an external force? Who is the "real" Bianca?

> *Bianca Morrison va a tomar un cigarrillo pero se golpea la mano delincuente con fuerza.*
> BIANCA. ¡No fumes Bianca Morrison! Perdón. Yo misma me asusté. Nunca grito. Mi propio grito me asustó. Es un ejercicio mental. Corrientazo sicológico lo llama el hipnotizador. Cuando me tienta el cigarrillo debo frenarme: No fumes Bianca Morrison. Y castigarme la mano delincuente. (iii: 32-33)

> [*Bianca Morrison is about to pick up a cigarette but slaps at her own delinquent hand.*
> BIANCA. Don't smoke, Bianca Morrison! Sorry. I scared myself. I never shout. My own scream frightened me. It's a mental exercise. The hypnotist calls it a psychological electric shock. When the cigarette tempts me I must stop myself: Don't smoke, Bianca Morrison. And I must punish my delinquent hand.]

This doubleness can be understood as Bianca's conflict of distinguishing between the self and the other, therefore opening the door to the complex and, in *Quíntuples*, metaphorical notion of incest as an introspective, self-conscious, paralyzing, and socially and legally unacceptable act inclined to focus on singularity and individualism rather than on plurality and the collective.

It can be argued that the plural realities represented in the quintuplicity of the characters and in their multiple masks collapse the instant the text is placed in the frame of incest. In the last scene, when Papá Morrison repeats with the slightest variation Dafne's initial speech–"Aplausos, aplausos, aplausos, que entra una mujer [un hombre] con causa. Gracias, muchas gracias por tan cálida ovación que no sé, francamente, si me toma por sorpresa o la esperaba" (i: 2; vi: 68) [Applause, applause, applause, a woman [a man] with a cause is coming on. Thank you, thank you very much for such a warm ovation. I don't know, frankly, if it takes me by surprise or if I expected it]–one is put in mind of a structure that is not only circular but also cancels the differences between the children and their father as well as the differences among the children. For they are, ultimately, "one." This linguistic and physical equivalence that surfaces between Dafne and her father, which is linked directly to incest, manifests the collapse of the conceptual and hierarchical differences that are the essence of individuality and the basis of the family structure: Dafne raises the oxymoronic nature of this relationship by stating about her father: "El Gran Divo Papá Morrison... heredó mi mundanidad y mi liviandad" (i: 9) [Big Stud Papá Morrison... inherited my worldliness and my frivolity], while Papá Morrison himself says: "Yo salí a Dafne Morrison" (vi: 71) [I turned out like Dafne Morrison]. Through these statements by daughter and father, one detects that *Quíntuples* problematizes the concept of otherness and subverts traditional family structures and hierarchies through the insistence on sameness and, indirectly, on incest.

This concept of otherness takes on artistic connotations when the reality of the six characters is erased onstage and the existence of two actors is revealed. At the moment when the Actor and the Actress abandon the parts they are playing, they manage to distance themselves from the forced otherness ironically incarnated in the transformation of six in one, played out in turn by two actor-characters. By way of this process of singularization, one not only recognizes the disappearance of the differences among the characters (movement from plural to singular), but sees the family as a microcosm of collectivity (movement from singular to multiple). Given this numerical structure and the dialectics between popular elements and classical traditions, it is pertinent to point out a possible link between *Quíntuples* and the Sophoclean tragedy *Oedipus Rex* with respect to the issues of duality, singularity, family relationships, and incest. As has been pointed out regarding *La pasión según Antígona Pérez*, Sánchez has explored in this play the origins of myths and their significance in contemporary Spanish American and Puerto Rican cultural reality. He has also investigated the characteristics that define Antígona Pérez (the absence of blood siblings) and her "family" relationship with the Tavárez brothers (her murdered political associates), with her uncle Creón Molina, with her mother, Aurora, and with her fiancé, Fernando. But, finally, reference to *La pasión* is justified by the need to discuss, in examining the source of Antigone's tragedy, the figure of Oedipus, her father.

Of interest here is René Girard's view in *Violence and the Sacred* of patricide and incest as a way of erasing distinctions between characters and actions. According to Girard, for example, the antagonism between Oedipus and Tiresias and their mutual accusations about the death of Laius, Oedipus's father, may serve only to unmask the "truth" about the other character without revealing a personal truth. However, their behavior cancels out the differences between the characters and makes them responsible for the destruction of a certain cultural order (71).[25] In the same way, the incest committed by Oedipus creates the image of a character who, in the most grotesque sense, plays at once all the possible roles in the family and dramatic structure: son, father, brother, husband. That is, Oedipus is a monster who kills his father, marries his mother, and begets his own siblings.[26] Girard points out:

> Incest is also a form of violence, an extreme form, and it plays in consequence an extreme role in the destruction of differences. It destroys that other crucial family distinction, that between the mother and her children. Between patricide and incest, the violent abolition of all family differences is achieved. The process that links violence to the loss of distinctions will naturally perceive incest and patricide as its ultimate goals. (74)

Dafne, Baby, Bianca, Mandrake, and Carlota represent a single child whose father–Big Stud Papá Morrison–creates and contains them all, just as Oedipus simultaneously creates and cancels out the paternity of his siblings through physical union with his mother and wife. In this vein, it is impossible to ignore the complex sexuality of the quintuplets, and the way in which the absence of a female progenitor–inevitably, their mother dies giving birth to them–is filled by

---

[25] Given Bermel's commentaries on the collapse of highly familiar social rituals provoked by farce, noted in the early pages of this chapter, one can see how farce and incest are converted into parallel structures that focus their attention on the breakdown of order.

[26] The epigraph to Luis Rafael Sánchez's play is from Tennessee Williams's *Sweet Bird of Youth*, which underscores the grotesque nature of the monster, particularly his relationship with and view of the self: "Monsters don't die early; they hang on long. Awfully long. Their vanity's infinite, almost as infinite as their disgust with themselves" (xi).

a pregnant daughter/sister, who will also give birth to quintuplets. Dafne's promiscuity, Baby's identity crisis, Bianca's homosexuality, Mandrake's narcissism, and Carlota's maternity constitute distinct and contradictory facets of the sex life, not just of the children, but of the father. Even the accident that puts the father in a fancy wheelchair is directly linked to an act of sexual desire and unfaithfulness.[27] This emphasis on the hypersexuality of the characters evidences the impossibility of separating each of these figures from its counterpart, from its identical and opposite image.

The second epigraph of this chapter–"Incestuous propagation leads to formless duplications, sinister repetitions, a dark mixture of unnamable things. In short, the incestuous creature exposes the community to the same danger as do twins" (Girard 75)– allows us to establish parallelisms with the origin and development of the characters in *Quíntuples*. In Sánchez's play the significance of this correlation between multiple births and incest is that its hyperbolic dimensions appear in the gestation not of two but of five.[28] To engender quintuplets, then, is to carry incest to its ultimate consequences, to its most absurd exaggeration. Therefore, although the close link between Dafne and her father synthesizes the incestuous nature of the relationships among the six family members, each of them, in a different way, is the creation and the victim of each of the others. In speaking of the "sacrificial lamb," Girard says:

> If violence is a great leveler of men and everybody becomes the double, or "twin," of his antagonist, it seems to follow that all the doubles are identical and that any one can at any given moment become the double of all the others.... A single victim can be substituted for all the potential victims, for all the enemy brothers that each member is striving to banish from the community. (79)

---

[27] As Papá Morrison is attempting to climb into the bedroom of Argentina Watson–the Jamaican mulatta who lives with her husband in Cristo Street in Old San Juan–Papá Morrison falls like an egg in a frying pan and is left physically incapacitated (vi: 76). The cleverness of this scene hinges on the combination of the fifteenth-century Spanish ballad "El Enamorado y la Muerte" and the folktale of Rapunzel (Papá Morrison is using Argentina's braids to climb into her house), with the allusion to Daniel Santos's highly sensuous music that encourages his sexual adventure.

[28] It does not seem to escape Sánchez that Mandrake the Magician happens to have an evil twin named Derek.

Dafne, as the double/opposite of Bianca, or Mandrake, as the reverse of Baby, finally blend into a single being, that is, the figure of their father, who in turn contains them all–"el padre es el padre y el padre es la madre" (vi: 70) [the father is the father and the father is the mother]–, and multiplies them in his seed as Big Stud Papá Morrison. But Papá Morrison is not the only one able to engender and contain them all simultaneously; Carlota too, pregnant with quintuplets, can do it–maybe with the help of her father, who has already "demonstrated" his generative and deforming filial love.

The mathematical and existential schema that represents the dialectic in *Quíntuples* between the plural and the singular, 1=5=2=1, has an important precedent in the analysis offered by Matías Montes Huidobro of *La hiel nuestra de cada día* (1961), another play by Sánchez with mythological antecedents. Both plays establish a numerical structure that refers to the problematic identity of characters who try to define themselves through another without realizing that they are the other–and therefore one. In the case of *La hiel*, Montes Huidobro points out two methods of existential annihilation based on the use of verbal as well as mathematical language (527). Part of the mathematical methodology is centered on the concept of "annihilation by addition" (Montes Huidobro 530), in which "numbers are part of a magical logic" (530):

> His addition challenges objectivity and is condemned to failure, a failure that signifies the final annihilation of the characters. . . . Numbers take on dramatic life and will lead to the very destruction of the characters. . . . At the end of the dramatic cycle, when adversity has carried out its mission, there is a poetic-existential reaffirmation of the characters expressed through numbers. This is achieved through a process of searching for the multiple and the integration of the essential. This essence is represented by the number one, the center towards which the protagonists are going. (531)

In a revealing way, and from a point of view that permits the establishment of parallels with *Quíntuples*, Montes Huidobro goes on to point out with respect to *La hiel nuestra de cada día*:

> This identification, the recognition of two (or more) in one, is what unexpectedly ends up saving the characters on their way nowhere. . . . The verbal and numerical subtraction to which the

characters have been subjected does not after all result in zero. . . . With profoundly human feeling, oneness becomes the essential number and overcomes the numerous subtractions. The process of numerical annihilation is inverted by the conversion of the two characters into one: subtraction of two, but with the wisdom of oneness. (532)

In *Quíntuples*, then, incest plays an obvious role. It is the generator of a multiplicity that is perceived and transformed–through its own introspective nature–into a unitary structure. Turning to a relative to procreate another relative implies the marginalization of the outside world as the source of life. Therefore, the complex interdependency among the six characters, their grotesque similarities, and the onstage "discovery" that the roles of the quintuplets and their father have been played by two actors who reveal their identity to the audience, dismantle both the concept of family and the concept of unity, creating at the same time an artistic and existentially dual and contradictory world.

Quíntuples's emphasis on numerical structures allows the play to establish intertextual dialogues with other literary expressions and traditions. Though differences in context must be recognized, it is appropriate to mention here Jorge Luis Borges's reference in his essay "El pudor de la historia" ["The Modesty of History"], from his collection *Otras inquisiciones* (1952) [*Other Inquisitions*], to the unsung contribution of Aeschylus to the history of the theatre. Borges describes how, while leafing through a history of Greek literature, his attention was caught by an enigmatic phrase: *"He brought in a second actor"*:

> I stopped; I found that the subject of that mysterious action was Aeschylus and that, as we can read in the fourth chapter of Aristotle's *Poetics*, he "raised the number of actors from one to two". . . . Originally, a single actor . . . shared the scene with the twelve individuals of the chorus. . . . [B]ut one day . . . the Athenians saw with amazement and perhaps with shock . . . the unannounced appearance of a second actor. . . . In the *Tusculanae* it is stated that Aeschylus joined the Pythagorean order, but we shall never know if he had a prefiguring, even an imperfect one, of the importance of that passage from one to two, from unity to plurality, and thus to infinity. (Rodríguez Monegal and Reid, 246-47)

In the final analysis, even as Borges recognizes Aeschylus's nod to plurality in increasing the number of actors onstage, he points out the obvious contradiction inherent in Aeschylus's membership in the Pythagorean order, as these two versions of reality are in conflict. Aeschylus's participation in this order suggests that he accepts a belief in the relatedness of all living beings and in some kind of a concept of the oneness of "life" in a world that Pythagoras considered dualist. The change from one actor to two, however, seems to insist on plurality.[29] The supposed antagonism between Pythagorean thought and the onstage appearance of two actors is parallel to the antagonism dramatized by Sánchez in the coexistence of six individuals who, even when they seem to establish a degree of onstage autonomy and authority, end up being dependent on one another and on the artistic process. And, as Sánchez's characters are deconstructed, they incarnate the issue of dramatic and existential identity.

The link of incest forged here between *Quíntuples* and a series of figures and events in mythical tradition and literature suggests a dual, bipartite reading in which this discourse and the discourse of farce share a common language, a common rhetoric. The concepts of origin, authority, and unity vs. duality are seen in the light of incest (in both its artistic and mythical-social context). The genesis of theatre (of art), then, coincides with the issues raised by incest. That is, incestuous acts as well as artistic ones (expressed in the genre of farce) call into question the origin of individuals and of their private means of expression. Moreover, they give rise to a conflict of authority and power in which conventional family structures are broken (allowing a single individual to be simultaneously husband and son to his mother, and brother and father to his children), and where the ideas of creator, creation, receiver, reality, and fiction are isolated from their traditional referents. The six characters of *Quíntuples* dramatize the issue of being one and many. As a result, the concepts of origin and authority (who engenders or creates

---

[29] G. S. Kirk and J. E. Raven cite Porfirius's text, *Vita Pythagorae*: "The following (declarations) came to be particularly famous: first, their affirmation that the soul is immortal; second, that it turns into other classes of living things, which, moreover, recur every certain span of time and that there is nothing absolutely new; finally, that *all living things must be considered to be related*. It seems that, in effect, Pythagoras was the first to introduce these beliefs into Greece" (315; my emphasis).

whom; who controls the actions and the speech of the others) appear in the framework of a dual reality that can be called mythical-artistic and whose plural nature is parallel to the contradictory codes of farce. The final anagnorisis achieved in the onstage unmasking of the two actors who have played the roles of the quintuplets and their father, reveals the magic that art, via farce, is capable of creating. Ironically, it also reveals the tragedy of the actor-characters who lose, or at least question, their identity in the "infinite" playing of roles.

The much discussed concept of identity in *Quíntuples* (artistic, psychological, sexual, social) is connected to the likewise much-discussed issue of national and political identity in Puerto Rican and Spanish American history and reality. In view of the persistent language of contradictions in *Quíntuples*, it is feasible to recognize the political implications of farce and its metaphorical links with incest. It is the conflictive dialogue between text and context, between inside and outside, between the singular and the plural, that allows farce to reveal its contradictory nature, and to incorporate other discourses into its complex profile. For example, parodying farce invites the audience to confront the notion that a new and humorous theatrical language is emanating from the stage. Nevertheless, this humor is conditioned by the audience's realization that a clash will take place not only onstage but metaphorically offstage. That is, the play's ambiguous and unexpected ending incites the audience to speculate beyond the world onstage. One wonders, for example, what has been the impact of the world outside the stage on the lives of the quintuplets. Will the Morrisons ever have the opportunity to act independently from the other members and from an authoritative father? Is personal and collective independence a possibility not only for the members of the family but for the community at large–particularly for that community where the quintuplets come from? If communication is hardly possible among siblings and father (emphasis on monologue rather than on dialogue), should we expect anything better among the members of a society? What is the reaction of the participants in the Conference on Family Affairs once they realize that they are bearers of an unorthodox picture of family life and of questionable advice? Is communication enhanced by the last scene of the play, or does it symbolize instead the diminishing possibilities of a collective dialogue?

Differing levels of physical, psychological, and sociopolitical uncertainty and aggression become the background constantly visible behind the artistic issues posed by the play, such as the controversial nature of acting. In *Quíntuples*, farce allows us to interpret various kinds of interplay both as a source of laughter and as a mirror image of our own grotesque interpersonal relationships and sociopolitical structures. In other words, both the concealment and exposure of multiple discourses that end up being interdependent, the fraternal closeness and distance among the quintuplets and their father, and the dichotomy between the exaggerated verbosity of the monologues and the absence of physical action become explicit manifestations of *Quíntuples*'s game of identity in which farce and humor focus on and question the political. These opposing expressions show the play's attempt to deconstruct discourse, and its tendency to unmask what seems to be beneath or beyond the theatrical. More explicitly, Sánchez's play portrays the conflict between the characters' rejection of the other and of other discourses. It also depicts the transformation into the other and the appropriation of those other discourses by those same characters.

Pushed to its very limits (as is always the case with farce), the play's characterization of theatrical instability can also evoke the unstable political context from which the characters emerge. Bianca, for example, explicitly alludes to the "coincidence" of the quintuplets' birth with important political events in Puerto Rican history, and later explicitly states that the Morrison quintuplets are natives of Puerto Rico (iii: 37):

> BIANCA. El nacimiento de los quíntuples Morrison fue un acontecimiento. Traspasó las barreras de la isla del encanto. Sólo el tiroteo al congreso norteamericano llevado a cabo por los nacionalistas puertorriqueños el mismo año desplazó el interés de los Quíntuples Morrison en la prensa mundial. ¡Perdón!
> ....
> ¡Papá Morrison insiste que jamás se toca la política! (iii: 36)

> [BIANCA. The birth of the Morrison quintuplets was a real event. The news reached far beyond the shores of the island of enchantment. Only the shooting at the U.S. Congress carried out by Puerto Rican nationalists that same year drew

away the attention of the world press from the Morrison quintuplets. Sorry!
....
Papá Morrison insists that one should never talk about politics.]

In addition to Dafne's encounter with Besos de Fuego on the well-known Puerto Rican beach of Isla Verde, the epithet *isla del encanto* is also an overt allusion to Puerto Rico as the birthplace of the quintuplets. Nevertheless, what is of significance is the reference to the event that overshadowed the quintuplets' birth, that is, the attack on 1 November 1950 by Puerto Rican nationalists on the Blair House in Washington, which was, at the time, the temporary residence of President Harry S. Truman.[30] The allusion to this controversial act places the Morrison family within an environment of political aggression and violence and brings to the surface the history of Puerto Rico's tense relationship with the United States during the twentieth century. What is significant about this relationship in terms of Sánchez's play is that many of the issues that the quintuplets have to deal with, such as their own independence from an oppressive family relationship, or the father's authoritative stands vis-à-vis his children, or the implications of incest within the socio-familial context, also shed light on the contextual Puerto Rican reality of the 1950s and subsequent decades. This reality included the establishment of the so-called Free Associated State, the beginning of the industrialized era in Puerto Rican history, the attempt to silence the independence and nationalist movements, and the political indecisiveness of the electorate and its inability to reach a consensus regarding its own future.

I am not suggesting that *Quintuples* is an allegory of Puerto Rico's colonial status, but that the search for artistic independence –from the Western tradition, from the marginalization of theatre within Spanish American literature, and from Spanish American theatre's lack of interest in farce–parallels the island's lack of power, or even desire, to create its own politically independent voice. This parallelism is dramatized by the creation of an inclusive environment (text and context) in which, on the one hand, existence on the margins of powerful literary structures lends credibility and indepen-

---

[30] For a brief description of the 1950 Nationalist revolt, see Francisco A. Scarano, *Puerto Rico: Cinco siglos de historia*, 729-32, and Blanca G. Silvestrini and María Dolores Luque de Sánchez, *Historia de Puerto Rico: Trayectoria de un pueblo*, 516.

dence to Spanish American farce, and, on the other, Spanish America's historical marginality and Puerto Rico's subordinate position with regard to the United States create tension between center and periphery. Ironically, this tension, portrayed through an unstable and grotesque family, represents both the laughable aspects of Puerto Rican history and the sorrowful consequences of–not coincidentally–five centuries of colonialism. As mentioned earlier, Spanish American farce takes from its Western counterpart its dual nature, but this duality reflects not so much the subjection of the marginalized other to the center, as the split identity of Spanish America's and Puerto Rico's artistic and political reality.

The aim of this chapter has been to explore the systems of opposites that *Quíntuples* portrays and questions, and the structures and discourses that are built and destroyed in Sánchez's piece. These systems of opposites reflect the dangerous, destructive, tormenting nature of farce while at the same time the genre is identified as "an ancient form of merrymaking" (Bermel 13). From this dual perspective, and using Sabina Berman's language, we can say that both *Quíntuples* in particular and Spanish American farce in general are linked to the so-called "pains of pleasure."

In this world of contrasts and contradictions, the spectator of *Quíntuples* is forced to deal with issues of identity and is confronted with the dilemma of reacting with a burst of laughter to the extremely humorous scenes and characters, or reacting with bewilderment before the tragic connotations of their existence. Will the audience focus on Bianca's comic ticks and nervousness, or on her painful need to hide her lesbian identity? Will they concentrate on the hypersexuality of Dafne, humorously described in the stage directions as a woman who carries in her mouth "the resolute promise of oral sex" (I: 2)? Or will they focus on her painful desire to have a new life, and on her recognition that no one can be who they want to be (I: 16)? Will they look at the family's interdependence or at its grotesque fragmentation?[31]

---

[31] Perivolaris, in stressing Sánchez's "exceptionally enjoyable humor" (17), underscores the emphasis of this humor in contemporary Puerto Rican literature: "Carmen Vázquez (*Por la vereda* 160-61) correctly concludes that one of Sánchez's most resonant achievements is to have opened the way for younger writers to write seriously through humor. In fact, so much so is this the case that the literary landscape Barradas sketched in monochrome in 1981 has now been colored by the arrival to full maturity of first-rate writers like Magali García Ramis, Edgardo Rodríguez Juliá, and Ana Lydia Vega, all of whose use and enjoyment of humor signals contemporary Puerto Rican literature's broader spectrum of expression" (18).

Quíntuples focuses on the dramatization of farce as a multifaceted communicative discourse. The examination of its farcical aspects and of the theme of incest in its literal and metaphorical dimensions have revealed this play's parodic reconfiguration of artistic, cultural, and sociopolitical discourses. Familial and social communication, sexual identity and relations, national identity and political instability, power struggles of individuals and the collective, and economic and social exploitation are some of the issues that *Quíntuples* playfully frames within the nontraditional discourse of farce.

The farcical elements of *Quíntuples* emphasize the contradictory character of family relations (family seen in social and political terms), and the dramatization of theatre's mask and falsehood. The play shows that neither the Morrison family nor the genre of farce are willing to conform to traditional expectations. Contradiction is at the heart of *Quíntuples* both as a strategy to examine the play's complex understanding of identity and power (artistic, communicative, social, sexual), and as a means of playing with and escaping from restrictive and authoritative forces (family, father, sexual codes, historical and political implications). As part of this complexity, *Quíntuples* dramatizes the explosive interaction between the overt elements of contemporary popular culture present in the play and the more oblique mythical and literary traditions of the classical past. The use of monologue in *Quíntuples*, for example, is linked to both traditions–ancient Greek tragedy and postmodern performance–, and also allows us to unmask the problematics of incest (notions of identity, familiarity, otherness, love, sexuality, plurality vs. singularity, parricide, and violence) in the context of farce. *Quíntuples* demonstrates how incest and farce represent grotesque and hyperbolic expressions of love and art that seek to radically transform social and theatrical communication.

Conclusions

BINDING THE UNBOUNDED

THE study of a literary genre in a postmodern era, as stated at the beginning, represents significant challenges as one confronts issues of establishing definitions, setting boundaries, categorizing discourses, tracing chronologies, reconciling contradictions, and identifying exceptions, among other demands. The challenge becomes even greater when the genre studied is placed "at the bottom of everyone's list of forms" (McDonald 77), and when some of its most acknowledged traits are related to the transgressive, the iconoclastic, the hyperbolic, the frivolous, and the marginal. Positionality has been then an important issue as we have examined farce's identity and characterization in the context of Spanish American literature in general and of theatre in particular. Traditionally considered a disparaged genre, farce in Spanish America becomes a postmodern theatrical expression that incorporates opposing discourses and follows multiple and contradictory paths in relation to its artistic formulations and to its historical development. We have attempted to show that farce's chameleonic nature is a mechanism to avoid fixation and to confront authority. And that is precisely why marginalization and transgression are among its most overt characteristics, which lead us to examine Spanish American farce's (marginal) relationship to other theatrical forms, to other Spanish American literary discourses, and to Western culture and literature as a whole. In other words, liminality is at the center of farce, and farce's strong presence in Spanish American theatre signals its capacity to simultaneously construct and question the categories of reality and fiction.

As part of this persistent concern with the marginal, Spanish

American farce has established an antagonistic relationship with artistic, sociocultural and political authority, and has not only avoided becoming part of the center, but has refused to be typified as meaningless and irrelevant, while questioning its own meaningful stands. As we have attempted to show throughout this book, Spanish American playwrights have recourse to farce as a way to communicate from the periphery and from an iconoclastic perspective, about central issues and concerns. Nevertheless, those very important concerns are not free from being parodied themselves.

In the context of exploring the identity, positionality and the communicative capacities of farce in contemporary Spanish American theatre, this study has embarked on the exegesis of four plays of the nineteen seventies and eighties from four different countries: Triana's *Revolico en el Campo de Marte*, Berman's *El suplicio del placer*, Vargas Llosa's *Kathie y el hipopótamo*, and Sánchez's *Quíntuples*. These farces' deep awareness of their iconoclastic stands regarding theatrical tradition and communication, their rebellious outlook toward social and political issues, their celebratory attitude towards polarization and unorthodoxy, and their overt intertextual conversations with critical and literary discourses suggest that they have not only placed marginality at the center of their identity, but that they have attempted to redefine their farcical identity in the context of Spanish American artistic, social, and political realities. It is possible to state that the ultimate contribution of these and other farces in the context of Spanish American theatre has been to question notions of power, authority and artistic prestige by problematizing this genre's own disparaged history as meaningless and non transcendental. The fact that many Spanish American contemporary playwrights have chosen to communicate their concerns and passions through farce–that is, through a fragmented, parodic, transgressive, and ambiguous genre–reveals their struggle against artistic and political fixation and hegemony, and against notions of dominance and hierarchy. In its attempt to constantly dismantle expectations, Spanish American farce has continued to underscore its physical dynamism and insist on juxtaposing the artistic with the political, the serious with the comic, the physical with the reflexive, the personal with the collective.

Throughout this study we have attempted to answer why Spanish American playwrights have taken recourse to farce more frequently than might be expected, considering that this genre lacks theatrical prestige and that Spanish American history is frequently linked more with political and socioeconomic turmoil, than with humor and merriment. Triana, Berman, Vargas Llosa, Sánchez and other Spanish American playwrights such as Argüelles, Buenaventura, Carballido, Castellanos, Gambaro, Ibargüengoitia, Leñero, and Marco Antonio de la Parra, to mention but a few, have recognized that one plausible way to exercise artistic freedom, to establish close links with a large popular audience, and to unmask social and political repression is through a discourse such as farce, known for its persistent breakdown of expectations. As we have seen throughout this study, Spanish American farce rejects fixation, is critical of its own past, plays with its various and not always prestigious identities, and underscores its lack of responsibility regarding artistic and political solutions.

Triana's *Revolico en el Campo de Marte* underscores its farcical dimensions by stressing its revolutionary approaches and stands, both towards art and towards politics. But the serious angles of dealing with revolutionary acts are themselves transgressed in this play by transforming everything (relationships, love affairs, friendships, economic deals) into a *revolico*, that is, into a chaotic, messy and apparently meaningless act. It is clear that these transformations are understood in the light of a genre that refuses to stay still and to be codified. As part of this *revolico* farce establishes a dialogue in Triana's play with other artistic and cultural expressions which have been frequently considered marginal, fragmented and evasive such as the absurd, the *esperpento*, the buffo and the *choteo*. Farce's insistence on sharing the stage with these theatrical and artistic forms can be seen as a mirror image of the various transgressive revolutionary acts which are themselves transgressed in Cuban history. It is not surprising then that in the context of farce the concepts of artistic and political revolution coexist with those of artistic and political *revolicos*.

In Berman's *El suplicio del placer* the use of farce is closely linked to a non conformist stand towards women's and feminist issues, even as we recognize that Berman's play takes a feminist stand. In this play both genre (farce) and gender (the female) issues reflect aspects of positionality (marginalization, repression) and identity (sexual, social, political). By transgressing everything that occupies center stage, *El suplicio* underscores the fact that prescriptive and fixed solutions represent an illusory end, and that ambiguity and exaggeration shed light into diverse and unorthodox realities. Berman's play demonstrates that rather than being unrelated issues, the problematics of genre and gender are deeply related, since both of these discourses have had to deal with issues of marginality and repression. In Vargas Llosa's *Kathie y el hipopótamo* the discourse of farce has been used to deal eloquently with the parodic aspects of communication and language (literal, metaphoric, symbolic, humorous), and to explore how these aspects relate to power, hierarchy and authority. The relationship between a creator and a scriptwriter, between a she and a he, between one with economic and social power and one without it, also underscores the play's own choice of farce as a source of artistic exploration and political criticism. Finally, in Sánchez's *Quíntuples* farce is used as a vehicle to expose a multiplicity of cultural, sexual, artistic, and political languages that range from the classical to the popular, from the intimate to the public, from the individual to the collective, from the passive to the radical, from the promiscuous to the frigid, from the traditional to the transgressive. Identity and power, and the interplay between reality and fiction are again issues closely related to the questioning of authority and hierarchy. The family structure becomes in Sánchez's play a loaded image of personal interactions and national conceptions, which are all questioned at the end of the play when the audience is confronted with two actors that have been performing the roles of the six members of the Morrison family. Through the use of two grotesque expressions of love and art–that is, through the relationship between incest and farce–Sánchez transgresses social, political and theatrical communication, underscoring the play's unwillingness to conform to traditional views and expectations.

It should be clear by now that in the light of an emphasis on farce's complex identity, the goal has not been to offer a straightforward definition of Spanish American farce, nor to explore *all* expressions of Spanish American farces. My interest lies in those farces that establish an extremely ambiguous artistic and sociopolitical relationship with their humorous character. The plays studied throughout this book emphasize the negative consequences of physical, psychological, sexual, political, linguistic, and artistic repression. But they do this with the ironic awareness that this denunciation is framed by a parodic game between what is meaningful and what is meaningless, and by the destruction of any form of authority, even one that, in farce's own (crossed) eyes, could seem constructive. Spanish American farce may continue to be "at the bottom of everyone's lists of forms," but since marginality is at the center of farce, we can now see from a new perspective both its strong artistic and political stands and its unfixed and antiauthoritative character.

WORKS CITED

Adler, Heidrun and Kati Rötter, eds. *Performance, pathos, política de los sexos: Teatro poscolonial de autoras latinoamericanas*. Frankfurt: Vervuert, 1999.
Aguilú de Murphy, Raquel. *Los textos dramáticos de Virgilio Piñera y el teatro del absurdo*. Madrid: Pliegos, 1989.
Ahern, Maureen, ed. *A Rosario Castellanos Reader: An Anthology of Her Poetry, Short Fiction, Essays, and Drama*. Introd. Maureen Ahern. Trans. Maureen Ahern et al. Austin: U of Texas P, 1988.
Aizenberg, Edna. "Historical Subversion and Violence of Representation in García Márquez and Ouloguem." *PMLA* 107 (1992): 1235-52.
Albuquerque, Severino. *Violent Acts: A Study of Contemporary Latin American Theatre*. Detroit: Wayne State UP, 1991.
Alston, William P. "Pleasure." *The Encyclopedia of Philosophy*. Vol. 5. Ed. Paul Edwards. New York: Macmillan and Free Press, 1972. 341-47.
Argüelles, Hugo. "(Nota introductoria del *Suplicio del placer* con apariencia de:) Prólogo." *Teatro de Sabina Berman*. Mexico: Editores Mexicanos Unidos, 1985. 211-13.
Artesi, Catalina Julia. "Una nueva forma para la farsa: *Fidela* de Aurelio Ferretti." *Latin American Theatre Review* 20 (1986): 49-56.
Atkinson, James B. "An Essay on Machiavelli and Comedy." *The Comedies of Machiavelli*. Bilingual edition. Ed. and trans. David Sices and James B. Atkinson. Hanover, NH: UP of New England, 1985. 1-34.
Aubrun, Charles V. *La comedia española (1600-1680)*. Trans. Julio Lago Alonso. Madrid: Taurus, 1968.
Bakhtin, Mikhail. *Rabelais and His World*. Bloomington: Indiana UP, 1984.
Barradas, Efraín. "Palabras apalabradas: Prólogo para una antología de cuentistas puertorriqueños de hoy." *Apalabramiento: Cuentos puertorriqueños de hoy*. Ed. Efraín Barradas. Hanover, NH: Ediciones del Norte, 1983. xiii-xxxi.
———. *Para leer en puertorriqueño: Acercamiento a la obra de Luis Rafael Sánchez*. Río Piedras, PR: Editorial Cultural, 1981.
Barthes, Roland. *The Pleasure of the Text*. Trans. Richard Miller. New York: Hill and Wang, 1975.
Benjamin, Walter. "The Task of the Translator." *Illuminations*. Trans. Harry Zohn. New York: Schocken Books, 1969. 69-82.
Bentley, Eric. "Farce." *Life of the Drama*. New York: Atheneum, 1967. 219-56.
Berman, Sabina. *El suplicio del placer*. Mexico: Grupo Editorial Gaceta, 1994. 159-217.
———. *El suplicio del placer*. *Teatro de Sabina Berman*. Mexico: Editores Mexicanos Unidos, 1985. 266-99.
———. *The Theatre of Sabina Berman: The Agony of Ecstasy and Other Plays*. Trans. Adam Versényi. Carbondale: Southern Illinois UP, 2003.

Bermel, Albert. *Farce: A History from Aristophanes to Woody Allen.* 1982. Carbondale & Edwardsville: Southern Illinois UP, 1990.

Bixler, Jacqueline. "From *farsa de verdad* to Farce as Façade: *El día que se soltaron los leones, ¡Silencio, pollos pelones, ya les van a echar su maíz!, Te juro, Juana, que tengo ganas,* and *Acapulco, los lunes.*" *Convention and Transgression: The Theatre of Emilio Carballido.* Lewisburg: Bucknell UP, 1997. 51-83.

———. "Games and Reality on the Latin American Stage." *Latin American Literary Review* 12.24 (1984): 22-35.

———. "Vargas Llosa's *Kathie y el hipopótamo*: The Theatre as a Self-Conscious Deception." *Hispania* 71.2 (1988): 254-61.

Bockus-Aponte, Barbara. "Estrategias dramáticas del feminismo en *El eterno femenino* de Rosario Castellanos." *Latin American Theatre Review* 20 (1987): 49-58.

Boling, Becky. "Reyes y princesas: La subversión del signo." *En busca de una imagen: Ensayos críticos sobre Griselda Gambaro y José Triana.* Ed. Diana Taylor. Ottawa, Canada: Girol Books, 1989.

———. "*El suplicio del placer*: 'Dos' by Sabina Berman." *Latin American Theatre Review* 24 (1990): 166-67.

Booth, Wayne. *The Rhetoric of Irony.* Chicago: U of Chicago P, 1974.

Borges, Jorge Luis. "Las versiones homéricas." *Discusión. Obras completas I: 1923-1949.* Buenos Aires: Emecé Editores, 1996. 239-43.

———. "The Homeric Versions." *Selected Nonfictions: Jorge Luis Borges.* Ed. Eliot Weinberger. Trans. Esther Allen, Suzanne Jill Levine, and Eliot Weinberger. New York: Viking Penguin, 1999. 69-74.

———. "The Modesty of History." *Borges: A Reader: A Selection from the Writings of Jorge Luis Borges.* Ed. Emir Rodríguez Monegal and Alastair Reid. New York: E. P. Dutton, 1981. 246-48.

———. "El pudor de la historia." *Otras inquisiciones. Jorge Luis Borges. Obras completas II: 1952-1972.* Barcelona: Emecé Editores, 1996. 128-34.

Boyd, Michael. *The Reflexive Novel: Fiction as Critique.* Lewisburg: Bucknell UP, 1983.

Brockett, Oscar G. *History of the Theatre.* 6th ed. Boston: Allyn & Bacon, 1991.

Burgess, Ronald D. *The New Dramatists of Mexico 1967-1985.* Lexington: UP of Kentucky, 1991.

Burgos, Norma. "Retorna un éxito teatral." *El Mundo* [Puerto Rico]. 12 April 1985: 53.

Burns, E. Bradford. *Latin America: A Concise Interpretive History.* 6th ed. Englewood Cliffs, NJ: Prentice Hall, 1994.

Butler, Judith. "Performative Acts and Gender Constitution: An Essay in Phenomenology and Feminist Theory." *Performing Feminisms: Feminist Critical Theory and Theatre.* Ed. Sue-Ellen Case. Baltimore: The Johns Hopkins UP, 1990. 270-82.

———. "Sexual Inversions." *Feminist Interpretations of Michel Foucault.* Ed. Susan J. Hekman. University Park: Pennsylvania State UP, 1996. 59-75.

Cabrera, Lydia. *Anagó: Vocabulario lucumí (El yoruba que se habla en Cuba).* Miami: Colección del Chihirekú, 1979.

"Camille Paglia." Ed Bradley. CBS News, *60 Minutes.* 1 August 1993. Transcript 25.45, 11-16.

Caputi, Anthony. *Buffo: The Genius of Vulgar Comedy.* Detroit: Wayne State, UP, 1978.

Carlson, Marvin. *Performance: A Critical Introduction.* London and New York: Routledge, 1996.

Carlson, Susan L. "Women in Comedy: Problem, Promise, Paradox." *Drama, Sex and Politics*. Themes in Drama Series. Cambridge: Cambridge UP, 1985.
Castellanos, Rosario. *The Eternal Feminine: Farce*. Trans. Diane E. Marting & Betty Tyree Osiek. *A Rosario Castellanos Reader*. Austin: U of Texas P, 1988. 273-367. [*El eterno femenino: Farsa*. Mexico: Fondo de Cultura Económica, 1975.]
Castellanos, Rosario. "La participación de la mujer mexicana en la educación formal." *Mujer que sabe latín...* 1973. Mexico: Fondo de Cultura Económica, 1984. 21-40.
———. *Tablero de damas*. *América: Revista Antológica* 68 (1952): 185-224.
———. "Woman and Her Image." *A Rosario Castellanos Reader: An Anthology of Her Poetry, Short Fiction, Essays, and Drama*. Ed. and trans. Maureen Ahern. Austin: U of Texas P, 1988. 236-44. [In *Mujer que sabe latín...* (1973).]
Castillo, Debra A. *Easy Women: Sex and Gender in Modern Mexican Fiction*. Minneapolis: U of Minnesota P, 1998.
———. *Talking Back: Toward a Latin American Feminist Literary Criticism*. Ithaca, NY: Cornell UP, 1992.
Castro-Klarén, Sara. "La crítica literaria feminista y la escritora en América Latina." *La sartén por el mango: Encuentro de escritoras latinoamericanas*. Ed. Patricia Elena González and Eliana Ortega. 2nd ed. Río Piedras, PR: Ediciones Huracán, 1985. 27-46.
———. *Understanding Mario Vargas Llosa*. 2nd ed. Columbia: U of South Carolina P, 1992.
Cervantes, Miguel de. *The Ingenious Gentleman, Don Quixote de la Mancha*. New York: Viking, 1967.
Chambers, Ross. *Room for Maneuver: Reading (the) Oppositional (in) Narrative*. Chicago: U of Chicago P, 1991.
Charney, Maurice. *Comedy High and Low: An Introduction to the Experience of Comedy*. New York: Oxford UP, 1978.
Cohen, Ralph. "Do Postmodern Genres Exist?" *Genre* 20.3-4 (1987): 241-57.
Cohen, Ted. "Metaphor and the Cultivation of Intimacy." *On Metaphor*. Ed. Sheldon Sacks. Chicago: U of Chicago P, 1979. 1-10.
Colón Zayas, Eliseo. *El teatro de Luis Rafael Sánchez: Códigos, ideología y lenguaje*. San Juan, PR: Editorial Playor, 1985.
Costantino, Roselyn. "El discurso del poder en *El suplicio del placer* de Sabina Berman." *De la colonia a la postmodernidad: Teoría teatral y crítica sobre teatro latinoamericano*. Ed. Peter Roster and Mario Rojas. Buenos Aires: Editorial Galerna, 1992. 245-52.
Cypess, Sandra Messinger. "Ethnic Identity in the Plays of Sabina Berman." *Tradition and Innovation: Reflections on Latin American Jewish Writing*. Ed. Robert DiAntonio and Nora Glickman. New York: State U of New York P, 1993. 165-77.
———. "From Colonial Constructs to Feminist Figures: Re/visions by Mexican Women Dramatists." *Theatre Journal* (1989): 492-504.
———. *La Malinche in Mexican Literature: From History to Myth*. Austin: U of Texas P, 1991.
———. "Spanish American Theatre in the Twentieth Century." *The Cambridge History of Latin American Literature. Volume 2: The Twentieth Century*. Eds. Roberto González Echevarría and Enrique Pupo-Walker. Cambridge: Cambridge UP, 1996. 497-525.
Dauster, Frank. "Bridging the Quantum Gap: Considerations on the Novelist as Playwright." *Latin American Theatre Review* 24.1 (1990): 5-15.
———. *Perfil generacional del teatro hispanoamericano (1894-1924)*. Ottawa: Girol Books, 1993.
———. "Vargas Llosa y el teatro como mentira." *Mester* 14.2 (1985): 89-94.

Davis, Jessica Milner. *Farce*. London: Methuen, 1978.
Dean, Joan F. "Joe Orton and the Redefinition of Farce." *Theatre Journal* 34.4 (1982): 481-92.
de Costa, Elena. *Collaborative Latin American Popular Theatre: From Theory to Form, from Text to Stage*. New York: Peter Lang, 1992.
de Man, Paul. *Allegories of Reading: Figural Language in Rousseau, Nietzsche, Rilke, and Proust*. New Haven: Yale UP, 1979.
———. "The Epistemology of Metaphor." *On Metaphor*. Ed. Sheldon Sacks. Chicago: U of Chicago P, 1979. 11-28.
de Valdés, María Elena. *The Shattered Mirror: Representations of Women in Mexican Literature*. Austin: U of Texas P, 1998.
Delany, Paul. *British Autobiography in the Seventeenth Century*. New York: Routledge and K. Paul, 1969.
Derrida, Jacques. "Des Tours de Babel." *Difference in Translation*. Ed. Joseph F. Graham. Ithaca, New York: Cornell UP, 1985, 165-205.
Donne, John. "Song." *The Norton Anthology of English Literature*. Ed. M. H. Abrams, et al. 3rd ed. New York: Norton, 1974. 1183.
Dougherty, Dru. "Poética y práctica de la farsa: *La Marquesa Rosalinda*, de Valle-Inclán." *Boletín de la Fundación Federico García Lorca* 19-20 (1996): 125-44.
Eichner, Hans. "The Eternal Feminine: An Aspect of Goethe's Ethics." Introduction in Johann Wolfgang Von Goethe. *Faust: A Tragedy. A New Translation. Background and Sources. The Author on the Drama. Contemporary Reactions. Modern Criticism*. Trans. Walter Arndt. Ed. Cyrus Hamlin. New York: Norton, 1976. 615-24.
Emmanuelli Huertas, Johanna. "*Quíntuples*: Las máscaras de la representación." *Revista de Estudios Hispánicos* (Puerto Rico) 17-18 (1990-91): 339-51.
Erlich, Victor. *Russian Formalism: History-Doctrine*. New York: Monton, 1980.
Escarpanter, José A. and José A. Madrigal. "El teatro popular cubano hasta 1869." Juan Francisco Valero. *Perro huevero aunque le quemen el hocico*. Eds. José A. Escarpanter and José A. Madrigal. Boulder, CO: Societies of Spanish and Spanish American Studies, 1986. 9-46.
Espinosa Domínguez, Carlos. "'Para mí el teatro es una ascesis, una cura de adelgazamiento': Entrevista a Mario Vargas Llosa." *Latin American Theatre Review* 20.1 (1986): 57-60.
Farrell, Joseph. "Fo and Feydeau: Is Farce a Laughing Matter?" *Italica* 72.3 (1995): 307-22.
Fernández de la Torriente, Gastón. "Vida y ficción en *Kathie y el hipopótamo* de Mario Vargas Llosa." *Selected Proceedings of the Thirty-Ninth Annual Mountain Interstate Foreign Language Conference*. Eds. Sixto E. Torres and S. Carl King. Clemson, SC: Clemson UP, 1991.
Ferrater Mora, José. "Placer." *Diccionario de Filosofía*. Vol. 2. Buenos Aires: Editorial Sudamericana, 1965. 422-23.
Figueroa, Alvin Joaquín. *La prosa de Luis Rafael Sánchez: Texto y contexto*. New York: Peter Lang, 1989.
Fiske, John. "Popular Culture." *Critical Terms for Literary Study*. 2nd ed. Eds. Frank Lentricchia and Thomas McLaughlin. Chicago: The U of Chicago P, 1995. 321-335.
Foley, Barbara. *Telling the Truth: The Theory and Practice of Documentary Fiction*. Ithaca: Cornell UP, 1986.
Foucault, Michel. *The History of Sexuality. Volume 1: An Introduction*. Trans. Robert Hurley. New York: Vintage, 1980.
———. *The Use of Pleasure. The History of Sexuality. Volume 2*. Trans. Robert Hurley. New York: Pantheon, 1985.

Fowler, Alastair. "Concepts of Genre." *Kinds of Literature: An Introduction to the Theory of Genres and Modes*. Oxford: Clarendon Press, 1982. 37-53.
Franco, Jean. "Beyond Ethnocentricity: Gender, Power, and the Third-World Intelligentsia." *Marxism and the Interpretation of Culture*. Ed. Cary Nelson & Lawrence Grossberg. Urbana: U of Illinois P, 1988. 503-15.
———. *Plotting Women: Gender and Representation in Mexico*. New York: Columbia UP, 1989.
Freedman, Barbara. "Errors in Comedy: A Psychoanalytic Theory of Farce." *New York Literary Forum* 5-6 (1980): 233-43.
García Márquez, Gabriel. *Cien años de soledad*. 4ª ed. Madrid: Espasa-Calpe, 1983.
———. "Los funerales de la Mamá Grande." *Los funerales de la Mamá Grande*. Buenos Aires: Editorial Sudamericana, 1975. 125-147.
García Pinto, Magdalena. Interview. "Sylvia Molloy." *Women Writers of Latin America: Intimate Histories*. Trans. Trudy Balch and Magdalena García Pinto. Austin: U of Texas P, 1991. 125-43.
Geis, Deborah. *Postmodern Theatric[k]s: Mondogue in Contemporary American Drama*. Ann Arbor: The U of Michigan P, 1995.
Geisdorfer Feal, Rosemary. "La ficción como tema: La trilogía dramática de Mario Vargas Llosa." *Texto Crítico* 13:36-37 (1987): 137-45.
Gerdes, Dick. "*La señorita de Tacna* and *Kathie y el hipopótamo*: Storytelling as Dramatized Art." *Mario Vargas Llosa*. Boston: Twayne, 1985. 154-67.
Gerdes, Dick and Tamara Holzapfel. "Melodrama and Reality in the Plays of Mario Vargas Llosa." *Latin American Theatre Review* 24.1 (1990): 17-28.
Gil, Alfonso M. "Notas e impresiones acerca del teatro de Benito Pérez Galdós." *Estudios Escénicos Cuadernos del Instituto del Teatro* 18 (1974): 155-64.
Girard, René. *Violence and the Sacred*. Trans. Patrick Gregory. 1972. Baltimore & London: The Johns Hopkins UP, 1989.
Gladhart, Amalia. *The Leper in Blue: Coercive Performance and the Contemporary Latin American Theatre*. Chapel Hill: North Carolina Studies in the Romance Languages and Literatures, 2000.
Goethe, Johann Wolfgang von. *Faust: Part One and Part Two*. Trans. and introd. Charles E. Passage. Indianapolis: The Bobbs-Merrill Company, 1965.
Golluscio de Montoya, Eva. "Los cuentos de *La señorita de Tacna*." *Latin American Theatre Reivew* 18.1 (1984): 35-43.
González, Aníbal. "Translation and Genealogy: *One Hundred Years of Solitude*." *Gabriel García Márquez: New Readings*. Cambridge: Cambridge UP, 1987. 65-79.
———. "Puerto Rico." *Handbook of Latin American Literature*. Ed. David William Foster. 2nd ed. New York & London: Garland, 1992. 555-81.
González, Patricia Elena. "Prólogo." *La sartén por el mango: Encuentro de escritoras latinoamericanas*. Ed. Patricia Elena González and Eliana Ortega. 2nd ed. Río Piedras, PR: Ediciones Huracán, 1985. 11-17.
González Echevarría, Roberto. "Big Mama's Wake." *Diacritics* 4.4 (1974): 55-57.
———. "The Dictatorship of Rhetoric/The Rhetoric of Dictatorship." *The Voice of the Masters: Writing and Authority in Modern Latin American Literature*. Austin: U of Texas P, 1985. 64-85.
Good, Carl. "Testimonio especular, testimonio sublime en *El eterno femenino* de Rosario Castellanos." *Gestos* 10.20 (1995): 55-73.
Gottlieb, Vera. "Why This Farce? *New Theatre Quarterly*. 7. 27 (1991): 217-228.
Greenblatt, Stephen. "Culture." *Critical Terms for Literary Study*. 2nd ed. Eds. Frank Lentricchia and Thomas McLaughlin. Chicago: The U of Chicago P, 1995. 225-232.
Hartsock, Nancy C. M. "Postmodernism and Political Change: Issues for Feminist Theory." *Feminist Interpretations of Michel Foucault*. Ed. Susan J. Hekman. University Park: Pennsylvania State UP, 1996. 39-55.

Hekman, Susan J. "Editor's Introduction." *Feminist Interpretations of Michel Foucault.* Ed. Susan J. Hekman. University Park: Pennsylvania State UP, 1996. 1-12.
Herbert, Christopher. "Comedy: The World of Pleasure." *Genre* 17.4 (1984): 401-16.
Hernández Vargas, Nélida and Daisy Caraballo Abréu, eds. *Luis Rafael Sánchez: Crítica y bibliografía.* Río Piedras, PR: Editorial de la Universidad de Puerto Rico, 1985.
Holzapfel, Tamara. "Evolutionary Tendencies in Spanish American Absurd Theatre." *Latin American Theatre Review.* 13.2 (Summer Supplement 1980): 37-42.
Howarth, W. D. "From Arlequin to Ubu: Farce as Anti-theatre." *Farce. Themes in Drama.* Ed. James Redmond. Cambridge: Cambridge UP, 1988. 153-171.
Hurrell, John Dennis. "A Note on Farce." *Quarterly Journal of Speech* 45.1 (1959): 426-430.
Hutcheon, Linda. *Irony's Edge: The Theory and Politics of Irony.* London: Routledge, 1994.
Ibsen, Kristine, ed. *The Other Mirror: Women's Narrative in Mexico, 1980-1995.* Westport: Greenwood Press, 1997.
Janson, H. W. and Samuel Cauman. *A Basic History of Art.* Englewood Cliffs: Prentice-Hall, 1971.
Johnson, Julie Greer. *Satire in Colonial Latin America: Turning the New World Upside Down.* Austin: U of Texas P, 1993.
Kierkegaard, Søren. *The Concept of Irony.* Trans. Lee M. Capel. New York: Harper & Row, 1965.
Knight, Franklin W. *The Caribbean: The Genesis of a Fragmented Nationalism.* 2nd ed. New York: Oxford UP, 1990.
Kronik, John W. "Invasions from Outer Space: Narration and the Dramatic Art in Spanish America." *Latin American Theatre Review* 26.2 (1993): 25-47.
Labinger, Andrea. "The Cruciform Farce in Latin America: Two Plays." *Farce. Themes in Drama Series.* Cambridge: Cambridge UP, 1988. 219-226.
Larrain, Jorge. *Theories of Development: Capitalism, Colonialism and Dependency.* Cambridge: Polity, 1989.
Larson, Catherine and Margarita Vargas. *Latin American Women Dramatists: Theatre, Texts, and Theories.* Bloomington: Indiana UP, 1998.
Leal, Rine. "Prólogo." *Teatro bufo: Siglo XIX. Antología. Tomo 1.* Havana: Editorial Arte y Literatura, 1975. 15-46.
Leñero, Vicente. *Vivir del teatro.* Mexico: Joaquín Mortiz, 1982.
Lima, Robert. "The Orisha Changó and Other African Deities in Cuban Drama." *Latin American Theatre Review* 23.2 (1990): 33-42.
Lindstrom, Naomi. "Rosario Castellanos: Pioneer of Feminist Criticism." *Homenaje a Rosario Castellanos.* Ed. Maureen Ahern and Mary Seale Vásquez. Valencia: Ediciones Albatros Hispanófila, 1980. 65-73.
Locke, John. *An Essay Concerning Human Understanding.* New York: Collier, 1965.
Lolo, Eduardo. "*La noche de los asesinos,* de José Triana, apuntes para una puesta en el tiempo." *Las trampas del tiempo y sus memorias.* Miami: Iberian Studies Institute, North-South Center [Letras de Oro], 1989. 19-47.
López-Baralt, Luce. "*La guaracha del Macho Camacho*: Saga nacional de la 'guachafita' puertorriqueña." *Revista Iberoamericana* 51.131 (1985): 103-23.
———. "La prosa de Luis Rafael Sánchez, escrita en puertorriqueño." *Ínsula* 31.356-57 (1976): 9.
López González, Aralia, Amelia Malagamba, and Elena Urrutia, eds. *Mujer y literatura mexicana y chicana: Culturas en contacto.* Vol. 2. Mexico: El Colegio de México and El Colegio de la Frontera Norte, 1990.
Luzuriaga, Gerardo. *Introducción a las teorías latinoamericanas del teatro: de 1930 al presente.* Puebla: Universidad Autónoma de Puebla, 1990.

Machiavelli, Niccoló. *The Mandrake*. *The Comedies of Machiavelli*. Bilingual edition. Ed. and trans. David Sices and James B. Atkinson. Hanover, NH: UP of New England, 1985. 153-275.
Magnarelli, Sharon. "Mario Vargas Llosa's *La señorita de Tacna*: Autobiography and/as Theater." *Mester* 14.2 (1985): 79-88.
———. "Tea for Two: Performing History and Desire in Sabina Berman's *Entre Villa y una mujer desnuda*." *Latin American Theatre Review* 30 (1996): 55-74.
"Mandrágora." María Moliner. *Diccionario de Uso del Español*. Vol. II. Madrid: Gredos, 1982. 327.
Mandrake the Magician. 29 Jan. 2001. <http://www.kingfeatures.com/features/comics/mandrake/about.htm>.
Mañach, Jorge. *Indagación del choteo*. Havana: Revista de Avance, 1928.
Marqués, René. *Carnaval afuera, carnaval adentro*. Río Piedras: Editorial Antillana, 1971.
Martínez, Jorge. "Sánchez trae de nuevo la magia a las tablas." *El Día*, "Sección Por Dentro." 5 October 1984.
Marx, Karl. *The Eighteenth Brumaire of Louis Bonaparte*. New York: International Publishers, 1981.
McCoy, Kenneth W. "Sex, Sin, and Storytelling: Eroticism in the Theatre of Mario Vargas Llosa." Doctoral Diss. Bowling Green State University, 1994.
———. "The Theatre of Mario Vargas Llosa: A Bibliography and Production History, 1981-1994." *Latin American Theatre Review* 28.2 (1995): 105-11.
McDonald, Russ. "Fear of Farce." *"Bad" Shakespeare: Revaluations of the Shakespeare Canon*. Ed. Maurice Charney. London & Toronto: Associated UP, 1988. 77-90.
McGowan, John. *Postmodernism and Its Critics*. Ithaca: Cornell UP, 1991.
McNab, Pamela J. "Humor in Castellanos's *El eterno femenino*: The Fractured Female Image." *Latin American Theatre Review* 33 (2000): 79-89.
Meléndez, Priscilla. "Creación y autocreación en *La señorita de Tacna* de Mario Vargas Llosa." *La dramaturgia hispanoamericana contemporánea: Teatralidad y autoconciencia*. Madrid: Editorial Pliegos, 1990. 155-171.
———. "El espejo en las tablas: Hacia una poética de la teatralidad en *Farsa del amor compradito* de Luis Rafael Sánchez." *La dramaturgia hispanoamericana contemporánea: Teatralidad y autoconciencia*. Madrid: Pliegos, 1990. 81-106.
———. "Lo uno y lo múltiple: Farsa e incesto en *Quíntuples* de Sánchez." *Latin American Theatre Review* 26.1 (1992): 7-22.
———. "Transgresión y transcripción: Ironía y ficción en *Kathie y el hipopótamo* de Vargas Llosa." *Revista Canadiense de Estudios Hispánicos* 15.1 (1990): 35-47.
Menchú, Rigoberta. *I, Rigoberta Menchú: An Indian Woman in Guatemala*. Ed. Elizabeth Burgos-Debray. Trans. Ann Wright. London: Verso, 1992.
Mesa-Lago, Carmelo. *Cuba in the 1970s: Pragmatism and Institutionalization*. Revised ed. Albuquerque: U of New Mexico P, 1978.
Meyerhold, Usevolod. "Farce." *Tulane Drama Review* 4.1 (1959): 139-149.
Moliner, María. *Diccionario de uso del español*. Madrid: Gredos, 1982.
Monleón, José. "El teatro de Vargas Llosa: La realidad del imaginario." *Antípodas* 1 (1988): 121-26.
Montes Huidobro, Matías. "Máscara familiar: Esquizofrenia mágica." *Persona: Vida y máscara en el teatro cubano*. Miami: Ediciones Universal, 1973.
———. *Persona: Vida y máscara en el teatro puertorriqueño*. San Juan, PR: Centro de Estudios Avanzados de Puerto Rico y el Caribe, Ateneo Puertorriqueño, Universidad Interamericana, Tinglado Puertorriqueño, 1986.
Morell, Hortensia R. "*Quíntuples* y el vértigo del teatro autorreflexivo de Luis Rafael Sánchez." *Latin American Theatre Review* 27.2 (1994): 39-51.

Muecke, D. C. *Irony and the Ironic*. 2nd ed. London: Methuen, 1982.
Nicoll, Allardyce. *The World of Harlequin: A Critical Study of the Commedia dell-Arte*. 1963. Cambridge: Cambridge UP, 1986.
Nigro, Kirsten. "Inventions and Transgressions: A Fractured Narrative on Feminist Theatre in Mexico." *Negotiating Performance: Gender, Sexuality, and Theatricality in Latin/o America*. Durham: Duke UP, 1994. 137-58.

———. "*La noche de los asesinos*: Playscript and Stage Enactment." *Latin American Theatre Review* 11.1 (1977): 45-57.

———. "Orden, limpieza y *Palabras comunes*: Otra vez los juegos prohibidos." *Palabras más que comunes; Ensayos sobre el teatro de José Triana*. Ed. Kirsten F. Nigro. Boulder, CO: Society of Spanish and Spanish-American Studies, 1994. 65-73.

———. "Para narrar la narrativa del teatro femenino: El paradigma mexicano." *Teatro y teatristas: Estudios sobre teatro argentino e iberoamericano*. Buenos Aires: Editorial Galerna/Facultad de Filosofía y Letras (UBA), 1992. 235-48.

———. "Rosario Castellanos' Debunking of the *Eternal Feminine*." *A Journal of Spanish Studies: Twentieth Century* 8:1-2 (1980): 89-102.
Ong, Walter J. *Orality and Literacy: The Technologizing of the Word*. London: Routledge, 1982.
O'Quinn, Kathleen. "'Tablero de Damas' and 'Álbum de Familia': Farces on Women Writers." *Homenaje a Rosario Castellanos*. Ed. Maureen Ahern and Mary Seale Vásquez. Valencia: Ediciones Albatros Hispanófila, 1980. 99-105.
Palls, Terry L. "El teatro del absurdo en Cuba: El compromiso artístico frente al compromiso político." *Latin American Theatre Review* 11.2 (1978): 25-32.
Pavis, Patrice. *Dictionary of the Theatre: Terms, Concepts, and Analysis*. Toronto & Buffalo: U of Toronto P, 1998.
Paz, Octavio. *Los hijos del limo: Del romanticismo a la vanguardia*. Barcelona: Seix Barral, 1987.

———. "Crítica de la pirámide." *El peregrino en su patria: Historia y política de México. México en la obra de Octavio Paz*. Vol. 1. Ed. Octavio Paz and Luis Mario Schneider. Mexico: Fondo de Cultura Económica, 1987.
Pelletieri, Osvaldo and Eduardo Rovner, eds. *La puesta en escena en Latinoamérica: Teoría y práctica teatral*. Buenos Aires: Galerna, 1995.
Pera, Cristóbal. *Modernistas en París: El mito de París en la prosa modernista hispanoamericana*. Bern, Switzerland: Peter Lang, 1997.
Pérez Blanco, Lucrecio. "El teatro: nueva y desventurada obsesión de Vargas Llosa." *Cuadernos Americanos* 252.1 (1984): 202-15.
Pérez Firmat, Gustavo. *The Cuban Condition: Translation and Identity in Modern Cuban Literature*. Cambridge: Cambridge UP, 1989.

———. "Riddles of the Sphincter." *Literature and Liminality: Festive Readings in the Hispanic Tradition*. Durham: Duke UP, 1986. 53-74.
Perivolaris, John Dimitri. *Puerto Rican Cultural Identity and the Work of Luis Rafael Sánchez*. Chapel Hill: U of North Carolina P, 2000.
Perret, Roy W. "Philosophy as Farce, or Farce as Philosophy." *Philosophy* 59 (1984): 373-81.
Pulido Jiménez, Juan José. "El humor satírico en *El eterno femenino*, de Rosario Castellanos." *Revista Canadiense de Estudios Hispánicos* 17.3 (1993): 483-94.
Pianca, Marina. *El teatro de nuestra América: un proyecto continental 1959-1989*. Minneapolis: Institute for the Study of Ideologies and Literatures, 1990.
Redmond, James, ed. *Farce. Themes in Drama*. Cambridge: Cambridge UP, 1988.
Reverte Bernal, Concepción. *Articulación temática en la narrativa y teatro de Mario Vargas Llosa: Visión del Perú*. Madrid, Melbourne, Auckland: VOX/AHS, 1994.

Ríos, Rubén. "El loro de Mario Vargas Llosa." *El Mundo* [San Juan, P.R.]. 13 Mar 1988, sec. Puerto Rico Ilustrado: 14-15.

———. "Del teatro ambulante al libro." *Diálogo* (U de Puerto Rico). Sept. 1992, 50.

Rivera-Rodas, Óscar. *El metateatro y la dramática de Vargas Llosa: Hacia una poética del espectador.* Amsterdam: John Benjamins, 1992.

Romano Thuesen, Evelia. "El humor en las farsas de Alfonsina Storni." *Alba de América* 15. 28-29 (1997): 374-388.

Rosmarin, Adena. *The Power of Genre.* Minneapolis: U of Minnesota P, 1985.

Ruiz Ramón, Francisco. *Historia del teatro español. Siglo XX.* 6th ed. Madrid: Cátedra, 1984.

Sackett, Theodore A. "Galdós dramaturgo, reformador del teatro de su tiempo." *Estreno* 7.1 (1981): 6-10.

Sánchez, Luis Rafael. "Cinco problemas posibles para el escritor puertorriqueño." *No llores por nosotros, Puerto Rico.* Hanover, NH: Ediciones del Norte, 1997. 127-166.

———. *La hiel nuestra de cada día.* Río Piedras, PR: Editorial Cultural, 1976.

———. *La pasión según Antígona Pérez.* 9ª ed. Río Piedras, PR: Editorial Cultural, 1985.

———. *Quíntuples.* Hanover, NH: Ediciones del Norte, 1985.

———. "Strip-tease at East Lansing." *No llores por nosotros, Puerto Rico.* Hanover, NH: Ediciones del Norte, 1997. 127-166.

Santos, Jesús M. "Vargas Llosa: 'El teatro fue mi primer amor'." Interview. *Antípodas* 1 (1988): 118-20.

Scarano, Francisco A. *Puerto Rico: Cinco siglos de historia.* San Juan, PR: McGraw Hill, 1993.

Schaefer, Claudia. *Textured Lives: Women, Art, and Representation in Modern Mexico.* Tucson: The U of Arizona P, 1992.

Schutz, W. Stanley. "The Nature of Farce: Definition and Devices." Unpublished doctoral dissertation. Michigan State University, 1967.

Schwab, Gustav. "Agamenón e Ifigenia." *Las más bellas leyendas de la antigüedad clásica.* Trans. Francisco Payarols. Barcelona: Editorial Labor, 1974. 289-98.

Sheridan, Alan. *Michel Foucault: The Will to Truth.* London: Tavistock Publications, 1980.

Sieber, Sharon. "The Deconstruction of Gender as Archetype in Rosario Castellanos' *El eterno femenino.*" *Letras femeninas* 25. 1-2 (1999): 38-48.

Silvestrini, Blanca G. and María Dolores Luque de Sánchez. *Historia de Puerto Rico: Trayectoria de un pueblo.* San Juan, PR: Cultural Puertorriqueña, 1987.

Standish, Peter. "A Novelist's Theatre." *Antípodas* 1 (1988): 133-41.

Stein, Stanley J. and Barbara H. *The Colonial Heritage in Latin America; Essays on Economic Dependence in Perspective.* New York: Oxford UP, 1970.

Szurmuk, Mónica. "Lo femenino en *El eterno femenino* de Rosario Castellanos." *Mujer y literatura mexicana y chicana: Culturas en contacto.* Vol. 2. Ed. Aralia López González, Amelia Malagamba, and Elena Urrutia. Mexico: El Colegio de México and El Colegio de la Frontera Norte, 1990. 37-47.

Taylor, Diana. "Framing the Revolution: Triana's *La noche de los asesinos* and *Ceremonial de guerra.*" *Latin American Theatre Review* 24.1 (1990): 81-92.

———. *Theatre of Crisis: Drama and Politics in Latin America.* Lexington: UP of Kentucky, 1991.

Thomas, Hugh. *Cuba: The Pursuit of Freedom.* New York: Harper & Row, 1971.

Todorov, Tzvetan. "The Origins of Genres." *Genres in Discourse.* 1978. New York: Cambridge UP, 1990. 13-38.

Triana, José. *Ceremonial de guerra.* Honolulu: Editorial Persona, 1990.

Triana, José. *La noche de los asesinos*. Havana: Casa de las Américas, 1965.
———. *Revolico en el Campo de Marte*. *Gestos: Teoría y Práctica del Teatro Hispánico* 10.19 (1995): 139-205.
Vanden Heuvel, Michael. *Performing Drama / Dramatizing Performance: Alternative Theatre and the Dramatic Text*. Ann Arbor: The U of Michigan P, 1993.
Vargas Llosa, Mario. *La Chunga*. Barcelona: Seix Barral, 1986.
———. *El hablador*. Barcelona: Seix Barral, 1987.
———. *Kathie y el hipopótamo*. Barcelona: Seix Barral, 1983.
———. *Kathie and the Hippopotamus*. Trans. Derry McKenney and Anthony Oliver-Smith. *Drama Contemporary: Latin America. Plays by Manuel Puig, Antonio Skármeta, Mario Vargas Llosa, Carlos Fuentes*. Eds. George Woodyard and Marion Peter Holt. New York: PAJ Publications, 1986.
———. *El loco de los balcones*. Barcelona: Seix Barral, 1993.
———. *Ojos bonitos, cuadros feos*. Lima, Peru: PEISA, 1996.
———. *La señorita de Tacna*. Barcelona: Seix Baral, 1981.
Vásquez, Mary Seale. "Rosario Castellanos, Image and Idea." *Homenaje a Rosario Castellanos*. Ed. Maureen Ahern and Mary Seale Vásquez. Valencia: Ediciones Albatros Hispanófila, 1980. 15-40.
Vázquez Arce, Carmen. *Por la vereda tropical: Notas sobre la cuentística de Luis Rafael Sánchez*. Buenos Aires: Ediciones de la Flor, 1994.
Vega, Lope de. *El lacayo fingido*. Madrid: Taurus, 1970.
Versényi, Adam. *Theatre in Latin America: Religion, Politics, and Culture from Cortés to the 1980s*. Cambridge & New York: Cambridge UP, 1993.
Villaverde, Cirilo. *Cecilia Valdés or Angel's Hill*. Trans. Sydney G. Gest. New York: Vantage Press, 1962.
Waldman, Gloria F. *Luis Rafael Sánchez: Pasión teatral*. San Juan, PR: Instituto de Cultura Puertorriqueña, 1988.
Walker, Nancy. "Do Feminists Ever Laugh? Women's Humor and Women's Rights." *International Journal of Women's Studies* 4.1 (1981): 1-9.
Webster's New Collegiate Dictionary. Springfield: G. & C. Merriam, 1981.
Weiss, Judith, Leslie Damasceno, et al. *Latin American Popular Theatre: The First Five Centuries*. Albuquerque: U of New Mexico P, 1993.
Williams, Raymond Leslie. *Mario Vargas Llosa*. New York: Ungar, 1986.
Williams, Robert I. "Play and the Concept of Farce." *Philosophy and Literature* 12.1 (1988): 58-69.
Wilt, Judith. "The Laughter of Maidens, the Cackle of Matriarchs: Notes on the Collision Between Comedy and Feminism." *Women and Literature* 1 (1980): 173-96.
Winnett, Susan. "Coming Unstrung: Women, Men, Narrative, and Principles of Pleasure." *PMLA* 105.3 (1990): 505-18.
Zachman, Jennifer A. "El placer fugaz y el amor angustiado: metateatro, género y poder en *El suplicio del placer* de Sabina Berman y *Noches de amor efímero* de Paloma Pedrero." *Gestos* 16.31 (2001): 37-50.
Zalacaín, Daniel. "René Marqués, del absurdo a la realidad." *Latin American Theatre Review* 12.1 (1978): 33-37.
———. *Teatro absurdista hispanoamericano*. Valencia & Chapel Hill: Albatros Ediciones Hispanofila, 1985.

NORTH CAROLINA STUDIES IN THE ROMANCE LANGUAGES AND LITERATURES

I.S.B.N. Prefix 0-8078-

Recent Titles

RAZA, GÉNERO E HIBRIDEZ EN *EL LAZARILLO DE CIEGOS CAMINANTES*, por Mariselle Meléndez. 1999. (No. 264). *-9268-8.*
DEL ESCENARIO A LA PANTALLA: LA ADAPTACIÓN CINEMATOGRÁFICA DEL TEATRO ESPAÑOL, por María Asunción Gómez. 2000. (No. 265). *-9269-6.*
THE LEPER IN BLUE: COERCIVE PERFORMANCE AND THE CONTEMPORARY LATIN AMERICAN THEATER, by Amalia Gladhart. 2000. (No. 266). *-9270-X.*
THE CHARM OF CATASTROPHE: A STUDY OF RABELAIS'S *QUART LIVRE*, by Alice Fiola Berry. 2000. (No. 267). *-9271-8.*
PUERTO RICAN CULTURAL IDENTITY AND THE WORK OF LUIS RAFAEL SÁNCHEZ, by John Dimitri Perivolaris. 2000. (No. 268). *-9272-6.*
MANNERISM AND BAROQUE IN SEVENTEENTH-CENTURY FRENCH POETRY: THE EXAMPLE OF TRISTAN L'HERMITE, by James Crenshaw Shepard. 2001. (No. 269). *-9273-4.*
RECLAIMING THE BODY: MARÍA DE ZAYA'S EARLY MODERN FEMINISM, by Lisa Vollendorf. 2001. (No. 270). *-9274-2.*
FORGED GENEALOGIES: SAINT-JOHN PERSE'S CONVERSATIONS WITH CULTURE, by Carol Rigolot. 2001. (No. 271). *-9275-0.*
VISIONES DE ESTEREOSCOPIO (PARADIGMA DE HIBRIDACIÓN EN EL ARTE Y LA NARRATIVA DE LA VANGUARDIA ESPAÑOLA), por María Soledad Fernández Utrera. 2001. (No. 272). *-9276-9.*
TRANSPOSING ART INTO TEXTS IN FRENCH ROMANTIC LITERATURE, by Henry F. Majewski. 2002. (No. 273). *-9277-7.*
IMAGES IN MIND: LOVESICKNESS, SPANISH SENTIMENTAL FICTION AND *DON QUIJOTE*, by Robert Folger. 2002. (No. 274). *-9278-5.*
INDISCERNIBLE COUNTERPARTS: THE INVENTION OF THE TEXT IN FRENCH CLASSICAL DRAMA, by Christopher Braider. 2002. (No. 275). *-9279-3.*
SAVAGE SIGHT/CONSTRUCTED NOISE. POETIC ADAPTATIONS OF PAINTERLY TECHNIQUES IN THE FRENCH AND AMERICAN AVANT-GARDES, by David LeHardy Sweet. 2003. (No. 276). *-9281-5.*
AN EARLY BOURGEOIS LITERATURE IN GOLDEN AGE SPAIN. *LAZARILLO DE TORMES, GUZMÁN DE ALFARACHE* AND BALTASAR GRACIÁN, by Francisco J. Sánchez. 2003. (No. 277). *-9280-7.*
METAFACT: ESSAYISTIC SCIENCE IN EIGHTEENTH-CENTURY FRANCE, by Lars O. Erickson. 2004. (No. 278). *-9282-3.*
THE INVENTION OF THE EYEWITNESS. A HISTORY OF TESTIMONY IN FRANCE, by Andrea Frisch. 2004. (No. 279). *-9283-1.*
SUBJECT TO CHANGE: THE LESSONS OF LATIN AMERICAN WOMEN'S *TESTIMONIO* FOR TRUTH, FICTION, AND THEORY, by Joanna R. Bartow. 2005. (No. 280). *-9284-X.*
QUESTIONING RACINIAN TRAGEDY, by John Campbell. 2005. (No. 281). *-9285-8.*
THE POLITICS OF FARCE IN CONTEMPORARY SPANISH AMERICAN THEATRE, by Priscilla Meléndez. 2006. (No. 282). *-9286-6.*
MODERATING MASCULINITY IN EARLY MODERN CULTURE, by Todd W. Reeser. 2006. (No. 283). *-9287-4.*

When ordering please cite the *ISBN Prefix* plus the last four digits for each title.

Send orders to: University of North Carolina Press
P.O. Box 2288
Chapel Hill, NC 27515-2288
U.S.A.
www.uncpress.unc.edu
FAX: 919 966-3829

The Department of Romance Studies Digital Arts and Collaboration Lab at the University of North Carolina at Chapel Hill is proud to support the digitization of the North Carolina Studies in the Romance Languages and Literatures series.

www.ingramcontent.com/pod-product-compliance
Lightning Source LLC
Chambersburg PA
CBHW020653230426
43665CB00008B/413